THE SPECTACLE OF VIOLENCE

'This is an excellent book in an incredibly under-researched area which will have a big impact on a range of debates. Gail Mason brings together sophisticated theoretical insights with well thought-out empirical material to offer new ways of understanding central issues such as power, subjectification, visibility and violence. It will make a major contribution to debates on sexuality and violence and may become a classic in the future.'

Beverley Skeggs, *University of Manchester*

The Spectacle of Violence explores the issues surrounding violence and hostility towards lesbians and gay men. Drawing on in-depth interviews with women reflecting a range of experiences of verbal hostility, physical violence and sexual violence, Gail Mason asks fundamental questions about where violence comes from and what effects it has. How do lesbians and gay men manage the risk of violence? And what is the relationship between violence and power?

Challenging current thinking, Mason highlights the ways in which different identities, different bodies and different systems of thought interact. She argues for the importance of thinking about homophobic violence in the context of other core issues such as gender and race. Examining the visual nature of violence, she demonstrates how violence infiltrates not just the daily experience of lesbians and gay men, but also the knowledge systems through which we construct and recognise sexual identities.

Focusing on 'real life' experiences of violence, *The Spectacle of Violence* is an important contribution to current thought about violence. Moving beyond issues of causation and prevention, it offers new ways of theorising the relationship between identity, knowledge and power.

Gail Mason is Lecturer in the Department of Gender Studies at The University of Sydney.

WRITING CORPOREALITES
Series Editor: Elspeth Probyn

This series seeks to encourage innovative writing about corporealities. It takes as a leading premise the fact that writing and studying embodied forms of sociality are intricately mutually informing. The type of work presented under the rubric of this series is therefore engaged and engaging, as it understands that writing itself is an embodied and social activity. The range of theoretical perspectives privileged may be wide but the common point of departure is a certain *parti pris* to study the materiality of contemporary processes and realities. Beyond discrete description, through different forms of writing, bodies, discourses, forms of power, histories and stories are put in play in order to inform other relations, other corporeal realities.

AIDS AND THE BODY POLITIC
Biomedicine and Sexual Difference
Catherine Waldby

FUR NATION
From the Beaver to Brigitte Bardot
Chantal Nadeau

WILD SCIENCE
Reading Feminism, Medicine and the Media
Edited by Janine Marchessault and Kim Sawchuk

THE SPECTACLE OF VIOLENCE

Homophobia, gender and knowledge

Gail Mason

London and New York

First published 2002
by Routledge
11 New Fetter Lane, London EC4P 4EE

Simultaneously published in the USA and Canada
by Routledge
29 West 35th Street, New York, NY 10001

Routledge is an imprint of the Taylor & Francis Group

© 2002 Gail Mason

Typeset in Garamond by Exe Valley Dataset Ltd, Exeter
Printed and bound in Great Britain by
Biddles Ltd, Guildford and King's Lynn

British Library Cataloguing in Publication Data
A catalogue record for this book is available from the British Library

Library of Congress Cataloging in Publication Data
Mason, Gail
The spectacle of violence: homophobia, gender and knowledge/Gail Mason.
p. cm.
Includes bibliographical references and index.
1. Homophobia–Australia.   2. Violence–Australia.   3. Gay men–Crimes
against–Australia.   4. Lesbians–Crimes against–Australia.   I. Title.
HQ76.45.A8 M37 2001
303.6′0994–dc21   2001031767

ISBN 0–415–18955–1 (hbk)
ISBN 0–415–18956–X (pbk)

CONTENTS

ACKNOWLEDGEMENTS

Many people have encouraged and influenced me during the time that I have been writing this book. I would like to thank my colleagues in the Department of Gender Studies, the University of Sydney, for providing a stimulating intellectual environment. Elspeth Probyn, series editor, deserves particular thanks. She respected my right to do this work how, and when, I liked, but provided critical feedback that enhanced it greatly, when it was needed the most. Rebecca Barden, at Routledge, supported the book and has shown true patience in waiting for it to arrive. A number of colleagues and friends have made the experience of researching and writing less lonely and more enjoyable. They have offered me invaluable ideas, feedback, hospitality, and challenging discussions and debates; many have also provided crucial comments on draft chapters. Thanks to: Stephen Tomsen, Beverley Skeggs, Julie Stubbs, Barbara Baird, Mariastella Pulvirenti, Linnell Secomb, Leslie Moran, Margaret Thornton, Andrew Sharpe, Bronwyn Mason, Anna Chapman, Jude Irwin and Nicole Asquith. Miranda Whale-Nagy has been a great research assistant; resourceful and astute, all at the one time. I owe a lot to the many opportunities that I have been given to present aspects of this work in Australian and international forums. I would like to thank the Centre for Women's Studies, University of Lancaster; the Department of Law, Birkbeck College, University of London; the Australian Institute of Criminology; the Human Sexualities Studies Program, San Francisco State University; and Women's Studies, the University of Tasmania. Martini Café, Newtown, sustained me with excellent coffee and relaxed ambience. The Sydney Lesbian and Gay Anti-Violence Project is responsible for bringing the issue of homophobia-related violence to public attention in many parts of Australia. I am grateful for the opportunity to have been involved with this organisation. Margaret Buchanan has been my soul-mate. She has shared with me unique insights, questions and passions that have profoundly shaped, not just this book, but also the way that I look at the world. Finally, I would like to thank the women who participated in this research. Their accounts of hostility and violence, particularly the ways in which they have resisted it, sustained this work in more ways than one.

INTRODUCTION

Impetus

It was amidst the heat and humidity of a women's shelter in the far north of Australia that I first began to think about violence. Working at the shelter was my initiation into the complexities and contradictions of assisting women and children whose lives had been disrupted, sometimes forever altered, by acts of violence. Physically, the shelter was located in an old wooden house. Like many houses in the tropics, it was built atop high stilts, designed to catch the slightest breeze. Anyone who has spent a summer in the tropics will understand the almost religious fervour with which locals approach the task of cooling their houses. In the shelter, this obsession had long since given way to the problem of over-crowding. The ground floor of the house had been converted into small, airless, box-like rooms, each housing multiple beds. This was the only means of accommodating the ever-escalating numbers of women and children in need of refuge. Added to this stifling atmosphere were the metal bars that encased every window and the security locks that were affixed to every door; devices that are rare in this part of the world. We could see out, but no one could see in. More importantly, no one could get in.

Although I was initially ambivalent about the necessity of this fortress approach to security, I soon learnt that it was indispensable. The address of the shelter was meant to be a secret. But you can't keep a secret in a small town. A couple of times, when I was working the over-night shift, I was woken at about three or four in the morning by an irate man banging on the door, shouting abuse and threats, shaking the bars, and demanding that his wife come home. Every time this happened, I would think that the recompense for feeling hot and confined in our boxed-in refuge was feeling safe and secure. This brought some relief.

During the time I worked at the shelter, I met a couple of women who have remained in my memory. They arrived at the shelter together, bringing their respective children with them. They came from a small outback town, and we were just one stop on a carefully laid route of escape. For some time, the two women had been having an affair. This had become general knowledge in

1

their home town. One woman's ex-husband had turned particularly vicious, embarking on a campaign of very public, and very loud, harassment. Having physically assaulted her, he then directed his attention to the other woman. He insulted and threatened her outside her house, her work, and even took to calling out abuse when she went to pick up her children after school. He taunted the women by calling them perverts, dirty lesbians, butch dykes, and many other names. Both women felt under siege, believing that neither they, nor their children, were safe. They started planning, and saving, for their escape. Months later, they made it to the shelter.

As this story unfolded, over endless cups of instant coffee, I remember remarking that it was, in fact, very similar to the situation of many other (heterosexual) women in the shelter. One woman's response was swift and sharp. Sure, she said, it is, but it's also different. Whilst I can't recall her exact words, I do know that she was at pains to make me see that the violence she described had as much to do with the demonisation of homosexuality as it did with gender inequalities between men and women. She resented my eagerness to categorise it in a way that failed to recognise this. The thing I remember most vividly was the strong feeling of discomfort this evoked in me. At the time, we were sitting in one of those airless cement boxes under the house. This may well have contributed to my physical discomfort. But I suspect that my sense of unease was triggered, or at least, intensified, by the intellectual and political challenge that I read into her remarks: was it enough to look at violence through the categories and boxes that brought me comfort, even relief, or did I need to recognise the ways in which different experiences of violence might exceed, or contradict, these snug interpretations?

A number of years later, this sense of discomfort returned. I had begun reading and working around the issue of homophobic violence, violence that is perpetrated against gay men and lesbians on the basis of their sexuality. *Déjà vu*. I felt like I was back in the shelter again, gasping for air, grappling with categories, identities, and concepts about which I felt uncertain or ambivalent: gay, lesbian, difference, hatred, prejudice, victim and so on. I felt uncomfortable about the representation of homophobic violence as a discrete problem of its own, one that had little to do with gendered violence, and one that could be adequately explained as the product of anti-homosexual culture and attitude alone. I also felt that, like the violence that is perpetrated against heterosexual women, the violence that lesbians and gay men report is likely to have implications that extend far beyond the question of individual or social control. Perhaps I had learnt something from my experience at the shelter, or perhaps I had learnt a few things since. Either way, I wondered how the issue of homophobic violence might look if I brought this sense of discomfort to bear upon it. What might I have to say about homophobic violence if I confronted the feelings of unease that these categories engendered?

This book is my attempt to come to terms with this sense of discomfort. It looks at the problem of homophobia-related violence and hostility. It highlights the ways in which different identities, different bodies and different knowledge systems interact in the enactment, experience, and effects of such violence. Simply put, the book is concerned with the contexts for, and the implications of, homophobia-related violence: where does violence come from, and where does it go; what produces violence, and what does it produce; what does violence do, and what does it not do? My responses to these questions – dual questions of context and consequence – are grounded in an empirical research project undertaken in Australia. This project involved a series of in-depth interviews with a diverse group of lesbian women. It focused upon their experiences and perceptions of verbal hostility, physical violence and sexual violence that was related, in some way, to their sexuality. I draw upon these interview accounts throughout the book. They offer me a means of looking at the issue of homophobia-related violence in ways that resist the static and categorical approaches that caused me uneasiness in the past. They highlight the interactive qualities and constitutive capacities of such violence. In particular, they reveal the importance of thinking about homophobia-related violence in the context of other specificities, such as those of gender and race. They emphasise the ways in which violence infiltrates not just the daily practices through which lesbians and gay men negotiate safety, but also the knowledge systems through which we construct and recognise sexual identities. In short, these accounts demand an analysis that is able to account for both the discursive and corporeal contexts, both the repressive and the productive implications, of violence.

As such, this book is positioned at a crossroads between different bodies of literature, particularly research on homophobic violence and feminist research on gendered violence. By forging some links between these two fields, I hope to make a contribution to each. Whilst my concerns may seem impossibly broad, they are made manageable by the focus that I take in individual chapters. I neither intend, nor desire, to provide a comprehensive analysis of the ins and outs of homophobia-related violence and hostility. More modestly, in each chapter I address a specific problematic, or question, that relates to the contexts for, or implications of, this violence. How do discourses of sexuality and gender interact in the violence that lesbians recount? To what extent is the concept of 'intersectionality' able to capture the interaction between the embodied differences that shape homophobia-related violence? How do lesbians and gay men 'manage' the risk of violence? Does the knowledge that we have of homophobia-related violence contribute to the formulation of particular subject positions? How might feminist and Foucauldian theory come together to theorise the relation between violence and power?

These questions are shaped by themes that appear, and reappear, throughout the book, linking the problematic of one chapter with another, sometimes closely, sometimes loosely. In particular, the metaphor of visuality – vision, evidence, surveillance, visibility, spectacle – is one that runs through much of my analysis. Notions of visuality resonate strongly in the discourse of homosexuality. Are lesbians and gay men invisible? Are you 'out' or 'open' about your homosexuality? Are you 'in the closet'? Should homosexuals 'flaunt' their sexuality? These are common questions. They all revolve around the idea that homosexuality should or should not, can or cannot, be visible. The concept of visuality also frames methodological debates about how we interpret experience, theoretical debates about the ways that we 'look at' and recognise different bodies, and epistemological debates about the relation between knowledge and power. All of these issues are central to the arguments of this book. Whilst the significance of visuality fluctuates between chapters, at times providing the over-arching analytical framework, at other times simply making a point of connection to other arguments, it is a bond that I use to eventually tie the chapters together. That is, I use the metaphor of visuality to argue that violence itself is a spectacle, a bodily experience and practice through which we see, and thereby come to know certain things.

Each chapter is designed to stand alone, and can easily be read on is own terms. However, I also intend the book to be cumulative; later chapters tend to build upon the arguments of earlier chapters. In this way, the analysis of the book develops as it moves along. For readers who are relatively un-familiar with the kinds of theory that I employ, I hope that the first chapter will lay some initial foundations, that subsequent chapters will add complexity to this, and that the final chapter will elucidate the major conceptual points.

In recent times, there has been much debate in western academic circles about the tendency of identity politics, including the feminist movement and the gay and lesbian movement, to exploit the desire for revenge amongst those who are subjugated (Brown 1995). Criticisms of the assumption that oppression provides an adequate moral ground upon which to construct claims for group recognition have produced a certain reticence amongst academics to conduct research into different forms of victimisation. Such research is often characterised as the product of a 'victim mentality' or 'victim politics'. It is often contrasted to research which emphasises the agency with which women, lesbians, or gay men also exercise power or, at least, resist their own subjugation. I agree that we would do well to hesitate, and to question the presumptions that motivate us, before we begin to conduct research on topics such as violence. However, I am not convinced that the most appropriate way to deal with our hesitation is to simply stop investigating practices that engender harm and injury; as if, the less we know about them, the more we can imagine that they do not exist. I believe that the point of this debate is to force us to seriously scrutinise the empirical and theoretical premises of our research. Ethically, I am unable to ignore violence, but I can look at it in different ways.

In this book I seek to open up the question of homophobia-related violence to different ways of thinking, particularly in terms of identity, knowledge, and power. I engage with theory that enables me to do this. This includes poststructural feminism, Foucauldian theory, and queer theory. However, like many academics who work in the field of violence, I am a firm believer in the importance of empirical research. Only through such research can we acquire the breadth of information that we need to understand violence on anything more than an individual basis; hence, my decision to investigate homophobia-related violence through interview accounts. It is my intention to bring these experiential accounts and this theoretical material together, so that they may bear upon, and inform, each other; only occasionally has such theory been used in the analysis of 'real life' accounts of violence. Methodologically this is a challenge in itself. It requires that I analyse (and maintain the integrity of) empirical accounts of violence through theory that often expresses scepticism for such research; as we shall see, I am motivated by a desire to explore possible methods of doing this. Theoretically, it means that I refuse to buy into a distinction between 'victim' and 'power' research. I prefer to work questions of victimisation and questions of empowerment with, and against, each other, looking for insights, challenges, and contradictions from both.

Some of the terminology that I use in this book requires explanation. To my mind, language is not a passive form of communication that simply describes the way things really are. It is a dynamic medium that both represents, and actively constitutes, that reality. We all use language differently, ascribing different meanings to different words. The language that I employ here reflects the assumptions that I make about a given incident or experience. It also shapes the ways in which I come to know and understand these phenomena. For these reasons, I believe it is important to clarify several terms from the beginning.

Violence is probably the word that I use the most. The concept of violence is sometimes used to denote a vast array of oppressions (in addition to physical force), that face particular groups of people. These might include various forms of discrimination, financial exploitation, institutional exclusion, and social marginalisation. I have never found this approach particularly helpful. I prefer to carefully distinguish between these different practices. Hence, my definition of violence is a fairly conventional, even legalistic, one. It refers to the exercise of physical force by one person/s upon the body of another. By physical force, I mean, pushing, shoving, hitting, punching, or otherwise harming or hurting the person who is targeted; which, in turn, often produces emotional and psychological harm. This may also include sexual assault, although I tend to signify the overt sexual nature of an act through more specific language, such as *rape*. Violence may be accompanied by threatening or abusive language; or it may not. It may be carried out with weapons; or without. It may be planned or spontaneous,

5

organised or disorganised. It may involve a one-to-one situation, or it may involve a group of individuals using physical force against one other individual or group of persons. My use of the word violence does not, however, encompass acts that are ordered by formal institutions, corporations, or the state (for example, warfare). To emphasise this, I often use the phrase *inter-personal violence*. The absence of consent is also crucial to my definition of violence. An act may wound the body of another, but it is only an act of violence if it is done so without the consent of that person. For example, acts conducted in the context of consenting sado-masochistic sex are not, for my purposes, acts of violence. Despite the fact that physical force sometimes causes death, much of what I have to say about violence assumes that this is not the outcome of a given incident. The contexts for such violence may be similar to those for less severe assaults, but the implications of homicide exceed the limits of the arguments that I make here. Although I do occasionally refer to homicide, I believe that the violent extinction of life demands an analysis of its own.

To seriously threaten another person with physical force can also be, to my way of thinking, an act of violence. It is likely to intimidate the person who is addressed, or to render them fearful in some way. In the main, however, I employ the term *hostility* to refer to verbal or written insults and threats. Whilst physical violence and verbal abuse may have similar discursive implications, the ways in which each is experienced may well differ. My use of the term hostility attempts to recognise this. Although acts of physical violence are usually accompanied by hostile language, such hostility often constitutes a problem in its own right.

I prefer the phrase *homophobia-related violence* to the more common *homophobic violence*. As I shall argue, anti-homosexual sentiment is rarely the sole explanation for the violence that lesbians or gay men report. Not only is homophobia itself infused with assumptions about gender, but the enactment and experience of such violence is also shaped by other specificities and differences, such as those of race, age, and class. In this book, I focus primarily on the interaction between sexuality, gender and, to a lesser extent, race. This reflects the particular articulations of identity that were explored in depth during the interviews I conducted. My use of the phrase homophobia-related violence is an attempt to remain alert to the ways in which different facets of identity interact in violence.

This begs the question of what I mean by *homophobia*. The term homophobia was first popularised in the early–mid 1970s (Weinberg, 1972; Lehne 1976). Weinberg used it to refer to an irrational fear of homosexuality, particularly the dread of being in close quarters with homosexuals. Soon after, the term *heterosexism* was also coined by Morin and Garfinkle (1978). Taking its lead from sociology, rather than psychology, it described a social belief system founded upon the assumption that heterosexuality is superior to homosexuality. Nonetheless, it is the term homophobia that has entered common vernacular, where it is now used to denote negativity towards homosexuality in general. There have, however, been numerous criticisms of the notion of homophobia. Kinsman, for example, argues that, although homophobia is an accurate description of the panic that some (male) hetero-sexuals experience in the company of gay men, by locating this reaction within a psychological framework it 'individualizes and privatizes gay oppression and obscures the social relations that organize it' (1987: 29). Kinsman reserves the term homophobia for particularly virulent personal responses to homosexuality. Similarly, Herek (1990) points out that the characterisation of anti-homosexual sentiment as a phobia implies that these attitudes are based on a fear, not unlike a phobia of spiders. For this reason he has advocated the concept of heterosexism, which he re-defines as an 'ideological system that denies, denigrates, and stigmatizes any nonhetero-sexual form of behavior, identity, relationship, or community' (316); more recently, Herek (2000) has also proposed the notion of *sexual prejudice*. This understanding of heterosexism seeks to emphasise the cultural and his-torical contexts which cultivate individual attitudes toward same-sex sexual desire.

Despite concerns about the phrase homophobia, I have chosen to use it in this book. I have several reasons for this. The currency that homophobia has acquired in public discourse means that it is more widely understood than the term heterosexism, particularly outside of sexuality studies and academia. Homophobia is thus the word that I used with interviewees. It is helpful for conveying the seriousness of violence, which is, after all, an extreme reaction to homosexuality. In adopting the term homophobia, I acknowledge that individual acts of violence can never be separated from the heterosexist culture within which they are situated; indeed, many of the arguments throughout this book seek to make this point. Whilst this choice of terminology is very much my own, the women I interviewed made the decision to describe a specific incident as homophobic in character. This proved to be far from straightforward. Indeed, it was in the course of discussing whether or not a particular encounter was actually related to homophobia that some of the most interesting issues emerged.

At different places in this book I also use phrases such as *gendered violence* and *racist violence*. In each case, I am talking about violence that is patterned by differences of gender or race. Gendered violence refers to the main forms of violence that are committed by heterosexual men towards women, particularly domestic violence, rape, and other forms of sexual assault; such violence is commonly called *violence against women* or *men's violence towards women*. The term racist violence refers to violence that appears to involve antipathy on the part of the perpetrator/s toward a particular racial group, to which the victim is assumed to belong. Such violence usually, but not always, follows patterns of racial privilege and subjugation; for example, violence committed by Anglo-Celtic Australians against Asian Australians, or by whites against blacks. Like violence that is related to homophobia, racist violence has been characterised as a form of hate crime. That is, as a form of violence that is motivated by prejudice, bias or hatred towards certain groups of people (Cunneen, Fraser and Tomsen 1997). Although it is outside the scope of this book to discuss whether or not violence towards women is also a form of hate crime, the possible links between these different 'types' of violence do raise some interesting issues about difference and power that I explore in various places. In particular, I will suggest that gendered, homophobic and racist violence are all shaped by hierarchical constructions of difference. In various places in this book I sometimes use the word violence on its own. It is important to note, however, that I am ever only referring to violence that is shaped by these regimes of difference.

Finally, the terms *sexuality, lesbian, gay*, and *homosexual* deserve some clarification. It is not unusual for sexuality to be used somewhat loosely, as if it were interchangeable with the act of sex, with heterosexuality or, even, with gender. In contrast, I use sexuality to talk about categories of sexual preference and identity; categories of lesbian, gay, homosexuality, or heterosexuality. This is very much a question of with *whom* we have, or desire to have, sex. Although the construction of sexuality is discussed in more detail in Chapter 1, it is worth noting now that the cultural processes that classify, normalise, and constitute sexual desire have engendered the idea that we all 'have' a discrete and classifiable sexuality. Yet, it is these very processes, which judge and accord a value to a given sexual practice, that underlie animosity towards those sexual preferences that do not fit the norm, such as homosexuality and other non-reproductive sexualities. Whilst I wish to challenge the normalisation and naturalisation of sexual categories, I am also committed to highlighting the negative, particularly violent, implications that flow from these categorisations. Within this context, the words lesbian and gay are self-defining. Someone, especially an interviewee, is lesbian if she chooses to identify in this way; some interviewees also called themselves gay, queer or homosexual. In most cases, we can assume that a woman describes herself as lesbian because her main sexual desires and/or practices are directed towards women. Primarily, I reserve the word gay to refer to men whose main sexual desires and/or practices are directed toward other men. Although the term homosexual has fallen out of use in recent times, I continue to employ it as a means of talking about lesbians and gay men together, and to highlight the hierarchical opposition between heterosexuality and homosexuality that conditions discourses of sexuality. Hence, to draw upon lesbian-identified narratives in the ways that I do, does not mean that I see sexual identities as stable or coherent. Rather, it is to attempt to recognise the profound, everyday implications that such categories have for individual lesbians and gay men, and for the discourses that shape our understandings of the sexual subject.

The book is divided into six chapters. The first is a methodological chapter. The next four chapters are equally split according to the two broad issues that I set out above. Chapters 2 and 3 look at the discursive and corporeal contexts for homophobia-related violence; where does violence come from? Chapters 4 and 5 look at the implications of such violence; where does violence go? Chapter 6 draws together these arguments to make a specific theoretical proposal of its own. Let me provide a brief outline of each chapter.

In Chapter 1 I lay out the methodological foundations, and tensions, of the book. I frame these within the notion of visuality. I suggest that there is a tendency in post-positivist and standpoint methodologies to treat experience as a self-evident form of knowledge which, in turn, relies upon a liberal-humanist model of the human subject. Taking sexuality as my example, and Foucault's notion of panopticism as my framework, I consider why this model of the subject is no longer convincing. I argue that we need to find ways of bringing empirical accounts of experience and poststructural theory into close proximity with each other. I discuss how I have gone about attempting to do this. I describe the research project which enables me to analyse homophobia-related violence; a qualitative interview study with over seventy lesbian women in Australia. My approach to the question of experience is a process of looking for, and analysing, 'statements' of violence in these interview accounts. My aim is to provide a basic template for engaging with accounts of experience in the remainder of the book.

In Chapter 2 I ask, what does hostility and violence towards lesbians look like? I set the scene for this discussion by providing a brief overview of the current literature on both homophobic violence and gendered violence. I suggest that lesbian experiences of homophobia-related violence need to be conceptualised as a conjunction of these fields of research; a question of both sexuality and gender. Towards this end, I argue that this type of violence makes a statement about the disordered, or dislocated, nature of lesbian sexuality. I identify four repertoires around questions of homosexuality, corporeality and gender that provide the discursive contexts for violence to do this; dirt; hetero-sex; butch; and boy/girl. These repertoires enable me to identify the kind of statement that violence makes. They also represent the mediums via which this violence is experienced as an expression of homophobic sentiment. Discussing each in turn, I look for the ways in which they connect to each other in order to produce a statement of lesbian disorder.

In feminist criminology and legal theory, the concept of *intersectionality* has emerged as a major means of conceptualising the relation between violence and difference. Chapter 3 picks up where Chapter 2 leaves off, by considering the extent to which intersectionality is able to conceptualise the interaction between regimes of difference in the enactment and experience of violence. I do this by drawing upon examples of violence that are shaped by specificities of race, gender and sexuality (which I refer to as 'territorial violence'). I suggest that although intersectionality is designed to overcome essentialist tendencies in violence research, this goal is restricted by an attachment to a social constructionist and intersectional model of the human subject. I suggest that a 'cultural' model of the body might assist us to recognise that the relation between violence and difference is an embodied and mutually constitutive one. Moreover, it might enable us to acknowledge that violence is not the produce of 'natural' bodily characteristics, but, rather, emerges from the hierarchical differences *between* certain bodies.

I begin addressing the implications of violence in Chapter 4. I suggest that, in order to understand the collective implications of homophobia-related violence, it is necessary to position this violence within the discourse of sexual visibility; that is, to consider how homophobic hostility functions through the ambiguous troupe of visibility. The knowledge that lesbians and gay men have of homophobia-related hostility interacts with other factors to engender practices of self-surveillance, particularly mapping one's body for visible expressions of sexuality. Yet, the pleasure that is derived from flouting the danger of homophobia suggests that it might be helpful to consider the implications of homophobic violence as a question of 'management'. In light of the contested nexus between homosexuality and visibility, the chapter concludes that the imperative to manage one's homosexuality, as a means of negotiating safety, is inevitably an imperative to manage that which is, ultimately, unmanageable.

Chapter 5 builds on the argument of the previous chapter by looking at the extent to which violence infiltrates the very discourses that construct the meaning of homosexuality. I suggest that the statements that violence makes cannot be confined to the insults that are hurled during an attack. Homophobia-related violence also marks the bodies of lesbians and gay men with signs of vulnerability and victimhood; signs that name the category of homosexuality as being 'in danger' of hostility. Does the injury implicit in this name insinuate itself into the normative processes through which lesbians and gay men are constituted as certain types of subjects? I address this question by arguing that, although violence may contribute to the definition of 'what' homosexuality is, it cannot tell lesbians and gay men 'who' they are as homosexuals; I appropriate the work of Hannah Arendt to make this distinction. In other words, violence has the capacity to constitute sexual subject positions but it cannot determine the subjectivities through which these identities are lived and reinvented by lesbians and gay men every day.

Finally, in Chapter 6, I draw upon the major arguments of previous chapters to establish a framework for conceptualising the nexus between violence and power, one that enables future research to bring together the insights of both feminist theory and Foucauldian theory. These are the two schools of thought with which I engage most consistently throughout this book. It has been suggested, however, that, when it comes to the question of violence, they are incompatible with one another. In this chapter I seek to dispute this assertion. By examining a series of key questions on violence and power, I argue that the tension between feminist theory and Foucault over this nexus is not so much a question of irreconcilable paradigms, but, more specifically, of the lack of an identifiable path between the two models; for instance, Foucualt's model of power need not be read to exclude the oppressive implications of violence that feminism highlights (the 'productive hypothesis' does not exclude the 'repressive hypothesis'). I pick up the idea, shared by both feminists and Foucault, that the nexus between violence and power is an instrumental one; that is, violence is an instrument of power. I suggest that we might think of instrumentality as a question of knowledge, of the capacity of violence to shape the ways that we see, and thereby come to know, certain things. In this way, the act of violence itself is a spectacle. This is not so much because violence is something that we observe, but, more, because violence is a mechanism through which we distinguish and observe other things. In other words, violence is more than a practice that acts upon individual subjects to inflict harm and injury. It is, metaphorically speaking, also a way of looking at these subjects.

In a 1996 paper entitled 'I am not a lesbian', Fiona McGregor writes about the launch of her new work of fiction, *Suck My Toes*. Upon hearing it described as book about 'lesbian Sydney', she recalls: 'It was like a cloud passing over a field of sunflowers. I wilted too' (1996: 31). How could the richness and diversity of her characters be so easily, and unproblematically, reduced to their sexuality? I understand these concerns. If the significance of one's work is restricted to its lesbian components, and its assumed lesbian readership, this can only mitigate its ability to contribute to broader fields of literature. Some might well ask, why write a book about lesbians, if you don't want it to be described as a lesbian book? In the context of violence, the answer is simple. In the literature on homophobic violence, it is the experiences of gay men that usually provide the benchmark for analysis. Not dissimilarly, in the literature on gendered violence, the experiences of heterosexual women commonly serve this same function. My focus upon lesbian women is an attempt to address the gaps in our knowledge left by this literature. In doing so, I realise that I tread a fine line between developing our understandings of the violence that is perpetrated towards lesbians, and reinforcing the lesbian's status as 'other'. I see my attempt to rectify this dearth of knowledge as a necessary, but not sufficient, research objective. Quite simply, I aim to do more. In focusing upon accounts of violence that do not match the 'typical' scenario of either homophobic violence or gendered violence, I hope to demonstrate that there is no standard case of either form of violence; the experience of the majority is neither normal nor universal. By exploring a very specific, but less routine, form of violence, I offer a slightly different perspective from which to think about both gendered violence and homophobic violence in general. It is in these ways that I attempt to come to terms with my discomfort over the categories that we use to analyse violence. So, yes, this is a book about violence towards lesbians. But, in it, lesbian women offer not only a knowledge of certain forms of violence, but, also, a way of examining that which we already know about violence. Such a text can, and will, speak for itself, but the way in which it is heard is 'ultimately the reader's province' (McGregor 1996: 39).

1

LOOKING THROUGH
EXPERIENCE

Letter II. Plan for a penitentiary inspection-house.

Before you look at the plan, take in words the general idea of it.

The building is circular.

The apartments of the prisoners occupy the circumference. You may call them if you please, the *cells*.

These *cells* are divided from one another, and the prisoners by that means secluded from all communication with each other, by partitions in the form of *radii* issuing from the circumference towards the centre . . .

The apartment of the inspector occupies the centre; you may call it if you please the *inspector's lodge*. . . .

Each cell has in the outward circumference, a *window*, large enough, not only to light the cell, but, through the cell, to afford light enough to the correspondent part of the lodge.

The inner circumference of the cell is formed by an iron *grating*, so light as not to screen any part of the cell from the inspector's view.

(Bentham 1962: 40–1)

In 1787 Jeremy Bentham, while visiting Russia, read an item in an English newspaper that captured his attention. The item advertised the proposed construction of a 'House of Corrections'. Employing ideas generated by his brother's exposure to a Parisian military school (Gordon 1980), Bentham responded to the advertisement by designing a building that he initially referred to as the 'Inspection House' but which later became known as the panopticon.[1] According to Bentham's original letters, the 'central-inspection principle' of this architectural design allowed it to be used for many, fundamentally identical, purposes: to guard the insane, reform the vicious, confine the suspected, employ the idle, punish the incorrigible, or educate the young (Bentham 1962: 40). In structural terms, the panopticon has a central tower with wide windows around its exterior. The tower is ringed by an annular building that is divided into cells and each cell occupies the full depth of this building. Within the central tower, a supervisor is located and, within each cell, a prisoner, patient, worker or 'madman' is housed. There are two windows in each cell, one on the inside facing the tower and one facing the outside world. In this way, sunlight is able to pass through the outer window to illuminate the interior space of the cell. This backlight effect is axiomatic to the design of the panopticon. By illuminating the cells it ensures that the occupants are visible from the tower. [2]

It was, of course, the architectural form and function of the panopticon that Foucault (1977) later transfigured into a visual and spatial metaphor for the disciplinary relations of modern western societies. Whilst Bentham and Foucault both express a deep respect for the panoptic schema, the rationale behind this respect is quite different for each. In Bentham's case, the panopticon is a practical means of observation that literally renders a whole group of human beings visible. The ingenuity of the design is found in the fact that those individuals who inhabit the outer cells of the panoptic structure, whether they be school children or convicted offenders, are visible at any given moment to those who supervise them from the central tower. It is the knowledge afforded by this visibility, the fact that inmates know that the supervisors can see what they are doing, that enables the panoptic institution to effectively control a large mass of people. In Foucault's panopticon, observation is also a medium to knowledge but the visibility it occasions has a figurative, rather than practical, significance to it. In appropriating the image of the panopticon to explicate his hypothesis on disciplinary power, Foucault suggests that human subjects become particular types of individuals according to the ways in which we are rendered visible within historically specific systems of knowledge. It is this visibility, the normative means via which we recognise ourselves and others, that facilitates the management and control of populations. In effect, this means that the very method through which Bentham sought to perfect his panoptic design – the production of a sense of abiding visibility – is the very feature that leads Foucault to characterise the panoptic schema as the symbol of an insidious form of power. The key to the panoptic mechanism, for both Bentham and Foucault, is found in this nexus between knowledge and visuality, in the idea that to render something visible is to make it knowable in ways that matter.

It is this correlation between knowledge and visuality that interests me in this chapter and, indeed, in many parts of this book.[3] Whilst panopticism is about much more than methodology, I believe that the different ways in which Bentham and Foucault engage with the idea that visuality is a medium to knowledge is indicative of one of the primary debates in empirical research methodology today. This is the question of how we employ accounts of the personal experience of individuals. On the one hand, we have the idea that observation is an effective means of learning details about the daily lives of a particular group of individuals. This was Bentham's assumption. So too is it the method by which the empirical researcher acquires forms of knowledge about his or her research subjects. Such observations might be made in the course of person-to-person interviews, ethnographies, participant observations, or the compilation of quantitative data. Although this approach to knowledge recognises that there are limitations on what can be observed, the overall intention is to treat empirical observations as visible evidence of that which took place. Indeed, in many cases, such observations may be the only means of attaining knowledge about a given phenomenon. On the other hand, we have Foucault's more ambivalent treatment of visuality. In this approach, phenomena are not simply observed. Instead, the practice of observation itself brings these things into being in specific terms: in the panoptic model the human subject becomes visible as a certain type of individual through the struggles between various knowledge regimes to define him or her. This way of thinking raises a fundamental dilemma for the researcher who wishes to observe everyday experience as a means of knowing the empirical world. If the individual who 'has' such experience is situated within various relations of knowledge and power, how are we to understand the accounts that he or she provides of the 'real' world? Is it possible to treat these experiences as a straightforward body of evidence or do we need to acknowledge the cultural contexts to which they are indebted (including the research environment itself) and the discursive functions they might perform? If so, how?

In this chapter I engage with these questions. This is because qualitative accounts of experience form the empirical backbone of this book. These accounts are drawn from an interview research project into the perceptions and experiences of homophobia-related hostility and violence among Australian lesbians (discussed in more detail below). In the chapters that follow, I draw heavily upon these accounts to make a number of arguments about homophobia-related violence, difference and power. They provide me with an invaluable means of 'observing' violence and hostility on a collective scale. It would not be possible for me to make these arguments without this body of knowledge. So, whilst my reading of Bentham's panopticon reminds me of the value of empirical observations of individual experience, my reading of Foucault's panopticon reminds me of the poststructural imperative to refrain from relying upon such experience as an unproblematic form of evidence. It is the tension between these two approaches that has raised the most consistent, not to mention troublesome, epistemological issues for my research. It is this tension that I primarily address in this chapter.

In order to begin considering how we might bring empirical accounts of experience and poststructural theory into close proximity with each other, I provide a brief overview of some of the methodologies that have prioritised empirical research, such as post-positivism and feminism. I suggest that there is a tendency in these methodologies to treat experience as a self-evident form of knowledge which, in turn, relies upon a liberal-humanist model of the human subject. Taking sexuality as my example, and panopticism as my framework, I consider why this model of the subject is no longer convincing. In endeavouring to respond to the proposition that accounts of experience do not represent a foundational knowledge of the 'real world', I propose that it is important to engage with both the fields of knowledge that feed into the experience of violence and the constitutive functions that such experience performs. In the last section of the chapter I discuss some of the more practical aspects of this approach to experience. I describe the research project that has enabled me to highlight women's experiences of homophobia-related hostility and violence. I then explain my approach to the critique of this experience as a question of looking for, and analysing, 'statements' of violence. My intention is to provide a basic framework for engaging with interview accounts of experience in the remainder of the book. Although the use of such material raises important methodological questions, I hope to demonstrate that these should neither discourage academic researchers from drawing upon observations of experience nor preclude us from taking a critical approach to such experience.

Experience as a question of evidence

The panopticon is a striking example of the importance ascribed to notions of visuality during the modernist era. Extending beyond the obvious fields of art and architecture, this fascination with sight and perspective infiltrated the development of western science (Foster 1988). Initially, it was the natural sciences that stressed the discovery of knowledge through disembodied and neutral observations. When social science later came to establish its own credentials, it emulated this approach by defining social facts as those observations that are independent of the knowing and/or experiencing subject. The dominant paradigm that has emerged relies upon a strict set of criteria for determining if a given form of knowledge is valid and reliable. Lennon and Whitford put it like this:

> Within that framework knowledge is referential – it is about something (the object) situated outside the knower. Knowledge is said to mirror an independently existing world, as that world really is. Putative knowledge reaches these goals by conforming to a set of criteria for testing and validation. These criteria are universal. . . . Genuine knowledge does not reflect the subject who produced it.
>
> (1994: 2)

Although challenges to this positivist ideal cannot be confined to any one historical period, it is fair to say that since the 1960s we have witnessed an

16

unprecedented groundswell of dissatisfaction with the epistemological foundations and methodological conventions of social science.[4] In the wake of commentators such as Thomas Kuhn (1962), a plethora of post-positivist methodologies have emerged. In general, these have sought to find ways of undertaking empirical research without buying into the tenets of traditional social science (Lincoln and Guba 1985; Reason and Rowan 1981). For example, they have attempted to: recognise the influence of the researcher in the knowledge that is produced; value the subjectivity and heterogeneity of research participants; engage with competing versions of the phenomena under examination; and allow research participants greater control over the research process and outcomes.

In the last twenty years or so, these methodologists have also been drawn to broader theoretical dissections of, and challenges to, modernist knowledge claims. Before discussing how these challenges relate to the specific question of experience, the point I wish to briefly make here is that it is the poststructural disavowal of foundational (not to mention objective) accounts of reality that has probably held the most appeal for post-positivists seeking to recognise the discursive registers that frame empirical narratives. At the same time, however, the anti-empiricist tendencies of poststructuralism (Rosenau 1992) have generated the greatest source of tension for those researchers who maintain a stake in empirical research. This tension tempers the extent to which poststructural theory is taken up in the methodological design of empirical research. In academic spheres with strong political roots, such as feminism, this seems to have led to an epistemological rift between those who are committed to the empirical generation of experiential knowledge, and those committed to deconstructing the very concepts that provide such knowledge (and the research methods used to produce it) with epistemic value in the first place; concepts such as woman, lesbian, subject, experience, victim, violence, etc.[5] Given feminism's long-standing commitment to acknowledge, and assuage, the injury and harm of violence it is hardly surprising that the vast majority of feminist research on men's violence towards women falls into the former camp and, in some instances, expresses a deep suspicion of poststructural challenges to the authority of experiential knowledge and the identity categories upon which it usually relies (Hester, Kelly and Radford 1996). In order to begin to explore the sources of this tension let me look more closely at one of the major ways in which experience has featured in feminist research, particularly empirical research.

Feminism and experience

Feminist thinking has produced some of the most influential challenges to the positivist tenets of social and behavioural science (Harding 1986; Reinharz 1979; Roberts 1981; Stanley and Wise 1983). Just as feminists have impugned the androcentric foundations of many academic disciplines, so too have they critiqued the methodological praxis through which these disciplines define themselves and the epistemological conventions that underpin this practice. Having revealed that claims to transcendence, objectivity and universality merely served to camouflage the male-centred source of much academic knowledge, early feminist commentators sought to articulate a philosophical approach to research that was capable of rivalling this masculinist paradigm.

One of the most significant elements of this challenge to positivism – and of particular relevance to research accounts of experience – was the prioritisation of women's views of the world. Gradually, and borrowing from Hegel and Marx, these efforts crystallised into what become known as feminist standpoint epistemology.[6] By rendering women's experiences of the world more visible, standpoint epistemology sought to give a voice to those that had previously been silenced or marginalised. Although Hartsock (1983a) originally argued that a feminist standpoint was something that feminists had to achieve, many subsequent versions have adopted the concept of 'women's standpoint' as a social given. As we see in sociology, psychology and black feminist studies, standpoint epistemology argues that research should start with women's lives, or with particular women's lives, and treat women's experience as the grounds of feminist knowledge (Smith 1987; Gilligan 1982; Collins 1990). According to Harding, research that commences from this marginalised social situation is 'scientifically better' because it is capable of generating 'less partial and distorted accounts of nature and social life' (Harding 1993: 61, 65).

By juxtaposing alternate subjectivities, standpoint epistemology has been able to critique the supposedly objective and universal evidence of many disciplines. In addition, the prioritisation of women's experience has challenged the positivist insistence that only certain types of data constitute real or scientific knowledge. Although experience has always provided a key ontological basis to the politics of feminism (it has been used to generate perceptions of collective oppression), the propensity of standpoint feminism to accord this kind of epistemic privilege to women as a group has attracted much criticism from other feminist quarters. Such critics have noted both a tendency to equate knowledge with experience (as if the act of knowing could be reduced to the realities of being) and an inclination to concede primacy to restricted understanding of identity (such as woman, black woman, or lesbian woman). For example, it is now well accepted that global concepts such as 'women's ways of knowing' tend to essentialise the category of woman and minimise the way in which gender interacts with regimes of ethnicity, sexuality and class (Bar On 1993; Alcoff 1991/2). Although advocates of standpoint epistemology have responded to these criticisms in various ways, in the final analysis most empirical researchers who remain committed to a model of standpoint continue to position women's experience as the foundation or starting point for knowledge and, in some instances, a superior form of knowledge.[7]

One of the problems that this raises for empirical research interested in poststructural theory, and the problem that concerns me in this chapter, is that standpoint epistemology continues to assume that the reality of social life is a 'given', a 'preconceptual material fact', and that women's experiences provide us with access to these facts (Hekman 1999: 37).[8] It is only possible to privilege personal experience in this way, as a form of unmediated evidence, if we accept the liberal-humanist proposition that the subject who has these experiences is an original and coherent source of the meaning of reality; or, as Scott puts it, if we accept that the things that the subject 'sees', and thereby knows, are a 'direct apprehension of a world of transparent objects' (1991: 775). The difficulty, of course, is that it is no longer adequate to assume that the experiences that individuals recount are simply an unmediated version of what took place. In part, this is because the idea of a pre-discursive and self-knowing subject has come under increasing challenge in recent years. This shift in thinking has significant implications for the way in which we engage with personal accounts of experience. Before considering these implications it is first necessary to articulate the parameters of this challenge and to consider what an alternate model of the human subject might look like. It is helpful to return to the question of panopticism in order to do this.

Panopticism: Bentham and Foucault

Jeremy Bentham sought perfection in the design of the panopticon. In his eyes, this meant constant and unrelenting surveillance. Realising the impossibility of this architectural ideal, Bentham's solution was to contrive a structural means for the occupants of the tower to 'see without being seen'. This was achieved in two ways. In the cells, the ubiquitous backlight effect ensured that inmates were always visible from the tower, although such visibility was usually in the form of a small shadow rather than a fully featured person. In the tower, a complex system of windows and blinds guaranteed that the supervisors had a constant view of the cells without ever being visible themselves. Bentham went so far as to speculate that if a whole family were housed in the tower (of course, only the head of the family need be paid), they would be sufficiently 'amused' by the scene to observe it during every free moment: 'It will supply in their instance the place of that great and constant fund of entertainment to the sedentary and vacant in towns – the looking out of the window' (1962: 45). Inmates would thus have the sense that they were under continual surveillance and, importantly, be prevented from determining anything to the contrary. In stark contrast to this axial visibility was the plan for complete lateral invisibility. Cells were to be perfectly individualised so as to prevent all communication between inmates: 'He is seen, but he does not see; he is the object of information, never a subject in communication' (Foucault 1977: 200). In this way the panopticon was able to order a human mass into a neatly organised, segregated and manageable collection of individuals.

It is not surprising that Foucault was drawn to the image of the panopticon. Its allusion to a 'visible' yet 'unverifiable' means of correction provided a template for thinking about the interaction between corporeality, visibility and regulation on a much larger scale, leading him to argue that the panoptic schema was to spread throughout the social body as a 'generalizable . . . way of defining power relations' in terms of everyday life (Foucault 1977: 205). Unlike Bentham, however, Foucault employed the panoptic image in a metaphorical rather than ontological sense. Panopticism became a heuristic tool for unearthing and examining the relation between power and the human subject at a local, everyday level. It formed the basis of Foucault's hypothesis of disciplinary power, which he eventually integrated into later models of bio-power and governmentality.

Foucault argued that, just as the panopticon, in all its lightness, replaced the darkness of the dungeon as a preferred model of punishment, so too did the visual and spatial techniques of disciplinary power come to subsume the violence and coercion of sovereign power.[9] These techniques were primarily the historically specific knowledge regimes, formal and informal, that rendered humans visible as particular types of subjects. This condition of visibility, induced by a sense of perpetual inspection, was identified by Foucault as a trap through which subjects internalise the processes of individualisation and normalisation, thereby fashioning their own subjectivity and behaviour:

> He who is subjected to a field of visibility, and who knows it, assumes responsibility for the constraints of power; he makes them play spontaneously upon himself; he inscribes in himself the power relation in which he simultaneously plays both roles; he becomes the principle of his own subjection.
>
> (1977: 203)

Reduced to its most basic, this model suggests that we live in a society of surveillance where the very concept of the individual has been assembled via techniques and forces that act upon human bodies. Particular knowledge systems (such as psychiatry, science, or the law) prompt us to see, and thereby know, ourselves and others in particular ways; or, to put this in the more abstract terms that Rajchman uses, to see 'is always to think . . . [a]nd conversely to think is always to see' (1988: 92). When humans are rendered recognisable as certain types of individuals we assume responsibility for modifying and constraining our behaviour, and our sense of self, so as to conform to normalised expectations and conventions. Hence, disciplinary power is associated less with a particular institution or apparatus and more with the way in which we ourselves become the bearers of power: 'We are neither in the amphitheatre, nor on the stage, but in the panoptic machine, invested by its effects of power, which we bring to ourselves since we are part of its mechanism' (Foucault 1977: 217). Significantly, this is not simply a question of what is seen, but, rather, of 'what can be seen' (Rajchman 1988:92). Disciplinary power does not just make subjects visible, it fundamentally determines if and how we are to see such subjects.

Unlike Bentham's panopticon, surveillance in Foucault's panopticon does not stem from a singular or central source. It takes place through a complex web, or carceral, of spatial relations. Hence, power is to be found, not so much in the individual, who does not own the machinery of power, but more in the distribution of bodies, knowledges and gazes within which the subject is caught up. Although the panopticon represents the theoretical possibility that any subject may exercise the mechanisms of surveillance, the practical distribution of panoptic positionings means that 'certain positions preponderate and permit an effect of supremacy to be produced' (Foucault 1980: 156).

I would like to illuminate this brief overview by looking specifically at the social formation of the sexual subject. In taking this example, I hope to explicate what a model of disciplinarity means for our understanding of the subject, and, thereby, lay the foundation for my assertion that the experiences of my research participants are not simply a self-evident form of knowledge. Moreover, I hope that this discussion of the sexual subject will explain my own approach to the question of lesbian and gay identity (and, indeed, all identity).

Categories of sexual identity

Essentialist assumptions have dominated discussions of sexual desire and practice in the west since at least the last century.[10] Sexual essentialism assumes that sexual desire is a culturally independent and intrinsic property, a fixed and inner core that differentiates us all at an individual level (Stein 1992). Having flourished at the beginning of the twentieth century, sexual essentialism continues to monopolise professional and public perceptions of sexuality. In academic circles, contemporary versions can be found in research that seeks to locate the origin of homosexuality in 'gay genes', in analysis that reduces sexuality to a separate sphere of life, or in the assumed existence of a distinct homosexual or gay subject throughout history (LeVay 1996; Padgug 1992; Boswell 1980). Despite its dominance, the social effects of sexual essentialism have come under increasing attack in the west. Although challenges have originated in diverse quarters (Kinsey, Pomeroy and Martin 1948, 1953; McIntosh 1992), feminism appears responsible for prompting the most long-standing and far-reaching campaigns against dominant sexual presumptions, rituals and practices. Most recently, it is the many feminist and queer appropriations of the Foucauldian critique of sexuality itself that have had a profound effect on our thinking about sexual identities, and the hetero–homo dyad in particular (Butler 1990; Sedgwick 1990).

In bringing his hypothesis of the disciplinary society to the notion of sexuality, and developing it in the process, Foucault presents a version of western society that, from the nineteenth century onwards, began to impose order on the multiple manifestations of sexual desire by classifying individual preferences and behaviours according to newly created typologies. 'Peripheral' sexualities were not, as has been commonly argued, merely suppressed or prohibited, as if to exclude them from society altogether. Rather, they were sought out and regulated by being given an 'analytical, visible, and permanent reality' (1978: 44). For example, during a period of intense sexual research, turn-of-the-century sexologists such as Krafft-Ebing, Westphal and Carpenter sought to capture the sexual core of the human subject with scientific classifications and labels, often developing specific categories as a means of explaining the unconventional gendered and sexual behaviour they observed (Vicinus 1989). In particular, those men and women whose 'diseased' desires and practices fell outside the normative ideal of monogamous, procreative hetero-sex (sanctioned by the church and the state) were labelled as *invert, pervert, homosexual*, and later, *lesbian* (Weeks 1990; Faderman 1991). Via these systems of psychiatric and medical knowledge – and the struggles that went on between them to define the sexual subject according to the particular lens of their own disciplines – sexual behaviours which had once been viewed as forbidden acts came to be seen as inextricably tied to an individual's biology or, under the influence of Freud (1953), to his or her psyche. Foucault describes this complex play between power and pleasure in the (now celebrated) following terms:

> The nineteenth-century homosexual became a personage, a past, a case history, and a childhood, in addition to being a type of life, a life form, and a morphology, with an indiscreet anatomy and possibly a mysterious physiology. Nothing that went into his total composition was unaffected by his sexuality . . . It [sodomy] was consubstantial with him, less as a habitual sin than as a singular nature . . . The sodomite had been a temporary aberration; the homosexual was now a species.
>
> (1978: 43)

This was not, of course, a seamless or gender-neutral process. The medical, scientific and legal communities that were so ready to adopt the notion of the homosexual male hesitated before publicly naming homosexual behaviour among women, particularly 'respectable' middle-class women (Weeks 1990). Instead, they focused their attention on homo-erotic behaviours among working-class women and criminal somatotypes. Hence, public expressions of concern about lesbianism did not emerge in most English-speaking nations until the 1920s; the degree to which this shift reflected a reaction to the contemporaneous rise of the feminist movement has been a matter of much discussion (Faderman 1981; Jeffreys 1985).

The significance of disciplinarity for the historical construction of sexuality lies in the way in which categories such as heterosexual and homosexual are not just labels imposed upon the subject, but, rather, are processes of normalisation that insinuate themselves into the very fabric of the modern corporeal and psychic subject. Quite simply, it is through the production of these visible subject positions that we come to see, and thereby know, ourselves as specific types of sexual subjects. It is important to note, however, that this is not a one-way process. As Rose makes clear, '[h]uman beings are not the unified subjects of some coherent regime of domination that produces persons in the form in which it dreams' (1996a: 140). The integral role that resistance and contestation play in the emergence of these identities means that sexual constructions intended for a particular purpose are inevitably reconfigured by the ways we live our everyday lives.

Nonetheless, the sexual demarcations that first became visible in the nineteenth century soon entrenched a quite rigid bifurcation between the normality of heterosexuality (specifically the monogamous heterosexual family) and the abnormality of homosexuality and other non-reproductive sexual practices (such as masturbation and prostitution). One of the legacies of this historical process is that sexual identities currently represent a fundamental criterion against which we monitor and constrain our own sexual practices and lifestyles. Whilst the hierarchies signified by these normative divisions are now under constant erosion, the historical stigma attached to a category such as 'the homosexual' continues to have dramatic consequences for most people who experience same-sex sexual desire. As Plummer notes, such categories 'have rendered – in the main – whole groups of people devalued, dishonourable, or dangerous and have frequently justified monstrous human atrocities and the denial of human rights' (Plummer 1981: 53).

Critiquing accounts of experience

It should be apparent from the above discussion that, unlike Bentham, for whom observation provided a form of evidence, Foucault's investment in visuality was rather more ambivalent.[11] In seeking to challenge empiricist assumptions about the self-evident nature of the empirical world, he appropriated vision as a metaphor for looking behind phenomena that are said to be commonsensical or natural. His aim was 'to "see" the depicted events in a new light, or in a different way – in the light of their underlying, unseen concepts' (Rajchman 1988: 91). Unmasking the subject in this way – revealing the ways in which supposedly self-evident categories of sexuality are actually historically specific constructions – invites us to carefully appreciate the concept of experience.

If we understand the subject as the product of particular knowledge systems – or, more accurately, of the struggle *between* discursive regimes to name and define the 'truth' of the subject – then experience must, in part, emerge out of the same discursive relations within which the subject is formulated. This is both a determined and a determining process. By this I mean that an event or emotion is fundamentally shaped by the subject position through which it is experienced; for example the experience of violence is constructed, in part, through one's identity as man or woman, heterosexual or homosexual, black or white. Within these parameters (and often pushing the boundaries of them), the thinking and acting subject draws upon certain discourses (usually those that dominate) to give intelligibility to the things she sees and feels. In this way, the meaning of a violent event is never fixed or essential but, rather, is actively constituted through the distinctions and differences of language and discourse. These differences, however, are not confined to the realm of the discursive. As feminist theorists of the body have made clear (Gatens 1996), the experiences available to us are just as much the product of the specificities of the human body as they are of discourse; the subject may be formulated through discursively constituted identities but he or she can never be contained by, or reduced to, the discursive terms of those identities.

This has two main implications for my own engagement with personal accounts of the experience of violation. First, it is not possible to presume the existence of a pre-discursive individual – the lesbian – who possesses a foundational account of what 'really' took place. If an account of experience is not simply a raw or unadulterated reflection of reality, it is necessary to acknowledge the multiple ways in which it is mediated and rendered intelligible to the woman in question (as I shall shortly discuss, the processes of interviewing and analysing add another layer to this mediation). This does not mean that experience does not exist or is not important. But it does mean that accounts of experience give us access to a form of reality that is discursively constituted. Some time ago, Haraway identified the dilemma this raises for feminist researchers: how do we simultaneously undertake 'a critical practice for recognising our own "semiotic technologies" for making meanings, *and* a no-nonsense commitment to faithful accounts of a "real" world' (Haraway 1988: 579)?[12] Haraway's (1990) answer to this question (which she depicts through the partiality and hybridity of the cyborg image) has been to argue that it is not necessary to essentialise or ontologise the notion of women's experience, as an 'absolute' or 'given', if we commit ourselves to seeing it as a 'construct with important political implications for feminism' (Hekman 1999: 49). In other words, the 'realities' that women recount during interview represent neither the objective facts of violence, in the positivist sense, nor the origins for a superior knowledge of violence, as in some standpoint models. But they do represent a verbal communication of a specific form of violation, pain, insult or injury, as it was experienced through particular fields of knowledge, and conveyed during interview. In recognising the discursive histories that inform accounts of violation, this approach loosens experience from its foundational and humanist assumptions. At the same time, however, it acknowledges that the experience of violence has, what Butler (1993) might call, an 'undeniable' materiality that can neither escape discourse, nor be fully reduced to it; experiences of violation arise out of the perpetual negotiation between materiality and discourse. In this sense, it is irrelevant that accounts of experience do not represent an (ultimately non-existent) objective depiction of violence. It is the perception that one has been violated, and the particular ways in which this is understood, that represents the kind of 'evidence' that demands feminist critique.

The second implication of recognising the human subject as the product of a constitutive process is the requirement that this places upon us to acknowledge that identity is itself the manifestation of subjectivities that are 'produced at the intersection of meaning with experience' (de Lauretis 1986: 8). In other words, we need to recognise that experience is a fundamental 'technology' through which individuals develop a sense of self (for example, a sense of one's self as lesbian or gay). Accounts of experience thus enjoin us to critically examine not only their historical and cultural conditions of existence, but also their functions within the constitutive processes of subjectification. Scott, speaking from the academic discipline of history, puts it like this:

> It is not individuals who have experience, but subjects who are constituted through experience. Experience in this definition then becomes not the origin of . . . explanation, nor the authoritative (because seen or felt) evidence that grounds what is known, but rather that which we seek to explain, that about which knowledge is produced.
>
> (1991: 780)

For Scott, individuals do not simply 'have' experience because it is experience that produces the very sense of being an individual. In other words, experience is both a cultural construct and an ongoing process out of which the subject is constructed as a particular type of individual and takes on a particular identity. This leads Scott to argue that experience is 'at once always already an interpretation and something that needs to be interpreted' (1991: 797).

But how are we to go about the intellectual enterprise of interpretation? It seems logical to suggest that we first need to know what these experiences look like. We need to render them visible so that they are available for interpretation. Yet, Scott argues against this. She suggests that the 'project of making experience visible precludes critical examination of the workings

25

of the ideological system itself, its categories of representation . . . its premises about what these categories mean and how they operate' (1991: 778). In order to understand what Scott actually means we need to remind ourselves of the different ways in which the nexus between visuality and knowledge can be conceptualised. That is, we need to return to the distinction between different types of research that I drew in the beginning of this chapter. On the one hand, we have research that uses observation as a technique for discovering knowledge. Such knowledge is assumed to *be* self-evident. On the other hand, we have research that uses observation as a medium for thinking about the ways in particular knowledges *become* self-evident.

In the first instance, the project of rendering experience visible is assumed to be sufficient in itself; visible experiences represent a foundational and unmediated knowledge. It is this approach to the visibility of experience that, according to Scott, is insufficient to, and incompatible with, the project of critiquing that same experience. For Scott, the things that the subject sees and feels (experiences) are not direct or authoritative apprehensions of the real world. They are deeply mediated forms of knowledge, interpretations of events that contribute to the ways in which we develop a sense of identity. The academic project of simply rendering experience visible assumes that such knowledge does not demand some form of explanation. In doing so, it reproduces naturalised understandings of the subject who 'has' this experience; it 'establishes the prior existence of individuals' (Scott 1991: 782).

In the second understanding of the nexus between visibility and knowledge, visibility is the medium that makes experience, and the events depicted, available for critique. Critique and visibility are not mutually exclusive because visibility is *a part of* critique; it is encapsulated within it. In this way, the critique of experience encompasses, and is dependent upon, the visibility of that experience: in order to critique personal accounts of experience we must first look at what it is that we are critiquing. This involves highlighting the particular forms and characteristics of violence as they are experienced in a given account. This is especially so when we are talking about a phenomenon like homophobia-related violence, where the experience of violation is understood as the product of the hierarchical relations that exist between different categories. For example, for a violent incident to be experienced as homophobic the person recounting that experience must have a particular perception of the relation between homosexuality and heterosexuality. Identity is not the origin of this experience, but it is one of the mediums through which these events are interpreted (interpretations that, in turn, make their own contribution to the way in which identity categories are reproduced and occupied).

In effect, rendering experience visible, via the observations that are made in a research setting, is not an adequate project in itself. It demands that we recognise the interpretive mechanisms that produce that particular experience of violation and/or the ways in which these interpretations are taken up in the panoptic processes of subjectification; interpretive processes which are reinterpreted through the interview environment of academic analysis. Hence, research that makes accounts of violation visible also requires us to take a fresh look at the violating events depicted *in* those accounts so as to examine their 'underlying, unseen concepts'. This is not a matter of assuming that the accounts of those who experience violation provide us with a superior take on the 'reality' of violence, of the kind that Hartsock (1983a) might claim. But, rather, as Hekman suggests in her Foucauldian rendition of the 'vision' of the oppressed, that the partial and situated perspectives of those who experience violation represent a discourse, or counter-discourse, in themselves. This kind of counter-discourse may seek to 'break the hold of the hegemonic discourse', but this does not bring it 'closer to "reality" than the discourse it exposes.' At the most, it may be 'closer to a definition of a less repressive society' (Hekman 1999: 34).

Looking at homophobia-related violence: interviews and critique

I have suggested that my engagement with interview accounts of experience involves, in a very basic sense, two steps. First, is the task of rendering experience visible so as to make it available for critique: observing experiences of homophobia-related violence in some way, finding out what they look like, making them available for interpretation. Second, is the task of looking at this experience through the notion of subjectification: critiquing the cultural contexts that shape experiences of violence, and analysing the ways in which they feed into the constitution of sexual subject positions. The first step demands that the second be undertaken, while the second step cannot take place without the first.

This raises the question of how I actually translate this epistemological approach into the practicalities of empirical research. How do I do this research? These are methodological questions: questions of research design and analysis. In this last section of the chapter I would like to outline how I have gone about the tasks of rendering experience visible and looking for the interpretive mechanisms that produce, and emerge from, these experiences. In some ways, this discussion requires a slight shift in emphasis, a move away from the abstract approach to knowledge production that I have taken above, toward a more practical account of actually doing interview research (the question of how interview material is interpreted probably falls somewhere in the middle of these two styles). Reflecting the dual steps outlined above, I divide this discussion into two sections. The first is an overview of the research project that enables me to bring particular accounts of homophobia-related violence and hostility into our line of vision. The second section explains how I go about critiquing these accounts of violence.

Rendering homophobia-related violence visible

The research project upon which this book is premised was designed to explore the phenomenon of violence and hostility that is related to homophobic attitudes. I began this research with a desire to explore some of the more extreme states of dominance that emerge from particular relations of subjugation, and to do this from the perspective of those who perceive themselves to be on the 'receiving end' of such subjugation. This is why I chose to examine homophobia-related violence. I saw it as an excessive manifestation of the broader heterosexism that continues to infuse contemporary western societies. Although I sought to contribute to our knowledge of violence and homophobia in general, I responded to the dearth of research on women's accounts of homophobia-related violence by narrowing my interview subjects to lesbians alone. My intention was not to just add the experiences of those who had been excluded to an existing knowledge base. It was to engage with the formation and function of these experiences and, in doing so, to critique some common assumptions about this type of violence.

I decided that qualitative research offered the most effective means of 'observing' homophobia-related violence and hostility. I designed a project that would enable to me to undertake a series of interactive, recursive individual and group interviews with a diversity of participants across the Australian state of Victoria.[13] I used a multi-pronged strategy to locate these participants. First, I made public calls for participants through several avenues: I published articles in lesbian and gay community newspapers; I organised the insertion of a pamphlet in the mailout of a major gay and lesbian organisation; and I distributed the same pamphlet to all major lesbian and gay organisations in Victoria. Second, I delivered numerous public presentations at lesbian and gay community groups. Coming at various stages of the research, these presentations had a dual purpose: to call for further participants in the research, and to provide feedback to the lesbian and gay communities about hostility and violence. Third, adopting a chain referral technique, I was referred to several interviewees by women I had already interviewed.

A total of seventy-five women actively participated in semi-structured individual interviews or focus groups.[14] These were conducted between 1993 and 1996.[15] Forty-seven women were interviewed either on their own or as a couple. The remaining women participated in one of three focus groups.[16] These groups were designed to ensure that women who may otherwise have been under-represented were included in the research. They were conducted with a young lesbian group, an outer-suburban lesbian social group, and a provincial lesbian social group (which included a number of women who lived in rural areas). All of the women who participated saw themselves as lesbian, gay or queer at the time of their participation.[17]

The broad objective of the interviews was to archive experiences and perceptions of verbal hostility, written aggression, threats, physical violence, and sexual violence that appeared, in the eyes of the person interviewed, to be related in some way to negativity, on the part of the perpetrator, towards homosexuality. I refer to this as homophobia-related violence or hostility. The interviews also focused upon the ways in which these experiences and perceptions interacted with other facets of identity, such as gender and ethnicity. My questions were designed to elicit accounts of the kinds of hostilities that are experienced as violating, the corporeal and cultural factors that might feed into this violence, the implications of such violence for understandings of personal safety, and the ways in which these understandings are taken up in the subjectivities of this group of women. Within these general parameters, interview schedules were deliberately flexible in order to maximise participants' contributions and to take account of their diverse experiences and interpretations. My intention was for the participants to gradually highlight some of the ways in which the field of inquiry might usefully evolve, thereby allowing emergent issues to be incorporated into subsequent interviews.[18]

The women I interviewed were stimulating, challenging and generous. I am deeply indebted to them, not just for the stories they narrated but equally for the opinions they expressed and the questions they asked of me. As a group, these women ranged in age from 14 to 57 years. Most were more than 30 but less than 40 years old. They came from a broad cross-section of geographical and residential areas throughout the state. Some lived in inner-city and suburban areas spread across Melbourne, as well as satellite towns on the edges of the city. Others lived in provincial towns (both large and small) and rural areas of the state. At least sixteen of the women had biological children, most from previous heterosexual relationships. Others had become mothers (biological and nonbiological) since being in a lesbian relationship. There was great diversity among these women in terms of social and economic background and lifestyle. My knowledge of factors in the women's lives such as employment, education, area of residence, parents' background and classbased identity, leads me to characterise them as a group who represent a broad cross-section of class divisions in Australia (McGregor 1997). The main social-economic group not represented, to my knowledge, was the very wealthy sector of Australian society. In conducting the interviews, I was careful to avoid a heavy bias towards university-educated, middle-class, professional women. For example, it is interesting to note the diversity among these women in terms of occupation/income source, which included: cook, gardener, recipient of unemployment benefit, public servant, nurse, artist, cleaner, psychologist, recipient of supporting parent's benefit, clerk, postal worker, computer analyst, fitter and turner, engineer, teacher, carpenter-joiner, manager, community worker, and viticulturalist. Determining ethnicity or immigrant/non-immigrant status during group interviews was not feasible with all participants (this was the same for socio-economic background). This leads me to confine my characterisation of ethno-religious

and national background to the women who participated in nongroup interviews. Of these forty-seven women, the majority were from an Anglo-Saxon
or Anglo-Celtic background. Fourteen identified themselves as immigrants
to Australia (three of these stated that they were from the English-speaking
backgrounds of Great Britain, Scotland and New Zealand). The other eleven
women stated that they belonged to a non-English-speaking or 'non-Anglo'
background. They described their heritage as: Greek Australian (two
women); Chinese (two women); Hong Kong Chinese; Dutch Australian (two
women); Israeli; Jewish; Indian; and Anglo-Indian.

As should be apparent from the above discussion, I also commenced this
research from the premise that all knowledge is situated. This is not just a
question of the supposedly unconscious factors that shape experience, as if
individuals are somehow influenced by discourses of which they have no
awareness. The situatedness of knowledge also has implications for the
practice and outcomes of research itself. It means, among other things, that
the researcher (the knower) is directly implicated in the knowledge he or she
produces. In other words, my own subjectivity fundamentally shapes the
picture of homophobia-related violence that I produce, according to the
assumptions that I make, the questions that I ask, the concepts and excerpts
I prioritise, the analysis that I compose, and the interpretations that I generate. In addition, such knowledge is always situated within the particularities
of the interview environment itself. The dynamics of each and every
interview, including questions of personality and timing, will influence the
things that interviewees tell me, how they tell me, the slant they put on a
given event, what they leave out, what they forget, and what they remember.
As will become apparent throughout this book, the women I interviewed
frequently provided a theoretically and politically informed account of their
own experience. This does not mean that discursive contributions to subjectivity are always transparent. But it does mean that research participants
often engage in deliberate interpretations and analyses of their own
experience. In short, the research process itself plays a direct, yet indeter-
minate, function in shaping the knowledge that is produced.

Looking for statements of violence

Having rendered experiences of homophobia-related violence visible, there are
various methods that I could use to interpret these accounts. For example, if I
followed traditional discourse or conversation analysis I might seek to create
typologies that uncover the 'depths or hidden semantic weight' behind the
interview account (Rose 1996a: 178). The tendency of such analysis to assume
that there is a deeper or universal meaning to a particular text prompts me to
take a somewhat different approach. Borrowing from the archaeo-genealogical
tradition (Foucault 1980; Kendall and Wickham 1999), I look to interview
accounts for *statements* of the knowledge regimes that fashion, as well as

emanate from, the experience of violence. I identify these statements according to the connections and associations between *interpretive repertoires* within these accounts. Both facets of this analysis deserve some explication.

A statement, as I invoke it here, is not simply a word, phrase or sentence. It refers to the clusters, groupings and regularities of language and action that form around particular objects (Foucault 1972). If we take homosexuality as an example of one such object, we might choose to understand statements as the elements, facets or components of discourse about homosexuality. Certain events will become statements according to the way in which they are articulated within a web of associated fields of knowledge. To put this another way, things that are said and done – violent words and actions for example – are capable of making a statement about homosexuality, or other objects, because they are read and rendered intelligible via closely connected bodies of knowledge. Indeed, words and actions only become statements within the context of other associated statements. As Rose suggests, this is not a question of what 'a word, a sentence, a story, a book "means" or what it "signifies" but rather "what it functions with, in connection with what other multiplicities its own are inserted and metamorphised"' (Rose 1996a: 178).[19] It is these connections which facilitate the transformation of words and actions into statements:

> Every statement is specified in this way: there is no statement in general, no free, neutral, independent statement; but a statement always belongs to a series or a whole, always plays a role among other statements, deriving support from them and distinguishing itself from them: it is always part of a network of statements, in which it has a role, however minimal it may be, to play.
>
> (Foucault 1972: 99)

This relation between statements and wider fields of knowledge is, therefore, neither linear nor benign. As Deleuze puts it, statements tend to 'coagulate around a corpus' of power relations: for example, around the historical regimes of knowledge that have facilitated the emergence and regulation of 'the homosexual'. At the same time, however, statements are also formations 'thrown up by the corpus in question' (Deleuze 1988: 17–18); for example, the creation of 'the homosexual' as a particular type of individual has generated its own statements about sexuality and gender. In this sense, discourse is both an 'origin' and an 'effect' of regularities and groupings of statements.[20] In short, statements are conceptual formations that emerge from particular events (such as violent words and actions), and that simultaneously provide the discursive context for comprehension of those events. As we shall see, they are sometimes overlapping, sometimes contradictory formations that reproduce associated fields of knowledge and which cannot function in the absence of these fields.

Interpretative, or linguistic, repertoires provide me with a practical means of identifying these statements. The notion of linguistic repertoires was initially employed to denote 'a 'limited range of terms used in particular stylistic and grammatical constructions . . . [often] organised around specific metaphors and figures of speech (tropes)' (Potter and Wetherell 1987: 149).[21] Linguistic repertoires are, thus, reconstructions of the various discursive patterns that individuals draw upon to express themselves. In this way they signal the possible statements that make up a given discourse. Discourse, however, is never a question of language alone. An act itself, its context and characteristics, can also highlight discursive patterns and presumptions (for example, whether the violence depicted is sexual or not). We can refer to this combination of contextual and linguistic patterns as an 'interpretive repertoire' (Potter and Wetherell 1987).

I look to interpretive repertoires for visible signs, or clues, about the statements of violence. They allow me to unearth and highlight the fields of knowledge through which certain events are experienced as a form of violation and, in turn, enable such events to make statements of their own. That is, they allow me to critique the accounts of experience that I have made visible. Whilst my access to repertoires is always mediated through interview accounts, my interest is not confined to the ways that interviewees interpret that experience. I am also concerned with repertoires within the violent incident itself, with the patterns of perpetrator language and behaviour depicted in the women's accounts. Certainly, there is no pre-determined or universal reading to be made here. Given that violence is, by definition, intrinsically antagonistic, I am, nonetheless, prepared to look to these accounts for the kinds of social assumptions that enable violent statements to come into existence in the first place; for example, as I shall argue in Chapter 2, certain assumptions about sexuality and gender make it possible for violent assertions of disorder to be made about lesbian women.

This is not the same as asking, what 'caused' the violence? When we ask causation questions we assume that we can establish a direct relationship between causes and their effects, a relationship which depends upon our ability to know the 'real' motives of the individual who is violent. The language that perpetrators use and the patterns of their behaviour do not tell us this. But these repertoires do allow us to contemplate the cultural and political contexts that sanction the circulation of particular forms of language in relation to particular violent situations and, in turn, enable such situations to even begin to say something about the object of that violence. Highlighting violent encounters as the events of a discourse in this way must, in the long run, also demand that we ask how such events function as techniques and practices in the processes of sub-jectification.

Conclusion

Notions of visuality echo throughout contemporary practices of knowledge production in complex and contradictory ways. Panopticism is an example of this. The design of Bentham's original panoptic structure reminds me that methods of observation provide researchers with access to experience, such as the experience of violation, that might otherwise not be available to us. Yet, in Foucault's version of the panopticon, observation does not just tell us these kinds of things, it is simultaneously a practice that produces such things. Here, the notion of visuality is implicated in the very processes of subjectification, in the idea that we become certain types of individuals according to the ways in which we are made visible within particular knowledge systems. Panopticism thus reminds me that we cannot treat experience as a transparent form of knowledge. The project of rendering accounts of violence visible is not a project in itself. It is ever only part of a larger critique. This critique demands not just that we look *at* these accounts of experience, but that we look *behind* and *beyond* them; that is, that we critique both the discursive histories and corporeal specificities out of which the act of violence and the experience of violation is constructed, as well as the contribution such violence might make to the ways in which subject positions are formulated and occupied.

In a general sense, this leads me to engage with interview accounts of experiences around homophobia-related violence in two primary ways throughout this book. First, I seek to recognise the cultural contexts through which certain events are enacted and understood as a form of violation; remembering that these accounts of experience are always formulated within the research process and shaped by the ways in which the researcher represents and analyses them. Second, I consider the functions that such incidents perform in the constitution of, and resistance to, subjectivities and subject positions. In doing this, I attempt to remain attuned to the fact that it is not always possible to make a neat separation between that which produces the experience of violation (what goes into it), and that which the experience of violence produces (what comes out of it). Sometimes it is necessary to look at one through the other; for example, to look at the discursive implications of violence by looking at the cultural contexts that enable it to make a discursive statement in the first place. Often this may be a question of the processes by which accounts of experience flow into, and out of, particular statements. Hence, I explore some of the ways in which the events depicted in these accounts enact and reproduce the very fields of knowledge out of which the experience emerges; for example, how violence becomes a form of knowledge in itself.

In a less obvious sense, the panoptic diagram also brings to mind a significant issue in the analysis of violence. On the one hand, the panopticon stands as a template for a fluid and dispersed model of disciplinary power.

But, on the other hand, it is an image patterned by the many lines of delineation that constitute it: the lines that divide the tower from the cells, the cells from each other, the inside from the outside, the margin from the centre, the inspector from the inmate, and so on. It is this image of fluid, yet patterned, surfaces that reminds me of the importance of remaining attuned to the ways in which the discursivities of violence represent multiple and shifting configurations, at the same time that they so often mirror the very same patterns of subjugation that we see in other social relations. These are issues that arise throughout this book.

2

DISORDER

What does homophobia-related hostility and violence towards lesbians look like? Would we recognise it if we looked for the characteristics that are commonly associated with violence against women? Perhaps not. What if we looked at the popular profile of anti-gay violence? Again, perhaps not. In this chapter I bring lesbian accounts of hostility and violence within our field of vision. My purpose in doing so is quite simple. I wish to create a picture of the kinds of incidents that lesbian women recount when they talk about hostility and violence that is, in some way, related to homophobic attitudes. In particular, I am interested in the regularities of speech and action that pattern these violent incidents. By unearthing these regularities, I hope to highlight both the kinds of thinking that are conducive to the commission of such violence, and the comments that this violence makes upon the nature of lesbian sexuality within contemporary regimes of sexuality and gender.

I begin the chapter by considering what we can learn about homophobia-related violence towards lesbians from two broad fields of research: gendered violence and homophobic violence. As the previous chapter makes clear, I am willing to take 'the risk of objectivity' that comes with quoting some of the facts and figures of this empirical research in order to get a grasp – even if a very slippery one – on the parameters of the problem.[1] I discuss the contributions that this research makes to our understanding of this violence, as well as some of the presumptions contained within the literature. I suggest that lesbian experiences of homophobia-related violence need to be conceptualised as a conjunction of these two fields of research: a question of both gender and sexuality.

In order to think about some of the ways in which regimes of sexuality and gender come together in the enactment and experience of this type of violence, I consider interview accounts of specific incidents of violence. I draw these accounts from an Australian research project into lesbian perceptions and experiences of homophobia-related hostility and violence; this project is outlined in Chapter 1. The incidents recounted are diverse. They include hostile words, threatening behaviours and violent acts. As experiences of violation, they 'speak' to each of these women in different ways. As will become apparent, however, the connection between these incidents lies in the way each involves an expression of some kind of anti-homosexual or, more specifically, anti-lesbian sentiment. Indeed, given the ways in which presumptions around both sexuality and gender interact in these incidents, it might be more precise to describe them as anti-lesbian rather than homophobia-related. I have, however, chosen to use the latter, somewhat broader phrase. In keeping with the rest of this book, I believe that this terminology allows me to emphasise both the sexual and gendered facets of this violence, without over-determining the extent to which perpetrators are presumed to have one specific motivation (they are 'against' lesbians). My focus on gender and sexuality in this chapter is not intended to provide an exhaustive account of the kinds of violence that lesbians talk about. The idea that certain behaviours are *related* to homophobia paves the way for exploring how such violence might interact with other systems of difference. For example, in Chapter 3, I consider homophobia-related violence in the context of racial specificity.

In the previous chapter, I suggested that the project of making the experience of violence visible is insufficient in itself. This is because experience is always shaped by cultural and corporeal contexts and, simultaneously, gives rise to particular discursive products of its own. In other words, the experience of violence is both an interpretation of certain events and a form of knowledge that is itself in demand of interpretation. It is these interpretative processes that I focus on in this chapter. In particular, I am interested in the discursive functions that violence towards lesbians performs, and the sexual and gendered discourses that enable it to do this. As discussed in Chapter 1, this is a question of looking for the particular statements that violence makes. A statement, in the sense that I employ it here, refers to the conceptual formations that emerge from the enactment and the experience of violence. In other words, a statement is one of the things that homophobia-related violence 'says' about its lesbian object, the message that it sends. Violence is only able to send such a message because of the ways in which it is rendered intelligible within closely associated fields of knowledge. For example, it is the connections between sexual desire and gender identity which mould the kind of statement that violence makes. Unearthing these statements is a case of looking for 'interpretive repertoires' within the accounts of experience that are under examination. By interpretive repertoires, I mean the linguistic and contextual patterns that are found in the incidents of violence described: for example, the kind of language that perpetrators regularly use or the types of violence they engage in. It is these repertoires that allow me to highlight the kinds of sexual and gendered assumptions that transform the words and actions of violence into a statement about lesbian sexuality.

This mode of interpretation means that at the same time that I go about the task of rendering experiences of violence visible, I look to the interview accounts of these experiences for clues or signs of the particular statements such violence makes. Specifically, I suggest that the statement that homophobia-related violence makes about lesbian sexuality is one of *disorder*; that is, homophobia-related violence makes a comment about the supposed disordered, or dislocated, nature of lesbian sexuality within contemporary sexual and gendered relations. I identify four repertoires around questions of homosexuality, female corporeality, and gender bifurcation that provide the social and linguistic 'ammunition', so to speak, for violence to do this. These repertoires are significant not just because they enable me to identify the kind of statement that violence makes. They are also the means by which the women who recount these incidents come to experience the violence as an expression of homophobic or anti-lesbian sentiment; that is, they are the mediums through which this violence is interpreted and accorded particular meanings. I refer to these repertoires as: dirt; hetero-sex; butch; and boy/girl. I discuss each in turn. Whilst I look for the ways in which these repertoires connect with each other to produce a statement of lesbian disorder, I should note that I explore the contradictions within and between them only in very minor ways. This is not because I am committed to providing a fixed picture of violence towards lesbians but, on the contrary, because my specific purpose in employing these examples is to highlight the importance of positioning this violence between regimes of gender and sexuality. Whilst it would certainly be possible to produce other, more subversive, readings of these accounts, my attention in this chapter is directed towards the derisive tone of this statement. Although I look to accounts of the experience of violation to do this, I am mindful that there is much more to be said about the interpretive mechanisms that produce this experience and the ways in which these interpretations contribute to the constitutive processes of subjectification. These issues are taken up in later chapters.

Things we already know
Gendered violence

To paint a picture of homophobia-related violence towards lesbians we might first turn to the feminist material on violence against women. Since the early 1970s research on men's violence towards women in western nations has been nothing short of tremendous, in terms of size, quality and influence. Although pre-feminist understandings of violence continue to haunt many popular and professional accounts, feminism has had a profound influence upon contemporary attitudes to the violence that women recount and the ways in which the body politic responds to it (the problem of men's sexual violence towards children has also been brought into the public arena). Prior to the second wave of the women's movement, men's violence towards women was understood within an individualised and pathologised framework that tended to shift responsibility away from the perpetrator and toward the victim. In documenting the histories of male violence, feminists created a space for women to voice their experiences and perceptions of violence in ways that challenged this image ('breaking the silence'). Nowadays, we are only too aware that crimes such as rape, domestic violence, and child sexual assault are not isolated, strange occurrences that take place between people who are 'not like us' (Edwards 1987; Dobash and Dobash 1979; Radford and Russell 1992). Instead, they are long-standing problems of massive cross-national proportions, intricately linked to each other through culturally specific patterns of female subjugation and male hegemony.

In addition to providing us with a conceptual framework for positioning violence within broader regimes of gender inequality – primarily via a structural model of patriarchal power – feminism has also given us a language for talking about violence. For example, the evolution of concepts such as 'the continuum of violence' (Kelly 1988) expose the connections that women make between different types of aggression, the fear and concern this can generate, and the consequent ability of violence to effect a form of social control (Hanmer and Saunders 1984; Stanko 1993). Similar arguments can be made about feminist-inspired terms such as 'survivor', 'domestic violence' and 'sexual harassment': terms that have allowed us to push and prod the concept of violence until it no longer signifies physical acts alone, but also denotes psychological and financial forms of abuse. At the same time that feminism has been expanding the meaning of violence, it has also been interrogating the representations of violence that we find in concepts such as 'sex crime' (Caputi 1988), 'serial killing' (Cameron and Fraser 1987), and 'battered woman syndrome' (Stubbs and Tolmie 1994).

None of this is to suggest that the battle against violence has been 'won': whilst there have been great advances in individual and institutional responses to violence, there are few suggestions that incidents of gendered violence are any less pervasive today than they were thirty years ago. Nor do I wish to suggest that our interventions around violence have been smooth sailing. Some of the most heated debates and polarisations within feminism have centred upon questions of violence, such as the contested relationship between pornography and violence (Read 1989; Brown 1992; Dworkin 1981), the ability of a feminist model of patriarchy to account for the way in which violence is refracted through regimes of class and race (Patel 1997), and, more recently, the capacity of feminist theory to respond to the violence that women perpetrate (Kelly 1996).

Although it is often taken for granted that 'lesbians are everywhere' within western feminism, the degree to which the literature on men's violence towards women is informed by accounts from non-heterosexual women is minimal. There is a small body of feminist research that prioritises lesbian accounts of violence, to which I will shortly return. However, the vast majority of feminist literature on violence yields few insights into the specific problem of homophobia-related violence towards lesbians.[2] Ironically, it is possible that the strongest feminist recognition of violence in the lives of lesbians has come through recent research that addresses, not violence by men, but violence within lesbian relationships.[3] One of the implications of this lacuna has been the evolution of a series of feminist statements about the violence that men enact upon adult women. Take, for example, the feminist axioms that women are at greater risk of violence in their homes than they are on the street, or that women are most likely to experience violence at the hands of men they know, especially their partners, rather than strangers. These statements capture many heterosexual women's encounters with violence, but do they sit so easily with lesbian accounts of homophobia-related violence? Let me consider this question by looking at some of the things that we do know about homophobia-related violence towards lesbians.

Homophobic violence

There is now an important, albeit small, body of literature on what has become known as 'violence against gay men and lesbians' or 'homophobic violence'. Although violence that involves enmity toward homosexuality is not a recent phenomenon – the most notorious example in modern times being the Nazi persecution of homosexuals, particularly men, during the 1930s and 1940s – systematic knowledge about violence directed towards individuals, or organisations, on the basis of their assumed homosexuality, or homosexual affiliations, is still in its infancy stage. Recent explorations into the field can be seen as part of a broader movement towards the construction and popularisation of concepts of hate crime or bias crime.[4] While crimes of prejudice – especially racist violence and ethno-religious genocide – have long been recognised, concepts such as hate crime encourage us to make associations between forms of violence that are quite distinct, but which may find a common frame of reference in the intolerance of difference.

Although methodological limitations in this body of research prevent us from drawing the kind of firm conclusions we might like, it does provide a rough description of a type of hostility that many lesbians and gay men report having experienced at some point during their lives.[5] The results from large victimisation surveys undertaken on homophobic violence in a number of English-speaking countries are notable here for their sheer consistency. Surveys during the 1980s and 1990s in the United States, Canada, Great Britain, Australia, and New Zealand suggest, in approximate terms, that: 70–80 per cent of lesbians and gay men report experiencing verbal abuse in public on the basis of their sexuality; 30–40 per cent report threats of violence; 20 per cent of gay men report physical violence; and 10–12 per cent of lesbians report physical violence.[6] Most of these surveys also record incidents where lesbians and gay men have been chased or followed, pelted with objects, spat upon, have had their property vandalised and, in the case of lesbians, have been sexually assaulted. Even more disturbing is the

Australian and North American research that highlights cases of homicide, particularly against gay men, where the victim's sexuality appears to be a significant factor (Tomsen 1997; Brenner and Ashley 1995; Howe 1997). Although it is exceptionally difficult to be definite, anecdotal suggestions that violence towards lesbians and gay men is on the rise, perhaps specifically in relation to HIV/AIDS, also find some support in quantitative research (Anti-Discrimination Board of NSW 1992; Dean, Wu and Martin 1992).

In this body of research, a picture emerges of homophobic violence. The typical homophobic incident is said to be a random street assault perpetrated by a group of young males who are strangers to the victim. The victim is often alone or with one or two other friends at the time. In cases of physical violence or verbal abuse, the incidents are more likely to occur at night and tend to take place in public places such as the street, car-parks, parks, and beats. This picture appears to be consistent across nations (Cox 1994; The Safe Neighbourhood Unit 1992; National Coalition of Anti-Violence Programs 1999).

It is difficult not to be struck by the difference between this profile of homophobic violence and the picture of gendered violence that I referred to earlier; one of the few common denominators is that both types of violence are, like most violence, committed by men. If this image of homophobic violence accurately represents lesbian accounts of violence then it suggests that homophobic violence and gendered violence are such discrete phenomena that we will learn little about homophobia-related violence towards lesbians from looking at the literature on violence against women. I wish to suggest, however, that in addition to the obvious quantitative distinctions between lesbian and gay accounts of violence (for example, gay men report greater levels of physical assault from strangers than lesbians), there are also signs that this 'typical' incident of homophobic violence may be a more accurate depiction of the violence that gay men report, than it is of the violence that lesbians report. For example, several Australian and US studies on lesbian reports of homophobia-related violence indicate that although much of this aggression does appear to involve random street-based attacks, a significant proportion of incidents take place at home or work, involve on-going campaigns of harassment, and are committed by one, older man acting alone, who may be known to the woman (Lesbian and Gay Anti-Violence Project 1992; Baird 1997; Mason 1997b; von Schulthess 1992).[7] Given the exploratory and limited nature of much research in this field, it is not possible to say that gay men don't experience these types of incidents as well. It is only possible to say that the popular profile of homophobic violence, whilst certainly pertinent to a lot of violence towards lesbians, may fail to capture a not insignificant proportion of the problem.

Returning to my earlier question, regarding the extent to which the most prominent maxims about women's accounts of male violence are applicable to lesbian accounts of homophobia-related violence, two things seem apparent from this literature. First, much homophobia-related violence towards lesbians does fall outside of these parameters. Indeed, research that makes broad comparisons between violence towards lesbians and violence towards women as a whole suggests that the former is more likely to involve a stranger and, according to one study, may actually be more frequent (Comstock 1991; Price Waterhouse Urwick 1995).[8] Second, there is, nonetheless, a proportion of homophobia-related violence towards lesbians that does have much in common with other types of violence that women recount, such as sexual assault or domestic violence. These commonalities are most apparent in relation to: the 'private' domain in which the violence takes place, in particular at or near home; the existence of some prior relationship between the perpetrator and the victim (even if only as acquaintances or ex-partners rather than current partners); a perpetrator who acts on his own; a perpetrator who is not necessarily a teenager or young man; and the ongoing nature of some of the hostility. There is little doubt that these kinds of comparisons are fraught with methodological limitations – not the least of which is the fusion of physical violence and verbal abuse in some of the research – which minimise the extent to which we can rely upon any quantitative results. However, the significance of these comparisons has less to do with quantitative differences, and more to do with the implication that homophobia-related violence towards lesbians is typical of neither gendered violence nor homophobic violence. Neither is it atypical. This is not a problem in itself. It only becomes one when we try to sequester violence in ways that restrict its complexities and contradictions to the singularity of one identity-based power relation: either gender *or* sexuality.

Explanatory accounts of violence

A tendency towards singular, or universal, ways of thinking becomes noticeable in explanatory accounts of violence. In the case of research that focuses upon violence towards lesbians and gay men (whether it is within a psychological or socio-political framework), the inclination is to position anti-homosexual sentiment as the paramount context within which the violence erupts. This is not to say that gender is ignored but, rather, that it becomes a fairly neutral variable in the definition of homophobia. For example, whilst homophobic violence is often said to reflect the heterosexist belief that homosexuality violates gender norms, the different implications that gender, as a sexualised power relation *between* men and women, might have for violence towards lesbians and violence towards gay men are often glossed over (Harry 1990; Comstock 1991). With some notable exceptions (Herek 1986, 2000), the literature on homophobic violence continues to allow sexuality to subsume the relevance of gender.

The small amount of literature, primarily feminist in orientation, that focuses exclusively on homophobia-related violence towards lesbians often mirrors this kind of argument by reducing the violence to a question of misogyny or sexism, thereby minimising its connections to violence towards gay men (von Schulthess 1992; Pharr 1988). In arguing that gender inequality can fully explain all facets of homophobic sentiment that is directed towards lesbians, this approach presumes that regimes of sexuality are employed *by* regimes of gender, not that they function in tandem *with* them. This analysis is not unique to research on homophobia-related violence towards lesbians but, instead, takes its lead from the tendency of much feminist literature to engage with questions of sexuality only as they relate to heterosexuality. For example, it is true that 'compulsory heterosexuality' has long been identified as a crucial ingredient, sometimes *the* crucial ingredient, in men's violence towards women. Yet, the significance of hetero-sexuality, as an institution, has generally been restricted to its function as a medium in the subordination of women (MacKinnon 1983; Hanmer 1990; Rich 1980). In other words, regimes of sexuality are deemed to be relevant only in so far as they denote heterosexual practices and, in turn, the ways in which these contribute to the maintenance of traditional notions of mascu-linity and femininity. Concepts of 'heter-reality' and 'hetero-patriarchy' – and the ways they have been picked up in violence discourse – may seek to capture the importance of heterosexuality for gender relations but they still reduce the significance of sexuality to one of male dominance alone; it is merely a question of whether this dominance is articulated as hetero-sexuality, as masculinity, as patriarchy, or as hetero-patriarchy (Raymond 1986; Hester 1992; Hanmer, Radford and Stanko 1989). The articulation of sexuality solely as a matter of men's power over women leaves little room for considering the ways in which heterosexuality also represents the privileged half of a heterosexual/homosexual binary; a binary that provides a crucial cultural context for the violence that is directed towards lesbians and gay men. This does not mean that psycho-social systems of gender inequality, and/or the social construction of masculinity, are not cogent rationales for the vast proportion of men's violence towards women. But, to put it simply, it does suggest that they tell only one half of the story when it comes to the violence that heterosexual men commit towards homosexual women, where sexual preference appears to be a major contributing factor.

The different bodies of literature on gendered violence and homophobic violence, and the few places where the two come together, offer an invaluable form of knowledge about homophobia-related violence towards lesbians. They provide entry points for thinking about the cultural contexts out of which such violence emerges. If, however, we wish to pursue this line of inquiry, it is crucial that we resist the kinds of polarised distinctions that reduce violence towards lesbians to a question of *either* gendered violence *or* homophobic violence. This is not to suggest that these fields of literature are somehow wrong in their accounts of violence. It simply means that we must be careful to recognise the normative effects of any body of literature. We must always assess the extent to which 'typical' scenarios of violence pre-suppose a universal object of that violence, and to what extent these scenarios are indicative of the accounts of violence we wish to consider.

Enunciating the field: repertoires of disorder

I have suggested above that we need to understand homophobia-related violence towards lesbians as a question of an interaction between regimes of sexuality and gender. This begs the question of how these discourses actually come together in the enactment and experience of this violence. If, as I have suggested, it is important to recognise that violence is a form of behaviour that makes a statement about those it objectifies, this question then becomes: what kind of statement does homophobia-related violence make about lesbian sexuality? In this section of the chapter, I respond to this question by examining specific accounts of violent incidents. These accounts are drawn from the research project that I described in Chapter 1; this project involved a series of individual and group interviews with seventy-five lesbian women. The accounts that I discuss here have been selected because they are broadly representative of the incidents that these women talked about. I suggest that, when considered collectively, this type of violence endorses, and thereby maintains, the idea that lesbianism is an expression of disordered sexual desire and gender identity. I arrive at this position by looking at the assumptions that appear to undergird the enactment of this violence. I conceptualise these assumptions in terms of a series of repertoires: themes of language and behaviour that pattern the incidents described and which characterise lesbian sexuality as disordered. I refer to these repertoires as: dirt, hetero-sex, butch, and boy/girl. Before examining specific interview examples of each of these repertoires, I would like to make a few general comments about the ways in which hostility and violence featured in the lives of the women I interviewed.

Virtually every woman I interviewed stated that at some point during her life she had experienced a verbally, physically or sexually abusive reaction to her sexuality.[9] Accounts of hostility ranged from mildly annoying incidents, through to cases of extreme physical and sexual violence. These included: verbal insults on the street; physical and verbal abuse by family members; property damage; aggressive and insulting behaviour by neighbours; sexual assault by ex-partners; harassment and isolation at school; physical attacks by strangers; written insults and threats by work colleagues; and abusive mail. While some women ever only experienced occasional verbal abuse, others recounted a much more extensive history of abuse and/or physical assault. Generally speaking, this difference appeared to be primarily related to the extent to which the woman was 'out' about her sexuality; the less trouble a woman went to in order to hide her sexuality, the more likely she was to receive negative responses. As I shall argue, however, the logic of this correlation is tempered by other factors, particularly the woman's physical, or gendered, appearance.

Verbal insults and remarks feature prominently in this interview material. As might be expected, verbal abuse – whether from strangers, work colleagues or family – was much more pervasive than physical or sexual assaults. For some women, anti-lesbian insults and derogatory comments were so much a part of everyday life as to be readily dismissed, sometimes laughed away, as the 'price you pay' for being open about your sexuality. Although I will explore particular characteristics of this verbal hostility in more detail below, it is important to note initially that such remarks do not only insult or deride the woman they target, they also single her out as someone who is worthy of comment. Many women talked about receiving unwelcome remarks like 'Leso!', 'Hey, there's a couple of lesos!', or 'Check out the dykes' (such remarks typically arise when women demonstrate affection for other women in public). Whilst these kinds of comments may not be insulting *per se*, like their hostile counterparts they are an attempt to draw attention to the woman they address and, as such, they imply that lesbian sexuality warrants this kind of scrutiny. As Asquith (1999) suggests, this 'naming' only occurs because lesbian sexuality is perceived to be aberrant and, hence, noteworthy. For some women, the presumption of abnormality behind these acts of naming contains an implied insult in itself.

In keeping with the research results described earlier, men committed most hostile and violent incidents. In a small proportion of incidents, primarily verbal abuse, women were the aggressors. The exact age of perpetrators was not always known. In cases where it was known, many appeared to be quite young. Nonetheless, it was not unusual for hostility to come from men in their thirties, forties and fifties, especially in workplace, neighbourhood or family situations. Most incidents were perpetrated by one man acting alone, but, if the violence involved strangers or distant acquaintances, there were sometimes two, three or more involved. Hence, some women recounted incidents of random street violence where the aggressor was a complete stranger, while others positioned the violence in the context of a pre-existing relationship with the perpetrator. Whilst physically violent incidents tended to be one-off, verbal or written abuse was sometimes on-going. As might be expected, in on-going cases the woman was more likely to know the man responsible.

Dirt

One of the most common words used to insult this group of women was the adjective 'dirty': as in 'dirty leso', 'dirty lesbian'. This language was particularly prevalent in the more minor verbal hostilities that the women experienced, from time to time, in the school yard, on the street, at work, or at home. It was also a frequent accompaniment to acts of physical violence.

This association between lesbianism and dirt comes to the fore in the following account of violence. At the time of the incident, Julia was about 25 years old and had worked for some time in a shoe store. It was not unusual for Julia's girlfriend to meet her after work and they often kissed on the street. Once or twice, this had been observed by some of the men who regularly drank at the hotel next door. She recalls:

> I'd been working late and was waiting for Jill outside on the footpath. Both of these men came out and they started calling out stupid questions like: 'Are you waiting for your girlfriend?'; 'Are you a leso?'; 'Don't you know you can catch things that way?'; 'Would make anyone sick. Filthy habit.' So I told them to piss off and mind their own business. I was pretty rude about it. . . . So one of them walks up to me, lands his fist right in my face and says something like, 'I'm not gonna take crap like that from a dirty leso cunt like you.'. . . It was like they had just been egging me on so they'd have an excuse to lay into me.

Julia quit her job after this incident. She also made a complaint to the police. Despite the pain and humiliation inflicted, she felt 'hugely vindicated' when the man who assaulted her was convicted.

Julia's attackers coupled their physical assault with language that characterises lesbian sexuality as a dirty sexuality. In thinking about the sexual assumptions contained within this violent association between lesbianism and dirt, I am reminded of recent feminist appropriations of Douglas' (1966), originally anthropological, claim that human bodies are endowed with notions of dirtiness when they disrupt the expected social order. It is possible to trace this association to long-standing Judeo-Christian traditions surrounding marriage and procreation: traditions, which mark transgressive sexual practices such as homosexuality with the trope of physical and psychological dirtiness (Butler 1990). This characterisation of homosexual practices as unclean can be understood as both a means to achieve, and a consequence of, established regimes of sexual order. This is apparent in the way that Young (1990) applies Kristeva's (1982) argument about dirt, as that which marks the precarious nature of one's subjectivity, to the question of homosexual desire. She suggests that homosexuality is often understood as an in-between or ambiguous form of sexuality, one that represents a disruption to the sexual order of contemporary western societies. If this sexual order is to be maintained, homosexuality must be expelled from the realms of respectable sexual practices. Naming it as dirty provides the rationalisation for this to happen. In other words, once homosexuality is said to be unclean, the sense of personal revulsion that follows ensures that it will be excluded from legitimate social and political spheres.

Hence, the kind of violent denunciation that Julia describes is not simply an expression of the perpetrator's belief that homosexuality is dirty. The assertion that Julia is unclean is itself a product of the sense of disgust that emanates from the potential disruption that homosexuality represents to the sexual order, and which ensures that it will, in many instances, be rejected. Thus, the violent characterisation of Julia as dirty both reproduces cultural aversion for disorderly subjects – a repulsion of homosexuality – and provides the linguistic and interpretive justification for assuming that lesbians are deserving of violent treatment.

Yet, the sense of uncleanliness that attaches to the lesbian subject does not ensue solely from the 'unruliness and disorder' (Butler 1990: 131) that homosexuality represents for the institution of heterosexuality. When applied to lesbians, the adjective dirty also acquires much of its potency from images of unhygienic and secreting female bodies, images that have been primarily derived from western responses to menstrual blood, vaginal fluids, pregnancy and childbirth. Significantly, the cultural inscription of female corporeality in flowing, engulfing and leaking terms represents, according to Grosz, a sense of gendered disorder; a 'disorder that threatens all order' and that, in so doing, calls for confinement and containment (1994: 203). In short, the merger of femaleness and homosexuality embodied in the lesbian subject – the material exchange of female fluids that is assumed to take place in sexual acts between women – is likely to produce an intensified and duplex sense of disorder. In the words of Julia's attacker, 'cunts' are always dirty, but 'lesbian cunts' are likely to be excessively dirty.

Anxiety about unruly corporealities and transgressive sexual practices is not a matter of disorder *per se*. It is also a question of contagion. That is, it is tied to concerns that irregular subjectivities, such as homosexuality, might contaminate the minds and bodies of others. As Young (1990) has suggested, this fear may be acute in relation to homosexuality because of the perceived possibility that anyone can engage in homosexual practices. Whilst this fear may have more to do with maintaining the borders and boundaries of social order than it has to do with material notions of inter-personal contamination, it is important to note that anxiety about the polluting tendencies of homosexuality does play out in individual acts of violence. Thus, in Julia's account, lesbianism is a 'filthy habit' that will make 'normal people' 'sick' if they 'catch' it.[10] Moreover, this general anxiety now seems to have found a literal outlet in the fear that surrounds popular narratives of HIV/AIDS (Waldby 1996). Although gay men continue to bear the violent brunt of AIDS-phobia, there is plenty of evidence that the assumed nexus between homosexuality and AIDS also functions to 'dirty' lesbians in similar ways. This is apparent in the not uncommon taunts of: 'Dirty leso! Die of AIDS!'

Quite simply, acts of violence emerge from, and reproduce, established associations between lesbianism, dirt, and physical pollution. Dirty bodies and dirty sexual acts induce a sense of disgust. This disgust manifests in a fear of contamination, a fear that one may be polluted through close proximity to the source of this dirt. These negative associations are dependent upon assumptions about appropriate and desirable expressions of sexuality and gender. In evoking these connections, acts of violence are able to gesture towards the supposedly irregular nature of homosexuality in women.

Hetero-sex

The language of dirt functions as an effective insult because it invokes corporeally specific images of lesbian sexuality. Yet, as Grosz (1994) notes, the revulsion that greets female corporeality in western societies is matched by an ambivalent attraction to this same body. The implications for any woman who does not return the hetero-sexualised components of this attraction can, on occasion, be quite vicious. More specifically, lesbians, who by definition do not return such attraction, can find that they are placed in an awkward position simply by virtue of disclosing their sexual preference. I am thinking here of the tendency among some heterosexual men to respond to lesbianism as if it were a personal challenge to their own sexual desire and identity. In extreme circumstances this kind of response is played out in instances of sexual assault and attempted sexual assault. It is the sexual nature of these attacks that, together with accompanying language, forms a repertoire of its own about sex and gender. I call this repertoire 'hetero-sex'. Although it is difficult to generalise, this type of homophobia-related violence does not appear to involve the language of dirt that we see in earlier examples of violence. This may reflect an assumed, if ultimately unsustainable, antithesis between sexual desirability and the notion of dirt.

Fay worked for a major international environmental organisation. In the following interview excerpt she recalls an incident that took place at a work party, as well as the situation that developed subsequent to this. Several weeks prior to this party, Fay had disclosed her sexuality to some of her work colleagues. As a result, she had experienced uncomfortable questions from male colleagues, such as: 'Aren't you attracted to me?' and 'What do you "do" with your girlfriend?'

> On that night they had a party. . . . Jason [a work colleague] brought three friends with him. One of them came up to me. He asked me out and I turned him down and he was really quite okay about it. . . . And then about half an hour later, he came back and was saying to me, 'Oh my mate tells me you're gay and I want to do something about it' and 'All you need is a good fuck.' And he was drunk, but not staggering kind of drunk, but he was pretty drunk . . . and he attempted to rape me. It was pretty clear cut attempted rape, by which point I managed to get him off and get out of there. By the end of the next day it was public knowledge [at work] what had happened at that party. . . . And then within a week of that party, I started to get harassing phone calls at home: 'I know where you live.

47

I'm gonna get you.' This person knew that I'm a lesbian, knew that
I worked with _____, knew what hours I worked. . . . A man,
definitely a man. The phone calls were of a sexual nature and as time
went on they became more explicit. . . . I changed my phone
number and had it made silent and gave it to [no one but close
friends and the supervisor at work]. . . . Two weeks later the calls
started again. They were really threatening. . . . The calls centred
around my sexuality. And by this stage I was getting one of these
calls every night.

Fay recounts an experience of attempted rape and on-going harassment
and intimidation. Not surprisingly she became deeply distressed and fearful
for her safety. She located the source of the telephone harassment in her
workplace, resigned, and was eventually (after difficult negotiations) awarded
financial compensation by her employer. Although sexual assault was not
common among the women I interviewed, Fay is certainly not alone in her
experience. A small number of women recounted incidents of rape or
sexualised violence (such as touching a woman's breasts without her consent),
where questions of sexual preference were clearly implicated. The most
obvious of these involved sexual aggression by ex-partners upon being
informed that the woman was sexually involved with another woman or was
contemplating such involvement. For example, another woman recalled:

It's pretty typical that I didn't call it rape at the time, but the night
I told my boyfriend that I wanted to have an affair with Siobhan, he
forced me to have sex with him and to do things he knew I hated
. . . After he was finished he said something like, 'Well, at least
she'll never be able to do that to you'.

The implications of refusing heterosexuality come to the fore in this kind of
sexual violence. The behaviour itself is imbued with the perpetrator's
expectation that his own heterosexual desire should be reciprocated by the
woman in question. This is hardly unusual in acts of sexual violence. What is
noticeable about these incidents is that the violence appears to emerge out of
a belief that the woman's lack of interest in hetero-sex in general is an
unacceptable state of affairs that demands remedy: 'I want to do something
about it'; 'at least she'll never be able to do that to you.'
   Like other forms of sexual violence, this behaviour cannot be reduced to a
question of individual sexual desire but, instead, only takes place within
broader sexual economies. The history of these economies has been well
documented in terms of a 'sexual contract' that, in governing the institutions
of family and marriage, has positioned women as objects to be 'exchanged'
rather than subjects with full personal and civic freedoms (Pateman 1988;
Rubin 1975). Whilst this process of commodification has sometimes been

portrayed in overly determinist and universalist terms, it is possible that this history has an express legacy in extreme, seemingly atavistic, behaviours such as violence. Take, for example, Irigaray's assertion that the social and linguistic economies through which men attend to their own needs and desires endow women with a value according to the 'price' they fetch in the heterosexual market.[11] As objects of exchange, women are precluded from ever being agents of exchange in their own right: 'Men make commerce *of* them, but they do not enter into any exchanges *with* them' (Irigaray 1985: 172). This privilege is reserved for men. Despite Irigaray's assertion that this process of commodification is a deeply 'hom(m)o-sexual' practice between men, others have accentuated its debt to the institution of heterosexuality; a point Rubin made succinctly in 1975 when she said: 'Gender is not only an identification with one sex; it also entails that sexual desire be directed toward the other sex' (1975: 180). For Wittig, the social contract that governs the commodification of women is thus more accurately articulated as a 'heterosexual contract' (an interesting counterpart to Pateman's 'sexual contract'). This contract denotes a social economy where all human relationships, including gender, are ordered according to the demands of heterosexuality. Wittig refers to the obligatory dogma that flows into, and flows out of, this social order as 'the straight mind': 'you-will-be-straight-or-you-will-not-be' (1992: 28).

Whilst recent reformulations of gender have been highly critical of the way in which, among other things, Wittig's account of gender accords a material and linguistic primacy to heterosexuality (Hale 1996; Butler 1990), the indispensability of heterosexuality to gender intelligibility has, if anything, only become more obvious. Thus, Butler's notion of the 'heterosexual matrix' seeks to partly account for gender as that which is 'oppositionally and hierarchically defined through the compulsory practice of heterosexuality' (1990: 151). Although many feminists would agree that Butler provides us with a more fertile and less problematic account of gender and sexuality, I am interested in Wittig's more extreme notion of the straight mind. It seems to me that if we read the straight mind, neither as a universal and pre-determined account of social reality, nor as an individual psychological condition but, instead, as a limited field of knowledge that circulates around the notion of homosexuality, it may assist us in coming to terms with the sexual-gendered assumptions that are put into play in the repertoires of forced hetero-sex that we see above. Specifically, the over-inflated priority that the straight mind accords to the compulsory status of heterosexuality has, I think, a particular resonance in homophobia-related violence towards women. In short, I am interested in adapting – not adopting – 'the straight mind' as a means of thinking about the discursive contexts that surround the extreme behaviour of homophobia-related violence.

As a discourse, the straight mind does not see lesbian sexuality as a legiti-mate sexual preference with a value of its own. Rather, lesbianism represents the rejection of a social order, which decrees that only men should be entitled to sexually exchange women. Whilst the straight mind represents a way of thinking in which all of us may partake, like most discourses we don't all partake in the same way or to anywhere near the same extent. It is possible that the more validity one accords to these discursive shackles, the more one buys into the desire to ameliorate the sense of irregularity embodied in lesbianism. Take, for example, comments by Nerida regarding the time she spent living in university accommodation. Recalling one particular co-resident who periodically attempted to 'grope' those women who were known to be lesbian, she remarks:

> He made it very clear that dykes were a waste of space because we didn't 'take dick' as he put it. . . . Although he sure managed to make it clear that lesbians were one of his fantasies. . . . It's like we were a personal insult to him, that he had to fix that as some kind of fucking service to mankind.

There is a certain poignancy in Nerida's idea of sexual violence and harassment as a 'fucking service'. Judith Roof (1991) has written of the way in which some heterosexual pornography presents lesbian sex as a titillating foreplay to the 'main event', which is, of course, the entry of the penis into the script. In this way, lesbian sex serves not just as a source of arousal for male heterosexual desire, but also as a site of disorder that must be rectified by the act of 'real' sex. Similarly, by momentarily relocating lesbians (women) in their rightful (feminine) place in the heterosexual (gendered) order, these acts of hetero-sexualised violence may denote a wider cultural desire to remedy (even if only fleetingly and unconvincingly) the disturbance that female homosexuality poses to the sexual-gendered systems of the straight mind. Indeed, if we take a social view of desire as that which can 'reassure the established order of things' (Probyn 1996: 43), we might see this violent repertoire as the physical embodiment of desire for the continued maintenance of the heterosexual order: the desire to put things straight.

Butch

The discordance that lesbianism represents for the discursive confines of the straight mind exposes the extent to which the regime of gender is dependent upon compulsory heterosexuality. This means, of course, that heterosexuality is also dependent upon the ordering logic of gender. Sexual desire for one's opposite is never simply an attraction towards a body composed of XX or XY chromosomes. It is always underwritten by the expectation that certain cultural and physical traits go hand-in-hand with the nature of each sexed body. It is these gendered traits that allow us to determine whether a particular individual is a desirable sexual partner. In other words, heterosexuality is reliant upon understandings of the particular characteristics that are said to constitute each gender; characteristics which, in turn, are constructed according to the relative ways in which they differ from the traits associated with the opposite gender. Accordingly, same-sex desire not only mocks the rules and obligations of heterosexuality, it also disregards fundamental gender norms.[12] It is this disregard that prompts Sedgwick to point to the heterocentric assumptions that inhere in the very concept of gender; a bias that gives 'heterosocial and heterosexual relations a conceptual privilege of incalculable consequence' (Sedgwick 1990: 31).

Early twentieth-century sexologists minimised the conundrum that homosexuality posed for the established gender order by characterising it as a case of gender inversion. Simply put, they argued that female homosexuality could be understood as an inverted version of masculinity in the female body and male homosexuality as femininity in the male body (Vicinus 1989). Although Freud (1953) challenged this alignment between gender and sexual object-choice, this critique appears to have had a lesser influence on the construction of the lesbian subject than his overall model of female sexuality. The hierarchical order that the Freudian school established between the 'masculinity' of clitoral activity and the 'femininity' of vaginal passivity, has infiltrated our understandings of female homosexuality just as much as it has infiltrated our understandings of female heterosexuality. In particular, it has generated a cultural imperative for the mature well-adjusted woman to turn to the vagina, at the expense of the clitoris, as the authentic site of sexual stimulation. As Laqueur notes, this authoritative technique for tightening 'the web of heterosexual union' has profound implications for homosexuality (1989a: 93). Indeed, Irigaray suggests that the social 'infraction' of the lesbian is found in her very refusal to choose the penis over the clitoris (Irigaray 1985: 194). Whether or not we buy into Irigaray's own assumption that lesbians choose the clitoris, and not the vagina, over the penis, her overall point is well taken. To refuse heterosexuality is to refuse the gendered order that defines it. This infraction continues to engender the characterisation of women who express desire for other women, as masculine.

It is not surprising, then, that in addition to 'dirty', another common adjective used to insult lesbians is the word 'butch'. One woman put it like this:

> The 'butch lesbian' has been the big stick to hit all lesbians with . . . and heterosexuals. That's right, don't take on anything that's not our place or we'll hit you with the big butch lesbian stick.[13]

Lesbians are only accused of being butch because of the historical association between lesbianism and masculinity. At the same time, however, the adjective butch only functions as a form of derision because of the idea that it is inappropriate and undesirable for women to take up behaviours and gestures typically associated with masculinity. Hence, as this interviewee suggests, the butch denunciation is not reserved for lesbians alone. Heterosexual women who traverse the limited gendered boundaries of the straight mind may attract similar comments. This is perhaps most evident in the continued conflation of feminism and lesbianism. For example, several of the women I interviewed recounted incidents of verbal and written abuse where lesbianism and feminism were assumed to be synonymous; or, as one male protagonist wrote in his hate mail to a women's community centre: 'Leso equals feminist. Feminist equals leso.'

There is, however, an important anomaly contained within the butch insult. On the one hand, to call any woman butch is to conjure up the impression that something is not quite right, her gender is a little irregular. On the other hand, every time a lesbian is called butch the sense of disruption that she poses to the conventional gender disorder is explained away as a case of masculinity. This masculinisation of the lesbian appears to mirror the desire to feminise her that we see in acts of forced heterosexual sex. In the following repertoire it should become clear that these two discursive enunciations are, in fact, two sides of the same coin.

Girl/boy?

In 1978 Monique Wittig made the controversial contention that lesbians, as active desiring subjects, 'are not women' (1992: 32). For Wittig, as for many feminist theorists before and after her, what shapes our understanding of 'woman' is the specific ways in which she is assumed to be related to 'man'. Without buying into a debate about whether heterosexuality or gender is the more fundamental power relation, Wittig's point, which Butler reinvents in her notion of the heterosexual matrix, can be taken as a general comment upon the fact that compulsory heterosexuality forms a cornerstone in the definition of gender. In the absence of an in-principle commitment to hetero-sex, lesbian sexuality lacks at least one criteria for establishing a claim on the category of woman. Accordingly, Wittig proclaims, 'a lesbian *has* to be something else, a not-woman, a not-man, a product of society, not a product of nature' (1992: 13). It would be an understatement to say that Wittig's assertion has had its critics.[14] I would like to suggest, however, that as a hypothesis about the way in which sexual difference is positioned within the discursive rhetoric of the straight mind, it provides us with a conceptual tool – not an ontological fact – for thinking further about the premises contained within violent eruptions of anti-lesbian sentiment.

As something less than a reflection of 'real' femininity – 'can't you get a man?' – lesbian sexuality poses an epistemological conundrum for the straight mind. The lesbian might, to invoke Irigaray's terms, literally resist her own commodification by bartering with men for the sexual right to other women (instead of being an object of exchange herself). But this does not, as Irigaray sometimes seems to suggest, accord her entry into the category of man. Even if we accept that the hostile characterisation of lesbian sexuality as butch momentarily confers some kind of honorary masculinity, the corporeal basis of the notion of sexual difference precludes the straight mind from ever accepting lesbian sexuality as anything more than a masculine charade. Quite simply, a lesbian doesn't have the right body to be a man. This means that lesbian sexuality (and male homosexuality) is not easily accommodated in either the category of femininity or the category of masculinity. The diametrical model of gender which informs the straight mind also means that there is no comfort zone for lesbian sexuality *between* these mutually exclusive binaries. As an inverted fusion of female corporeality and sexual desire for other women – the 'wrong' gender with the 'wrong' sexuality – lesbianism represents an irregular amalgam of subjectivities, perhaps an excess, within the gendered order of the straight mind.

I wish to suggest that this irregularity, this dislocation, inscribes lesbian sexuality with a sense of gender ambiguity that augments the sexual ambiguity manifest in repertoires of dirt. The way in which this plays out in violence and hostility is most apparent in one particular repertoire of homophobia-related sentiment. Time and time again, the women I inter-viewed told of verbal comments and harassment, by women as well as men, that often took the form of a question: 'Are you a boy or a girl?'; 'How can we tell what you are?' Perhaps in some instances these questions reflect a genuine confusion. In most, however, and certainly where the person asking is actually acquainted with the woman, there is an obvious awareness that they are addressing a woman. The problem is that she does not look, talk or act like a woman should: 'What are you? Women don't behave like that.' Take, for example, the following brutal incident recounted by Sue. At the time of the attack, Sue was working night shift and was on a meal break:

> I was walking down the street . . . [when] these three boys approached me. I could see them and I knew something was gonna happen. They were looking at me and it was fairly dark, and I thought of running across the car park behind the building, that was about 500 metres probably . . . I said to myself, no if they're gonna do something it'd be better out in the open. That was pretty scary. And then, as I was about to walk past them, I walked out into the road 'cause they were walking three abreast, and just to avoid them mainly. And then one guy on the end he just shouldered me as I passed and then I got probably a metre past and he just yelled out something to me, oh, 'Apologise for that you dirty fucking lesbian!' and stuff, 'Apologise for bumping into me' and stuff. I didn't know what to do. He actually hit me, he turned around and grabbed me and hit me . . . I just didn't really know what was going on. Then he

had another hit and I fell to the ground and they were kicking me and hitting me and stuff to my head and upper body and just all the time saying, they had bottles of beer, stubbies, and they were saying they were gonna cut me up and kill me and, 'You're a dirty lesbian', 'You're disgusting' and all this stuff, like 'What do you think you are, a boy or a girl?' and 'How do we know what you are?' . . . At one stage I nearly passed out and then I think I got kicked or hit or something in the ribs and I came to a bit more. I was glad I did. And then they tried to drag me into that car park and then I just heard someone screech on their brakes and this guy who was travelling in the opposite direction, he turned around his car and as I could hear the brakes screeching, one of the guys asked me for money and was trying to get my wallet which was in the pocket of my jeans. And this guy jumped out and hit one of them. They didn't run off they just sort of walked off, as if, oh well, we're finished now.

This type of physical violation has a profound effect upon the survivor's sense of bodily integrity and safety. Prior to the attack Sue felt safe on her own at night in public places, something she put down to her strength, size, and no-nonsense body language. The random nature of this attack smashed this sense of independence and security. Months later, Sue was still experiencing difficulty going out alone at night and had postponed returning to work. She was hopeful that these reactions would eventually pass.

Sue's attackers formed the opinion that she was lesbian, and, in familiar terms, characterised her as dirty and disgusting. Exactly how they arrived at this conclusion is unclear. Presumably, there was something in Sue's appearance and/or demeanour that signalled her sexuality to them (which could, of course, be present if she was heterosexual). Despite knowing, therefore, that Sue *was* a woman they persisted with the assertion that they couldn't tell whether she was 'a boy or a girl'. Is this because Sue's assumed lesbianism functioned as an automatic cue for an ambiguous gender or is it because there was something else about Sue that not only told them she was lesbian, but that also constituted a gender infraction in itself? I wish to suggest that the first possibility actually applies to all homophobia-related violence towards lesbians, in one way or another, and that the second is a variable peculiar to some instances of homophobia-related violence. Let me explain.

I have argued above that the discourse of the straight mind constructs the lesbian as a site of ambiguity within the regime of gender. It is very likely, then, that violent expressions of homophobia-related sentiment contain within them wider cultural anxieties about gender identity. Amongst the women I interviewed, aggressive questions and comments about being a boy or a girl, a man or a woman, were experienced, irrespective of how 'feminine' or 'masculine' the woman appeared to be. Merely holding hands, kissing, or expressing intimate affection with another woman can be enough to prompt this kind of pugnacious outburst. In some instances, telling family members about one's sexuality may produce unwelcome comments about not being a proper woman or girl: 'My father wanted me to have a sex change so that everything would be fixed.' Whilst this sense of dysphoria is most apparent in the girl/boy repertoire, there is little doubt that all repertoires of homophobia-related violence towards lesbians contain some vestige of the straight mind's tendency to read lesbianism as a fundamental infraction of the gender order. Furthermore, it is possible that the different attempts to feminise and masculinise the lesbian that we saw in earlier repertoires are merely momentary assertions of the desire to rectify this anxiety, to reassure the established order of things, by repositioning the lesbian in one or other of the more disciplined gender polarities, whether it be masculinity or femininity.

Against this backdrop – lesbianism as a signifier of disordered gender – it is possible that there are instances of homophobia-related violence where one's gender image plays an additional role. For example, a small group of women stood out amongst those I interviewed for the fact that they experienced higher levels of verbal abuse and physical violence in their everyday lives. If I had to find a common link between these women I would say that, like Sue, they are women who make few concessions to conventional codes of feminine appearance and/or demeanour, particularly in terms of clothing, hair, jewellery, cosmetics, walk, speech, gestures, etc. Certainly, it is possible that this group of women experienced higher levels of hostility than others simply because the association between lesbianism and masculinity allowed their attackers to read their 'less feminine' appearance as a sign of lesbianism, thus allowing them to be more easily identified. Yet, it is just as likely that they attracted more hostility than those lesbians who adopt a conventional 'femme' appearance because of their very refusal to mark their gender in the expected ways.[15] If homophobia-related violence as a whole gestures towards the assumption that lesbians 'fail to *do* their gender right' (Butler 1990: 140, emphasis added), it is possible that a particular abhorrence is reserved for those (lesbian or heterosexual) women who, in contrast to the recent emergence of lesbian chic, fail to *display* their gender right. Given that these kinds of assessments are always in the eye of the beholder, and always historically and culturally specific (that is, there is no *one* straight mind), I am loath to specify exactly what a disordered gender image looks like, except to say that it is unlikely to be a question of exactly how a woman *does* look in any particular context, and more to do with how she does *not* look; that is, she does not look like a woman is expected to look according to the restricted understandings of gendered body image that bolster the various discursive spaces of the straight mind.

Conclusion

Violence makes a statement about the disordered nature of lesbian sexuality. It does this through the language and action of a series of repertoires – dirt, hetero-sex, butch and boy/girl – that tell us that there is a fundamental irregularity about lesbian sexuality. By marking lesbianism in this manner, violence implies that heterosexuality is the preferred mode of sexual subjectivity, as well as the normative position from which to experience one's gender identity. In this way, homophobia-related violence towards lesbians makes a statement about the relative value of different sexual desires and gender functions. As we have seen throughout this chapter, none of these repertoires function in isolation from each other. While the notion of disorder weaves its way through all of them, providing a consistent conceptual link, each repertoire connects to others. For example, notions of dirt denote a form of sexual ambiguity that is reproduced in the gendered logic of the straight mind. Similarly, accusations of butchness emerge out of the same historical associations between homosexuality and inversion that shapes hostile queries about whether the lesbian is a girl or a boy. It is these connections that reinforce statements of disorder.

These connections are matched by a number of contradictions. For example, how can the lesbian be the subject of heterosexual desire if she is butch, or for that matter, dirty? How can we reconcile the assumption of masculinity that undergirds violent characterisations of the lesbian as butch, with acts of sexual assault that depend upon the assumed femininity, and hence, heterosexuality, of the female body? It seems to me that these contradictions reflect the differing enunciative fields through which violence erupts; that is, they reflect the fact that different acts of violence contain different points of emphasis. Despite these contradictions, each repertoire emerges out of highly rigid dichotomies of heterosexuality/homosexuality and masculinity/femininity. The way in which these regimes come together in any given act will differ according to the specificities of the situation at hand and the individuals involved. Nonetheless, the co-dependent relation between gender and sexuality that we see in all of these repertoires demands that we attend to the complex, sometimes incongruous, ways in which homophobic actions are framed and authorised by both of these regimes.

In bringing these repertoires together, I do not seek to account for the origins of this violence. Rather, in rendering visible the distinct, yet interactive, character of these repertoires I hope, in some small way, to reveal the contours of the normative sexual and gendered economies that undergird them: to see what it means for statements of lesbian disorder to come into existence. These repertoires are not necessarily unique to homophobia-related violence towards lesbians. In different ways, each are likely to shape both violence towards gay men and the other forms of violence that women experience. Nor are these repertoires intended to be exhaustive. They are examples that arise from particular empirical accounts of violence. It is likely that there are many other repertoires through which violence is able to make a statement about the disordered nature of lesbian sexuality; just as there are other statements, apart from disorder, that it may make.

Whilst it is crucial to acknowledge the capacity of violence to denigrate lesbian sexuality in the ways that I have suggested, it is also important to keep in mind the sense of anxiety that lesbianism appears to generate within the discourse of the straight mind. Every time violence enunciates lesbian sexuality as a disordered expression of sexuality and gender it must, simultaneously, reveal the very vulnerability of these regimes to transgressive practices and subjectivities. In other words, violence may function to remind us that lesbian sexuality breaches the norms of sexual and gendered life, but, in doing so, it betrays the permeability of the very boundaries and categories that maintain this view of life.

3

DIFFERENT TERRITORY

A question of intersectionality?

'[T]he color of our gender mattered.'
(Alexander and Mohanty 1997: xiv)

Let me begin this chapter by recounting an incident of violence told to me in interview by a woman, Jo, who identifies as gay and Chinese Australian:

> I was walking to a friend's place, somewhere in the inner city, and it was like broad daylight on a Sunday. I was on my own and these three young men and one woman came up to me. . . . Anyhow, I might have been taking up a bit of space on the road and they literally came up to me, pushed me backwards against this wall and one of them put his fist right up in my face and he said something fucked like, "I can't believe this place sometimes. We have to put up with Asians invading our country, our 'TVs'." – He used a different word for Asian but I don't want to say it. Then it was like, god, he realised I was a girl and then he said something about Asian chicks who look like lesos, trying to act like they've got a right to be here. He was kind of shoving me, like, back against the wall, with his hand squeezing my breast, and pissed off. . . . They took one look at me, everything about me told them I was someone they didn't want in their territory. And suddenly, wham, it was like I knew it too.

The profoundly disturbing nature of this violent attack prompted an immediate desire for retaliation from Jo. Her first impulse was to amass a group of friends into an impromptu 'team of avengers', who scanned the adjacent streets in an attempt to locate the perpetrators. Only when this proved unsuccessful did Jo report the incident to the police. In the hours, days and months following the encounter she experienced intense feelings of fear, humiliation and anger. Although I can never hope to do justice to the pain of this experience, I believe that we can learn a lot by looking closely at Jo's story. She describes an incident of violence that pivots on the perpetrator's outright hostility towards 'Asians'. At the same time, however, this hostility appears to be shaped by certain assumptions about sexuality and gender. This strikes me as significant. It is an example of the way in which different categories of identity – those of sexuality, gender and race – 'come together' in both the enactment and the experience of inter-personal violence. It raises the question of how we conceptualise and represent the relation between violence and the construction of difference. In this chapter I address this question.

In feminist research on violence the concept of *intersectionality* has emerged as a means, if not the primary means, of understanding the relation between violence and difference. Intersectionality has been defined as an 'anti-essentialist' tool, designed to assist us to recognise and represent difference in multiple rather than singular terms; for example, to recognise the ways in which differences of gender *and* race, rather than gender *or* race, shape certain types of violence.[1] Despite the obvious importance and value of a concept such as intersectionality, the issues I wish to explore in this chapter centre upon the possibility that intersectionality might not actually take us far enough in conceptualising *how* identities work together in the context of violence and, further, may even hinder us in moving away from essentialised understandings of violence. My concerns about intersectionality as a concept are flagged in Jo's account of violence. First, in looking at the violence that Jo describes I am less than convinced that race simply *intersects* with gender or sexuality in either the act of violence itself or in the way that Jo experiences it. It seems to me that the process by which these particular categories of identity 'come together' may be more effectively conceptualised as a matter of mutual constitution, than one of intersection. Second, Jo suggests that her attackers only needed 'one look' to know that she was not welcome in 'their territory'. In doing, so she hints at the embodied nature of the relation between difference and violence; that is, at the way in which her physical appearance tells the perpetrators that she is different from them in ways that they believe warrant aggression and hostility. As it currently stands, intersectionality has difficulty acknowledging the question of embodiment. In attempting to escape the essentialism of many feminist accounts of violence, intersectionality tends to rely upon a social constructionist understanding of the individual who enacts and/or experiences violence. As I shall argue, social constructionism is itself dependent upon a model of the human body as natural and prior to discourse. This restricts the ability of intersectionality to account for the embodied character of violence, without reproducing the very essentialist assumptions it is designed to avoid.

In the previous chapter I argued that violence towards lesbians be understood neither as a problem of homophobic violence nor a problem of gendered violence. I suggested that it embodies an interface between the two. In this chapter I develop this argument. I do this by making racial specificity a visible factor in this equation. In an empirical sense, it is important to recognise that racial difference, like gender, shapes the prevalence and charac- teristics of homophobia-related violence; for example, there are suggestions that lesbians and gay men of colour report higher levels of homophobia- related violence than do their white counterparts (Comstock 1991; National Coalition of Anti-Violence Programs 1999). I address this fact not so much by detailing racial variations in Australian accounts of such violence, but, more, by considering how we theoretically formulate this increasingly complex picture of violence. In particular, I am interested in how we con- ceptualise the interaction between race, sexuality and gender in the com- mission and experience of violence.

This focus demands that I take a different approach to the idea of homophobia-related violence than I did in the previous chapter. To make my argument, I draw upon a small number of violent incidents, drawn from interview accounts, where homophobic attitudes are apparent. However, homophobia is far from the dominating sentiment in these incidents. Indeed, race, gender and sexuality intermingle in these accounts to an extent that defies conventional categorisations of 'racist violence', 'homophobic violence' or 'gendered violence'. The incidents recounted are all of these things. As a consequence, I have chosen to engage with these interview excerpts by drawing upon the notion of 'territory'; the notion that Jo uses to explain her own encounter. Territory, as I employ it here, has both material and discursive facets to it. It refers to particular locations about which people have a sense of ownership or belonging (as in 'my' neighbourhood or 'my' nation), and the conceptual categories through which people achieve this sense of belonging (as in categories of whiteness, femininity or heterosexuality); each is depend- ent upon the other. I adopt the term territorial violence simply to signify the way in which this understanding of territory shapes the particular incidents of violence that I recount; whilst the notion of territory seems to have a particular pertinence to racial violence, as we shall see, it also resonates in the homophobic and gendered aspects of these accounts as well. Although I wish to draw attention to some of the ways in which violence may be infused by a sense of territory, my purpose is to employ this empirical material as an example for revisiting the concept of intersectionality. It is not my primary purpose to theorise territorial violence itself. Indeed, in the following chapter, the question of territory becomes integrated into a more general discussion about the ways in which lesbians and gay men map personal safety. Hence, my use of the term territorial violence should not be taken to imply the existence of a distinct or new form of violence.

Among the women I interviewed, quite a few talked about racism as well as homophobia. I have, however, chosen to focus upon a selection of excerpts from two interviewees only: Jo and So Fong. I make no claim that the incidents of territorial violence they recount are typical of any particular form of violence. This is not why they are significant. By providing us with overt examples of ways in which several regimes of difference interact in the one violent event, these accounts offer us a rare opportunity to see quite clearly, blatantly in fact, the way in which different specificities 'come together' in the enactment and experience of violence. They highlight a process that is present in other incidents of violence, but which is often difficult to capture and reproduce in a research context. In so doing, they remind us that intersectionality is always pertinent to those forms of violence that are invested with constructions of difference (and, perhaps, to many other forms as well). As I shall argue, this includes all gendered, racist and homophobic violence.[2]

My argument in this chapter moves through three sections. First, I suggest that certain forms of violence – racist violence, homophobic violence and gendered violence (by gendered violence, I mean the kinds of violence that are predominantly committed by men against women, such as sexual assault or domestic violence) – are inevitably, if loosely, linked to each other, in the sense that they are all undergirded by hierarchical constructions of difference. This leads me to consider the contribution that intersectionality has made to representing difference in multiple, rather than singular, terms. Second, I draw upon examples of territorial violence, recounted by Jo and So Fong, to argue that categories of gender, race and/or sexuality do not just intersect with each other in incidents of inter-personal violence. Rather, they are the 'vehicles of articulation' for each other. Finally, if certain forms of violence are always underpinned by difference/s then they must also be grounded in the bodily specificities through which these differences are constructed. In assuming a social constructionist model, intersectionality risks tying the relation between difference and violence to the idea of an essential body. As an alternative, I suggest that we might turn to what I call a cultural model of the body. This model enables us to recognise that the relation between violence and difference is an embodied one. At the same time, it assists us to acknowledge that such violence emerges, not from properties intrinsic to any particular body, but, rather, from the difference *between* these embodied constructs.

Before I do this, however, it is important to recognise the ways in which my analysis is conditioned by questions of representation. In particular, I am thinking of the intense debates that have taken place over the last couple of decades, both in and outside of feminism, about whether or not the experience of racial or ethnic subjugation brings with it an intrinsic form of epistemic privilege about that subjugation (Bar On 1993). Certainly, as an Anglo-Australian, who is unlikely to be on the receiving end of racism, I can never really know racist violence from the perspective of someone who experiences it. However, my reading of these debates leads me to value the academic interview as one means of 'listening to', and 'speaking with', those women who experience the implications of racism in their daily lives (Felton and Flanagan 1993). I value this methodological strategy not simply because it provides a means for these experiences to be told to others. Indeed, to believe that my research could, or should, simply provide a space for the voices of 'the racially subjugated' to be heard is to assume, first, that such speech is dependent upon my own intellectual benevolence and, second, that it has an authenticity that precludes me from critiquing it. As Spivak and others have argued, the latter assumption merely reproduces the ethnocentric premise that it is only the experiences of racially privileged subjects that demand deconstruction (Hollinsworth 1995; Spivak 1988). Instead, I believe that this interview material is valuable precisely because it *does* enable me – requires me – to actively critique the kinds of discourses that facilitate and maintain racist violence.

As with the representation of all identity categories, the language of racial difference is replete with conceptual tensions (in the Introduction I noted these same kind of tensions in relation to the categories of gay and lesbian). In writing about racial difference, I have chosen to reproduce the same language that the women I interviewed used to talk about their own racial or ethnic identities. For Jo and So Fong, this means either Chinese, Chinese Australian or Asian.[3] Although this approach avoids the arbitrary imposition of racial categories at the point of analysis, it is still beholden to the fact that these categories represent neither neutral nor naturally arising identities. They are very much the product of contemporary racial and ethnic relations in Australia in the 1990s, and the history of immigration and colonisation out of which these relations emerge.[4] On the one hand, such categories provide a critical means of challenging the oppressive effects of this history. But, on the other hand, we must not forget that, in doing so, they inevitably 'consort' with the very ethnocentric constructions that have enabled the white western world to name others as 'outsiders', 'alien', and 'different' to begin with (Mirza 1997: 15–16).

Non-indigenous, English-speaking-background Australians tend to be less adept at identifying their own racial and ethnic heritage. I have taken the liberty of referring to individuals who are from a predominantly Anglo-Celtic background via the shorthand term Anglo and through the notion of whiteness. In a more general sense, I tend to employ the concept of race rather than, say, ethnicity. Given the problematic, and interwoven, nature of these terms (Brah 1993; Frankenberg 1993), my selection of one over the other is again a decision that reflects the preferred language of the women I interviewed.

I am aware that my reliance upon these forms of racial classification (whether Asian or Anglo) ties my analysis to homogenisations and generalisations that, in another context, I might seek to resist. Such categories are rarely capable of capturing the ambivalence and hybridity between, and among, different racial groupings. Moreover, they tend to reinforce simplistic distinctions of self/other that, in themselves, facilitate the production of racial hierarchies. Hence, it is important to emphasise that my intention in invoking these pared down and simplified constructs is not to suggest that they are foundational or unproblematic descriptors of the way things are. Rather, my purpose is to expose them as constructions that actively shape the enactment and experience of violence. By looking at the way in which racial categories function *through* other categories, such as those of gender and sexuality, I hope to contribute to the on-going deconstruction of the hierarchies that characterise them.

Intersectionality and the construction of difference

When we take the step of naming violence as either racist, homophobic or gendered, we need to recognise that the historical, cultural and local contexts peculiar to each of these 'isms' will shape that violence in distinct ways. There is no sense in which the specific ingredients of one (e.g. racism) can be reduced to the terms of the other (e.g. sexism). There is, however, one common denominator that they share. Broadly speaking, each pivots on hierarchical constructions of difference. Indeed, it is these constructions that provide the justification for naming a given act as gendered, homophobic or racist in the first place. For example, decades of feminist research has revealed the innumerable and nuanced ways in which acts of rape, domestic violence and sexual harassment are imbued with assumptions about appropriate and desirable notions of femininity and masculinity. Not dissimilarly, the prejudice, fear and intolerance that lie at the core of homophobic or racist violence only makes sense in the context of regimes of sexual or racial order that attach notions of superiority and inferiority to particular sexual acts or racial categories (not to mention other forms of hate crime such as ethno-religious violence and violence towards people with disabilities).

I do not want to draw an overly simplistic comparison between these forms of violence. The diversities and distinctions are too numerous. However, I do want to suggest that to characterise a violent act as gendered, homophobic or racist is to suggest that the act itself turns on hierarchical constructions of a particular form of difference (e.g. gender difference) and the identity categories associated with it (e.g. identities of woman and man).[5] These regimes of difference run like a fine thread through these diverse forms of violence, linking them in a delicate, yet persistent, manner.

In this sense, difference provides both the rudimentary context that distinguishes one form of violence from another (for example, that which distinguishes racist violence from sexual assault) and a point of connection that allows us to see the broad links between these forms of violence (for example, that which allows us to see the ways in which both racist violence and sexual assault pivot on a sense of superiority and concomitant devaluation of the personal integrity of the racial or gendered other). Consequently, every time we describe certain acts of violence in terms of singular regimes of gender, race or sexuality, the existence of this link should alert us to the shortcomings of homogeneous formulations of violence. For example, every time we categorise an act of violence as gendered, how are we to account for the racial specificities through which that violence is enacted and experienced?

In the fields of law, discrimination and violence, the concept of inter-sectionality has emerged as one response to this question. Whilst its specific origins can be traced to the interface between critical race theory and feminist legal theory, the broader circumstances of its emergence are, of course, found in the highly charged movement towards anti-essentialism within, and outside of, western feminism (Spelman 1988; hooks 1981). In highlighting the tendency of white feminism to engage with the category of woman as if it embodied racial and ethnic (and associated class) privilege, women of colour have called for recognition of the ways in which regimes of gender and race work with, and against, each other to produce manifold, sometimes irreconcilable, differences in the experiences of women. Parallel critiques of the gender neutrality of anti-racist discourse have revealed the ease with which the experiences, for example, of black women and Asian women become lost between concerns about sexism and concerns about racism (Crenshaw 1991). For feminism, these issues have crystallised into a critique of the assumptions that gender is a self-contained modality of difference, and that the identity of woman has a singular, universal (read white) core. This shift away from essential subjectivities has dovetailed with, and in some cases been fuelled by, poststructural critiques of the unified human subject (the Enlightenment subject). In this context, the anti-essentialist appreciation of difference has come to be understood as a question of the indeterminacy and instability of the identity categories that configure all human subjects.

In the context of violence, resistance to the 'imposition of a singular identity category' has engendered political campaigns that highlight the racial and ethnic specificity of women's experiences of violence, whilst simultaneously making connections between different ethnicities (Patel 1997: 256). This movement has taken innumerable paths and been articulated in a variety of ways, depending upon: the type of violence under consideration; the contemporary cultural and national contexts in question; and the histories of race relations and colonisation that shape them. By examining the different histories of racial privilege and oppression among women, research has revealed the ways in which the particular forms of violence that are committed against women, such as sexual assault and domestic violence, are embedded in interlocking systems of race, gender and class inequalities (Wilson 1993; Southall Black Sisters 1994; Cunneen and Stubbs 1996). In some instances, differences between women's experiences of violence have been recognised and accommodated within a patriarchal model of gender relations (Hester, Kelly and Radford 1996). Although this approach recognises difference at the experiential level, its preference for assimilating that difference into existing, somewhat uniform, theoretical formulations means that it is better able to account for the homogeneous, rather than heterogeneous, features of violence. In other instances, a refusal to reduce women's experience to a question of gender alone has prompted careful consideration of the way in which multiple identities come together in the context of violence; what Mama (1989) might call the 'colluding interaction' between sexual, racial and institutional oppression. This is not simply a matter of adding race to gender. The problem with an additive analysis is that it assumes that the individual is composed of a proliferation of 'subject positions along a pluralist axis' which, as Butler points out, requires one exclusionary identity to be repudiated, in order for another to be enacted (1993: 14); that is, one can only be raced when one is not gendered, gendered when one is not raced. Instead, the intention has been to formulate this 'coming together' of multiple identities (and the power relations that feed into, and off, them) in a way that neither dismisses different identities, assimilates one into another, nor requires one to be prioritised over another.

I am interested in how we represent this process. The way in which we signify the 'coming together' of particular categories is determined, in part, by the assumptions we make about the subject who enacts violence, the subject who experiences violation, and the particular socio-political relations that produce a climate conducive to violence. Whilst various concepts have been adopted to articulate this process,[6] it seems to me that the notion of intersectionality has acquired a notable currency – perhaps most obviously in North America and Australia – in the literature on men's violence towards women, especially that which is influenced by feminist legal discourse (Abrams 1994; Scales-Trent 1990; Stubbs and Tolmie 1994). Intersectionality replaces singular or universal notions of experience, identity and power with a model that positions the subject at the intersection of categories of identity, such as those of gender and race. In this model, different axes of power intersect to produce qualitative distinctions between the experiences of white women and the experiences of women of colour. Thus, for women of colour, experiences of violence are the product of 'their intersectional identity as both women *and* of colour' (Crenshaw 1991: 1244). Intersectionality thereby allows us to think about the enactment and experience of violence as the product of multiple, sometimes contradictory, often shifting, but always intersecting identities. Importantly, intersectionality is not just a word that we use to talk about differences. It represents a particular mode of conceptualising these differences that is larger than the actual usage of the term itself. It is a *type* of analysis that seeks to understand the subject as the product of intersecting categories of identity and difference, in order to move beyond essentialist or universalist accounts of violence. For example, in Razack's terms, difference is a 'set of interlocking social arrangements that constitute groups differently, *as subordinate and dominant*' (1994: 899). Hence, research on violence may be framed by an intersectional analysis without ever invoking the phrase intersectionality.

Despite the enthusiasm with which intersectionality has been greeted in feminist circles, I am concerned that its utility may eventually be hindered by what, to my mind, is an unresolved tension between some of its premises and its major purpose, which is to 'denote the various ways in which race and gender *interact*' (Crenshaw 1991: 1244, emphasis added). I wish to suggest that there are two primary sources of this tension. First, is the assumption that the subject is constituted at the *intersection* of autonomous structures of gender, race, sexuality and so on. Crenshaw expressed her own reservations about this in 1991 when she characterised intersectionality as a 'provisional concept'. Although it allows us to make the conceptual shift away from singular or universal notions of gender and race, it continues to 'engage dominant assumptions that race and gender are essentially separate categories' (Crenshaw 1991: 1244). Second, in seeking to move beyond essentialist accounts of the human subject, proponents of intersectionality have been deeply suspicious of attempts to characterise difference as a matter of corporeality. In the context of violence, they have largely taken their lead from social constructionism (MacKinnon 1987). According to social constructionism the body is characterised as a biological object upon which culture, psychology or ideology is imposed. For example, within feminism, the sex/gender distinction has emerged as a means of representing the process by which social meanings (gender=masculinity and femininity) are imposed upon the natural, pre-discursive body (sex=male and female). By challenging violence at the level of the social, constructionism has attempted to neutralise the effects of specific forms of embodiment (such as sex). However, the dilemma for constructionism is that no matter how far it attempts to distance itself from essentialism, it is framed by the mind/body distinction of traditional philosophy. This distinction presupposes a human subject who, in essence, is tied to the natural world because his or her body is presumed to exist prior to, or outside of, discourse.

In the following sections of this chapter, I address both of these issues in turn. Through examples of territorial violence, I consider why an intersecting model of identity (of the human subject) is insufficient, and how we might go about developing it. I move on to provide an overview of the argument that difference is inevitably a question of embodiment. I suggest that acts of violence that pivot on questions of difference cannot escape this. To my mind, this raises the question of how we recognise the deeply embodied relation between difference and violence without investing in essentialist premises about that body.

Territories of violence

So Fong emigrated to Australia from Hong Kong with her family in the early 1980s. She identifies as Chinese but, in the Australian context, also describes herself as Asian. So Fong's primary sexual and emotional relationships are with women, and she identifies as lesbian. During the course of our interview, she recounted an incident that took place at a football game in Melbourne a year or so beforehand. During half-time, So Fong left her seat to make a visit to the women's toilets, which were marked by a sign that read 'Ladies'. When she got there, she found that her path was physically blocked by three young, Anglo women who appeared to be quite drunk.[7] They informed her that she could not enter the toilets and risked getting her 'head bashed in' if she tried to do so. Initially, So Fong presumed that everyone was receiving the same treatment. But it transpired that each woman was being assessed according to the extent to which she looked like a 'lady'; some passed, some did not. As So Fong turned to leave, one of the young women forming the barricade called out something along the lines of: 'Does she look like a lady to you? Looks like a slanty-eyed boy. What's a ching-chong doing at the footy, anyhow?'

There are many facets to this incident. I would like to consider the question of race first. Like the violence directed towards Jo, the hostility So Fong recounts is stamped with ethnocentric assumptions about racial difference, national borders, and local boundaries. It reproduces a long history of anti-Asian sentiment and violence in Australia (Human Rights and Equal Opportunity Commission 1991; White 1997). This sentiment can be traced, in part, to the tendency of 'white settler societies' (among others) to construct a sense of nationalism in terms that are explicitly racial; in particular, through the entrenchment of a national identity that is exclusively white and, often, Anglo-Celtic (Ang and Stratton 1998).[8] For Anglo-Australians with strong nationalist tendencies, this identity is dependent upon the sense of belonging that comes from being 'at home' among people who are like oneself; familiar people in familiar spaces. In a racially and culturally diverse nation, such familiarity is readily eroded by the presence of racial and ethnic others. Indeed, according to Hage, the presence of these others can make a strong nationalist feel 'that he or she can no longer operate in, communicate in or recognise the national space'. A sense of discord is likely to surface (Hage 1998: 41). A multicultural society like Australia is, of course, full of quite ordinary places and situations where this discord might emerge. These are spaces where, for example: the football is no longer the province of predetermined racial groups; Asian images 'invade' the television; Asian men and women have a visible urban presence; and Chinese lesbians think they are ladies.

Just as nations seek to control global boundaries by fostering a sense of national identity, individuals within a given state may simultaneously engage in informal systems of regulation and control (Stasiulis and Yuval-Davis 1995). Hage refers to these attempts to establish control over one's assumed territory as acts of 'spatial management': acts that enable individuals to police the movement of racial others as if they were 'mere object[s] to be removed from national space' (Hage 1998: 44). The familiarity that acts of spatial management are designed to achieve often manifests as a desire to return to the past, to the idealised image of a former 'White Australia'. One of the most telling examples of this desire is found in the offensive 'Asians Go Home' street graffiti that has plagued Australian cities for decades.

Violence can also be understood as an act of spatial management. In the incidents recounted by both So Fong and Jo, we see assertions from the perpetrators about the ownership of local and national territory: statements of territory. A sense of racial familiarity determines who has the 'right' to be in 'their' country which, in turn, determines who is out of place on a particular street, at the football, or in the Ladies toilets. In this way, So Fong's exclusion from the territory of the women's toilets can be understood, in part, as a direct response to the significance that these young Anglo women attach to the fact that she is Chinese. Indeed, it was not just So Fong's possible entry to the Ladies that disturbed these young white women, it was also her presence at the football; a disturbance that So Fong put down to 'a sign of the typical ethnocentric view that anyone who looks Asian doesn't "belong" in certain places, the football, the beach . . . but we're right at home in an "ethnic" restaurant or a "Chinese laundry"'.[9]

Violent acts of spatial management have a particular pertinence to racially defined notions of territory, but they are not confined to them. Attempts to exclude women and homosexuals from material and discursive spaces that are traditionally masculine and/or heterosexual have a long history that needs no rehearsing here. Hence, it is also possible to read So Fong's account as an example of a symbolic attempt to police the feminised category of lady, by literally controlling the material space of the Ladies. Similarly, Jo's attacker also makes reference to 'lesos' (as well as Asians) who act like they have the right to be in 'his' territory. Whilst this is significant in itself, I am particularly interested in these different statements of territory because of the way in which they appear to reinforce and rely upon each other. In both of these incidents the management of territory – whether it be territories of race, gender or sexuality – takes place through one or more other specificities, other constructions of difference. For example, the hostility directed towards So Fong followed several intertwined trajectories. So Fong offers some insight into this:

> It's ironic, because they were kind of right. I'm not a lady. Ladies are very feminine and I'm not . . . I look butch and I know that my looking butch is part of being a dyke for me. It's kind of a sexual thing really . . . But then sexual culture is also about race isn't it? I think Asian women are stereotyped as more feminine than non-Asian women. But I don't buy into the expected image of a subservient Asian woman. . . . I think I'm seen as a bit of a contradiction because of that.

Although So Fong ties the hostility against her to the fact that she does not look like a lady, this butchness is, in turn, a conscious expression of her lesbianism. In this way the gendered readings that the young women make of So Fong's body are inevitably dependent upon the ways in which sexuality shapes So Fong's body image. But, more than this, So Fong goes on to make the point that just as there are no *sexually*-neutral readings of femininity, neither are there *racially*-neutral ones. Historically, in western discourse, white femininity has been valorised as the typical, the purest, and the most desirable form of femininity (Dyer 1997). These racialised readings of gender have variable and often contradictory implications for women who are neither western nor white (for example, the masculinisation and/or hyper-sexualisation of African American women and Aboriginal Australian women). In Australia, South-East Asian women continue to be stereotyped through images of a passive, yet exotic, hetero-femininity (Yue 1996; Ang 1995).[10] In the eyes of her Anglo aggressors, So Fong probably does not look like a lady because she does not embody this image, she does not look the way they expect an *Asian lady* to look: 'Does she look like a lady to you? Looks like a slanty-eyed boy.' So Fong reads her exclusion from the category of lady not simply as an automatic rejection of all Asian women, but, rather, as the exclusion of someone who did not live up to the Anglo stereotype of Asian femininity. Although it is likely that these young women would have rejected any woman who looked too butch, we can never know whether an Asian woman who looked more conventional would have met their criteria, or whether all Asian (or non-white) women were excluded. Nonetheless, what *is* clear is that these young women managed the idealised territory of femininity, the definition of lady, *through* criteria that were racially and sexually specific. This is how their hostility was acted out and this is also how So Fong experienced it.[11]

We can see this same kind of process operating, in a different direction, so to speak, in the violence that Jo recounts. Here the incident appears to commence as a racist attack. This is quickly augmented by anti-homosexual attitudes: 'Asian chicks who look like lesos, trying to act like they've got a right to be here.' Significantly, the physical expression of this racism-homophobia changes when the attacker realises Jo is a woman: he squeezes her breast. To say that the incident becomes gendered at this point would be to assume that his initial response is not also gendered. In fact, the whole incident is gendered in the sense that when the perpetrator assumes that Jo is a male his physical contact with her is not sexualised. The difference that gender makes is evident in his transformation of this non-sexual act into one with threatening sexual overtones. Whilst a random encounter with an Asian man would, no doubt, have also produced a racist response, it is unlikely that it would have been sexualised. If it were, such sexualisation would probably have been acted out in quite a different manner.

The concept of intersectionality is designed to represent the deeply inter-active process between race, gender and sexuality that we see in these accounts of violence. My concern, however, is that there is a gap between that which intersectionality aims to do and that which it is able to do. In an intersectional model, race, gender and sexuality intersect with each other in a grid-like structure. Particular subject positions emerge at the junction of the interlinking axes of identity that make up this grid. Grosz (1994) makes the point that this kind of gridlike formulation is always problematic, because it conceptualises differences of race, sexuality or gender as solid, autonomous structures external to the individual subject. The problem is that before one axis can intersect, cross, cut, or pass over another, it must already exist, elsewhere, in a state of divergence or separation from the others. Each axis must function independently from, outside of, or prior to, its intersection with other axes. To see identity categories in this way, as 'fully separable axes', is, as Butler notes, to attribute a 'false uniformity to them'. This uniformity is at the heart of the very exclusionary practices that produce discrete 'categories' and 'positions' in the first place (Butler 1993: 117). In other words, to assume that categories of gender and race merely intersect with each other at certain points, is to assume that they also function elsewhere in neutral terms that are mutually exclusive of each other. This means that intersectionality unavoidably contains within it the premise that race is *not* always gendered, gender is *not* always raced, or sexuality is *not* always gendered.

This is clearly not the case in the accounts of territorial violence that I have reproduced above. For example, the hostility directed towards So Fong's butchness may reflect an amalgam of assumptions about sexual and gender differences, but these understandings are produced *through* a racially specific discourse. Similarly, the racist violence that Jo describes is enacted in a way that is fundamentally gendered. To my mind, this violence is less a question of the way in which identities intersect *with* each other and more a question of the way in which they operate as 'the conditions of articulation *for* each other' (Butler 1993: 117). When understood as the 'vehicles' for one another, categories do not simply traverse each other, they encode each other: race is always 'lived in the modality of gender', gender is always 'lived in the modality of race', and so on (117). Grosz refers to this alternative understanding of identity as one of 'mutual constitution', a process whereby each category of identity, each construction of difference, is inevitably implicated in another (1994: 20).

It seems to me that intersectionality might be better able to represent the co-dependent relation between categories of identity if we re-articulate it – if we refine our thinking about the actual processes of this interplay – as a question of mutual constitution; or, to put this more simply, as an *interaction* instead of an *intersection*. Whilst territorial violence is the example which prompts me to make this suggestion, the significance of this distinction between intersection and interaction is not confined to this example alone. The very purpose of intersectionality is to enable us to conceptualise *all* forms of violence in ways that are neither reductionist nor universalist. Importantly, this means that the violence that we tend to label gendered, racist or homophobic is inevitably infused not just by the most visible or dominant difference that exists between perpetrator and victim, but also by the ways in which this difference is shaped by other modes of difference and the categories of identity they produce. This is not to suggest that all regimes of difference contribute in equal proportions to any given act of violence or to the experience of being violated. Violence may be, and often is, dominated by one modality of difference. But it is configured by others.

One of the dangers of the (intersectional) premise that individual modes of difference *can* operate independently of each other is the ease with which this allows us to assume that the 'coming together' of differences is only relevant to positions of subjugation.[12] For example, the very idea that gender is not always raced has allowed white western feminism to assume that race is only pertinent to the experience of Asian or black women (i.e. gender is essentially white because whiteness is not a racial or ethnic category in itself). If, however, the relation between various regimes of difference is cast as a question of mutual constitution – if gender is always raced – it becomes intellectually perverse not to acknowledge that a particular mode of difference shapes those it privileges as well as those it subjugates. So Fong talks of this privilege in the following terms:

> If I were a white woman, if I were you, for sure I'd still have to be worried about all the violence that is handed out to women. But I wouldn't also have to worry that every time I step off my own bit of turf I might be entering racist territory, or that men might be more sexist to me because they're also racists. The difference of race is as simple as that.

So Fong's point is that, in the context of violence, whiteness most commonly functions as a freedom: the freedom to rarely need to worry about the risk of racist violence; the freedom to know that you will not have to personally deal with the racism of the law or the criminal justice system. Standpoints of masculinity and heterosexuality bring their own comparable, yet unique, prerogatives and immunities (although, as we see in acts of territorial violence, this sense of privilege is easily threatened).

The process of mutual constitution is not, therefore, a stable or un-troubled one (it is *not* a return to a unified model of the subject). As Ahmed (1998) has argued, racial and gendered identifications do not simply collude with each other in the construction of subject positions. They also 'collide', in a shifting series of contradictions and incommensurabilities. This means that conflicting readings of the interaction between particular facets of identity may co-exist with one other. For instance, our experiences of violation may be configured by our knowledge of the perpetrators' perception of us, but we may also hold a very different sense of self from those who objectify us in this way (a point I return to in Chapter 5). Moreover, it is likely that this interrelationship will be experienced, and reacted to, differently over time and across contexts; one facet of identity may predominate in one situation, but not in another. For example, although Asian-ness may represent a vulnerability to racist violence, femininity may actually heighten the likelihood of such violence in a given situation (or possibly mitigate it). Similarly, some of the 'joys' of white immunity to racist violence (or masculine immunity to sexual violence) may be undermined by the threat of homophobic violence if one is gay or lesbian (Moraga 1983; Martin and Mohanty 1986). Nevertheless, it is important to remember that whilst one form of subjugation may dull the privilege associated with another (or vice versa), it rarely extinguishes it. To borrow again from Ahmed, no singular construction of difference is ever a complete 'guarantee for determining who does and does not have the right to walk in the leafy suburbs' (1998: 63).

The cultural body

Articulating difference as a process of mutual constitution takes us that bit closer to capturing the interactive relation between race, gender and sexuality, without seeing these as structures that operate independently of each other. In this way it furthers the aim of intersectionality, which is to push the representation of difference beyond essential or universal accounts of identity and/or power. But working towards this goal is not just a matter of being able to represent the interdependent relation between particular categories. It is also a question of being able to recognise the mediums through which this interaction takes place. If those mediums are tied in other ways to an essential notion of the human subject then this overall goal remains elusive.

As I have already noted, social constructionism seeks to challenge ways of thinking that validate hierarchies of gender, sexuality and race as a matter of biological difference (if something is natural it cannot, or should not, be altered). It does this by distinguishing difference at the social level from difference at the corporeal level, and prioritising the former. At the risk of losing some complexity, it is fair to say that this distinction, in turn, is dependent upon the philosophical dichotomy that Cartesian dualism draws between the body (nature) and the mind (culture) of the human subject.[13] In this formulation, the body is a pre-discursive, essential and biological object. If difference *could* be confined to the social level then this understanding of the body, and the relation between mind and body, might not present a particular problem for an anti-essentialist account of violence. But what if it is not as easy to separate the social from the biological (the mind from the body) as constructionism would have us believe? What if difference is inescapably an embodied, and not just a social, construct? What does this mean for an analysis of violence that values the aims of intersectionality?

In light of these questions, it should come as no surprise that I wish to suggest that the body is probably the most immediate and visible signifier of difference. Not only is it marked *by* difference, the body is also a mark *of* difference (Ahmed 1998). It is the appearance of our bodies (skin colour, breasts, absence of breasts, hair texture, shape of the eyes, genitals), as well as how we use our bodies (the ways we have sex, the ways we eat, the ways we work, the ways we worship) that provides the matter out of which differences of race, gender and sexuality are constructed. Although this understanding of difference is 'concerned with the mechanisms by which bodies are recognised as different', this is 'only in so far as they are constructed as possessing or lacking some socially privileged quality or qualities' (Gatens 1996: 73). In other words, the body is the medium through which human subjects are differentiated from each other and value is accorded to particular subject positions. These value judgements contain within them assessments of superiority and inferiority which, in terms of the latter, may manifest in attributes of 'alien', 'slanty-eyed boy', 'primitive', 'passive', 'dirty', 'sick' and so on (Young 1990; Rothenberg 1990).

In relation to the question of territorial violence, Hage (1998) reminds us that nationalism is a way of imagining one's location within the nation and, hence, is very much an embodied frame of mind. As the medium through which attributes of national otherness are constructed, the body thus represents a crucial, and visible, site of knowledge for the enactment of racist violence; it is not just the physical means by which it is carried out. The violent management of particular territories is likely to turn on the extent to which the bodily images, gestures and practices of others accord with the nationalist's desire for familiarity and homogeneity. Quite simply, the physical appearance of a given individual will determine the assumptions that are made by strong nationalists about the 'rights' of that individual to be in a certain place, to act in a certain way, at a certain point in time. For example, in Jo's account of violence, it is the way in which the perpetrators read her body that enables them to deduce that she is someone who they do not want in 'their' territory. Jo is well aware of this:

> You know ever since that incident I can't get it out of my head that my body tells it all. My body tells a story. They look at me and they see I'm different. They see I'm Chinese, female, gay . . . You know that Jeanette Winterson book, what's it called, *Written on the Body* I think? That's me.

Jo suggests that her body 'tells a story'. It tells a story to the perpetrators of violence because it marks her 'as possessing or lacking some socially privileged quality or qualities'. It is a visible site for the fields of knowledge that enable the enactment of this violence. In so doing, Jo hints at the fact that the knowledge systems through which she interprets her own experience of this violation are also embodied. Certainly, the experience of physical violation is, by very definition, an embodied one: an experience of flesh and bone. However, the body's role in producing this experience is not confined to somatic forms of harm and injury. Specificities of Chinese-ness and female-ness construct Jo's understanding of this harm by configuring the kinds of knowledge systems that she draws upon to interpret it as a particular form of violation:

> I *feel* it as a Chinese woman . . . no, not just because I experience everything as a Chinese woman but because of what being Chinese means [in Australia] . . . I know that there are some people out there who hate me for being different.

In other words, Jo's body fashions the kinds of discourses through which her particular experiences of violation are produced. This is because her understanding of difference itself is corporeally specific. In short, the interpretations of difference that mould both the act of violence and the experience of violation are always embodied.

It is here that the difficulty lies for an intersectional analysis of the relation between violence and difference. As I have suggested, intersectionality is designed to move beyond essentialist understandings of violence. It tends to do this, however, by relying upon a social constructionist framework. This framework avoids articulating difference as a question of embodiment because it does not wish to tie it to a natural or biological essence; after all, it is this kind of thinking that has accorded an inferior status to black bodies, Asian bodies, female bodies, homosexual bodies and so on. However, constructionism itself presumes the existence of a mind/body distinction, the same distinction that reproduces an essential interpretation of the human body. This means that every time an intersectional account of violence prioritises difference at the social level, to the exclusion of the corporeal level, it also buys into this interpretation.

However, the question of embodiment really only presents this kind of a problem if we accept the constructionist premise that there are 'real' bodies beneath the cultural veneer of racial, gendered and sexual identities, if we accept that the body is a fixed and pre-cultural object of nature. It seems to me that recent challenges to constructionism – to the body/mind distinction that frames it – provide an alternative model of embodiment that might assist us to move beyond this impasse. In this model – which I refer to as the cultural model – the body is not just a passive biological object overlaid with social meaning. The identity categories that emerge from particular constructions of difference do not simply attach themselves to pre-existing bodies, as if they were blank slates waiting to be written upon. Instead, identities represent specific regulatory norms through which history, culture and discourse forge our understandings and experiences of the human body. In a Foucauldian sense, the body is still acted upon, but this action is part of the process of subjectification through which knowledge systems envisage and formulate that body in certain ways; or, as Probyn puts it, 'very different bodies will be produced under very different discursive regimes' (1998: 9).[14] There is no shortage of arguments about the specific ways in which the discourses prevalent in a given culture, at a given time, do this. Pertinent examples include: the historical reproduction of two primary categories of sex through social practices designed to 'breed out' hermaphroditic or inter-sexed infants (Laqueur 1989b); the maintenance of racially distinct and 'pure' bodies through social taboos against inter-marriage (Dyer 1997); and the shaping of western female bodies through surgery, beauty regimes, eating practices and fitness programs designed to achieve a slimmer, whiter, or more attractive body (Caraway 1991; Bordo 1993). Simply put, this model suggests that the body is a product of culture, not just of nature.

The idea of a cultural body has prompted many feminists to rethink the sex/gender distinction, and many queer theorists to deconstruct the notion of essential sexual desire (Gatens 1996; Probyn 1996). Similarly, post-colonial theorists also question the supposedly self-evident traits of racial difference by arguing that race is the 'effect', not just the source, of racist ideology (Gunew and Yeatman 1993; Bhabha 1994). Whilst theorists of race, such as Fanon (1952) and Said (1978), have highlighted the capacity of racism to infiltrate the experience of one's body, the notion of a cultural body takes this further by arguing that racial categories do not just describe immutable differences between naturally raced bodies, they also function to 'figure the body as the bearer of immutable difference' (Brah 1993: 13). In this way, the body is still a signifier of difference, but it is also *a product of* that difference.

To suggest that the body is formulated within culturally specific know-ledge systems is not the same as suggesting that the body is 'somehow made of discourse pure and simple' (Butler 1995: 229). Physical differences in skin colour, hair, genitals, or sexual desire *do* exist. The point is that they exist neither completely separate from, nor prior to, discourse and power; for the cultural body, 'materialization and investiture are coextensive' (Butler 1995: 235).[15] It is significant for the present argument that this is a normative process. Bodies ever only take on a sense of individuality and identity through the way in which they are positioned in relation to other bodies. This means that it is the value-laden notions of inter-personal alterity – the exclusionary kinds of logic that produce hierarchical constructions of self/other, masculine/feminine, white/black, occidental/oriental, heterosexual/homosexual and so on – that give bodies 'their own concreteness and specificity' (Grosz 1994: 209).[16] In this model, difference is said to emerge in the exchanges *between* bodies, in the contested space between self and other

[17] It represents a cultural, commonly hierarchical, *relation* bodies come to be understood as distinct *from* one another.

articular implications for the way that we think about those violence that turn upon the construction of difference. We need no further than the common refrain that individuals are assaulted and violated because they *are* homosexual, Asian, or female to realise how easy it is to slip into locating the source of hostility in fixed subject positions, usually those associated with the victim. Conversely, to understand difference as an ordered relation *between* bodies is to shift the emphasis away from qualities intrinsic to a particular body, and towards the cultural processes through which those bodies come to be understood as different from each other. These processes are apparent in earlier interview accounts of violence, where perpetrators determine who is 'welcome', and who is 'not welcome', according to the meanings attached to the differences between what they are, and what others are. For example, So Fong was not excluded from the Ladies because she *is* a Chinese lesbian. She was excluded from the Ladies because the perpetrators recognised her as being different *to* them in various ways; and to their minds these differences pointed to an inferiority, or lack, that demanded her exclusion. Hostility was a way of achieving this.

To understand the body as a cultural product is to be able to recognise it as a site for the kinds of knowledges through which gendered, racist and homophobic violences are enacted and experienced; and, indeed, to speculate about the possible ways in which violence itself might invest corporeality (the subject matter of Chapter 5). Loosened from the pre-discursive foundations of constructionism, the body functions as a mark of the differences that undergird these forms of violence without reducing them to a question of natural, authentic or fixed essences. The model of the cultural body thus provides a starting point for revisiting the anti-essentialist goals of intersectionality, enabling them to be pursued as a question of the ways in which *embodied specificities* are *mutually constitutive* of each other. Here, the body remains a *site* of knowledge for the enactment and experience of violence, but it is never the *source* of that knowledge. If race, gender and sexuality are always the vehicles of articulation for each other, then neither is that knowledge conceived in unitary or universal terms. Every act of violence that emerges out of assumptions about fixed and rigid categories of difference is dependent upon a body, or bodies, that, in its very multiplicity, must ultimately expose the incoherence and fluidity of those categories.[18]

Conclusion

In this chapter, I have considered accounts from two women regarding encounters with violence that appear to be related to territories of race, gender and sexuality. Taking these accounts as examples, I have sought to revisit and revitalise the concept of intersectionality. I have no issue with the intention behind the concept of intersectionality itself; that is, with the goal of moving away from essentialist and universal accounts of violence. My concerns have more to do with the language through which we seek to do this, and the kinds of assumptions that this language encourages us to make. In particular, I am not convinced that intersectionality is the best tool for achieving this goal. Indeed, it may actually restrict our ability to do so. I have two main reasons for saying this. First, I do not believe that the notion of an intersection fully encapsulates the highly interactive way in which categories of identity are articulated through each other and enacted in violence. Second, the tendency of intersectional accounts of violence to take a social constructionist approach to difference makes it difficult to move beyond an essentialist notion of both the subject who enacts, and the subject who experiences, violence.

I have suggested that we might overcome the first of these difficulties by rethinking the issue of intersectionality as a matter of mutual constitution. This might help us to represent the way in which differences are articulated, and identities are lived, through and within each other. I have not suggested that a given incident of violence cannot be dominated by one prejudice, one facet of identity, or one power relation. In some instances, it may be appropriate, and necessary, for an analysis of violence to prioritise one particular construction of difference. Nor have I suggested that the process of mutual constitution denotes a seamless interaction, free of contradictions. I have, however, suggested that we need to recognise, on the one hand, that racist, homophobic and gendered violence are all undergirded by particular constructions of difference and, on the other hand, that these constructions are produced through other forms of specificity that preclude such violence from being reduced to a single or universal category.

This shift in thinking directs our attention towards the place of the body in constructions of difference. I have suggested that recognising the body as one of the primary sites through which difference is identified, and violence erupts, need not be a case of 'fossilising specificity into determinate body-types' (Cheah and Grosz 1996: 211). Recent notions of what I call the cultural body allow us to locate both the enactment and the experience of violence in the interactive particularities of embodied identities, without being trapped by essentialist versions of that body. Moreover, they enable us to recognise that the body is the origin of neither difference nor violence. Instead, violence erupts out of the hierarchical, and visible, relation *between* bodies, the connections and disconnections, the values that this relation attributes to particular bodies, the way that some bodies are assumed to be superior to others, and so on. This sense of superiority requires that others be managed to a certain degree. Violence provides one means of doing this. Hence, it is no coincidence that violence is so often patterned by systems of gender, sexuality and race. These patterns reflect some of the most normative and value-laden lines of difference between human subjects.

4

BODY MAPS

Envisaging homophobia, violence and safety

Several years ago I presented a paper at an international victimology conference held in Adelaide, Australia.[1] My paper was part of a session on hostility against members of the gay and lesbian communities. Prior to our presentations, a signed letter of complaint was submitted to the conference administration. The author of the letter objected to the inclusion of the gay and lesbian session in the program. Expressing both anger and disappointment at our presence, which she described as an 'advertisement' for a 'deviant pressure group', she asserted: 'If gays and lesbians give public witness to their sexual preferences their "acts" are no longer in private, and cannot be said to have a private connotation any longer.' Although the session proceeded unimpeded, I was struck at the time by the particulars of this grievance. The writer seemed less concerned with gay and lesbian sexualities *per se* and more concerned with the 'public witness' of such sexualities. The open admission of a (presumed) preference for certain sexual 'acts' appeared to arouse her anger rather than the acts themselves. Ironically, her certainty that this breakdown of privatised homosexuality provided a legitimate ground for complaint seemed to find some fuel in the 'right to privacy' arguments that have marked many claims by the gay and lesbian movement for social and legal reform.

The emergence of one complaint within the context of a large and diverse international conference is hardly significant in itself. Nor is disdain for the public acknowledgment of gay and lesbian sexualities in any way peculiar to this complainant. What interests me, however, is the framing of these sentiments within a trope of visibility: that is, the way in which heteronormative attitudes are articulated as a question of the degree to which we can 'see' same-sex sexualities. This trope is, to my mind, the crystallisation of assumptions that circulate in contemporary western nations regarding the appropriateness, or otherwise, of expressions and representations of homosexuality. We need look no further than the popular and longstanding refrain against those who 'flaunt' their homosexuality to realise that the very suggestion that homosexuality *can* be flaunted is itself the product of the social and political hush that has historically enveloped the subject of same-sex sexuality. Whilst the cultural mandate to conceal one's homosexuality may have waned, the knowledge that it is possible to do so continues to serve as the favoured benchmark against which all representations of homosexuality are measured.

In this chapter I pick up on the unspoken question that this letter of complaint posed for those of us at the victimology conference who sought to highlight the problem of homophobia-related hostility and violence: how is this hostility marked by notions of visibility and invisibility that circulate within contemporary discourses of sexuality, and homosexuality in particular? Specifically, how are the implications (or effects, if you like) of hostility and violence configured by the trope of visibility?

The effects of homophobia-related hostility upon the individual are a source of on-going concern. For many lesbians and gay men these include not only the emotional and physical pain of the immediate incident but also long-term psychological distress and trauma (Garnets, Herek and Levy 1990; Hunter 1990; Ryan and Futterman 1998; van den Boogaard 1989). Without wishing to downplay the harm that homophobia-related violence inflicts upon those who are personally targeted, my purpose here is to explore the implications of this hostility as they are amplified beyond the question of individual injury. Feminism has shown us that gendered violence has the capacity to affect the lives of women, irrespective of whether they have direct and personal experience of it. I pick up on this argument by premising this chapter upon the idea that violence does not have to be experienced to have repercussions. Hence, the interview excerpts that I draw upon focus not so much on the details of actual encounters with hostility, but more upon the women's responses to the *possibility* of a hostile or violent reaction to their sexuality. I will suggest that, in order to understand the cultural, or collective, implications of homophobia-related hostility, it is necessary to position this hostility in the wider context of discursive statements of sexual visibility: that is, to see how homophobia-related violence functions through the relation between homosexuality and visibility. To my mind, the collective implications of violence can be understood as a question of knowledge. What does it mean for lesbians and gay men to *know*, whether through individual experience or not, about the risks and possibilities of homophobia-related hostility and violence? One answer to this question is found in the specific techniques that lesbians and gay men use to negotiate a sense of safety from inter-personal violence. By looking at the contribution that lesbian and gay knowledges of homophobia-related violence make to the construction of these 'safety maps', I hope to be able to say something about the significance of the homosexuality–visibility nexus to the capacity of violence to infiltrate the lives of lesbians and gay men.

One of the significant issues to emerge from Chapter 2 was the central role that gender plays in violence that is commonly characterised as homophobic. In Chapter 3, I sought to build on this by considering the extent to which the concept of intersectionality is able to account for the ways in which constructions of difference infuse the enactment and experience of inter-personal violence. My examination of violence that is shaped by racist, homophobic and sexist sentiment led me to suggest that it might be helpful to conceptualise this as an embodied process of mutual constitution, rather than one of intersectionality. Both of these chapters highlight the fact that identities will always interact with each other to produce differences in the characteristics and experience of homophobia-related violence. However, in this chapter I consider personal safety primarily as it relates to homosexuality. This focus on sexual preference prompts me to look at the congruence, rather than the variance, between anti-lesbian and anti-gay violence. Although I canvass some of the ways in which safety from homophobia-related violence is refracted by relations of gender, ethnicity, class, and age, I am willing to wager that the relation between homosexuality and visibility marks all forms of violence where homophobia comes into play, albeit in varying ways. Hence, I draw upon perceptions of homophobia-related hostility among women as a medium for thinking about the implications of homophobia-related violence for both men and women.

The trope of visibility

There is a vexed relationship between discourses of sexuality and notions of visibility. Historically, the obligation to confess one's sexual desire as a means of revealing the inner truth about oneself lies side by side with the imposition of silences and secrecies about all forms of sexual behaviour. In western cultures, this tension, between 'the obligation to tell the truth' and the cultural convention of 'verbal prohibition', continues to engender a bifurcated understanding of sexual desire, as both a means for 'deciphering who one is' and the source of an imperative towards 'hiding what one does' (Foucault 1988: 16). The historical classification of sexual desires and practices into observable categories of sexual identity thus represents a technology through which one comes to know and speak of oneself as a certain type of sexual being, for example, as heterosexual or homosexual. At the same time, however, the production of these visible identities also functions as a 'trap' (Foucault 1977: 200). [2] In providing us with the means to recognise ourselves, and others, as certain types of subjects, sexual identities prompt us to assume responsibility for curtailing, confessing and regulating our own behaviour so as to conform to the expectations attached to these particular subject positions. While all sexual subject positions are vulnerable to the sense of personal and social scrutiny that prompts us to monitor our own behaviour in this way, the extent to which we feel the need to hide what we 'do' will be shaped, in part, by the uneven implications of being visible as a specific type of sexual person. Despite the recent recognition of heterosexuality as an identity in itself — most likely bringing with it new constraints as well as freedoms – the historical privilege accorded to monogamous heterosexual marriage means that hetero-erotic desires continue to be seen as unremarkable and unproblematic expressions of sexuality. While the very normativity of the institution of heterosexuality inevitably constrains the sexual subjectivities of those who choose it as a lifestyle, the negative implications of openly identifying as heterosexual remain minimal. In contrast, visibility can operate to 'trap' the many women and men whose sexual desires and practices deviate from this benchmark (for example, gay men and lesbians, sex workers, or those who engage in sado-masochistic sexualities) not only because it restricts their sense of sexual subjectivity, but also because it brings with it the threat of social or legal sanctions, including discrimination, incarceration, violence or personal rejection.

Sedgwick captures the importance of the trope of visibility to the particular politics of homosexuality when she argues that the privacy of 'the closet', and the demarcation between being in or out of the closet, is the 'defining structure' for lesbian and gay oppression in the twentieth century (1990: 71–2). The very idea that 'coming out' is a *possible* moment for any lesbian or gay man exemplifies her point well.[3] Although western nations are currently witnessing the burgeoning emergence of an undisguised and unapologetic homosexuality into the public domains of law, media, culture and politics, the legacy of a history of disapprobation and pathologisation is found in the continued heteronormative predilection for censoring certain expressions of same-sex sexual desire. This permeates the everyday lives of lesbians and gay men in routine yet heterogeneous ways. Surveys, interviews, fiction and personal anecdotes all reveal pervasive and complex pictures of veiled, sometimes secretive, homosexualities, including: the refusal of some (certainly not all) heterosexual women and men to legitimate, or even acknowledge, the homosexuality of others; the perception among gay men and lesbians that they need to masquerade or 'pass' as heterosexual in situations of work, family or even friendship; the tendency to ignore or trivialise the act of coming out; and the recent promotion of acceptable expressions of monogamous or 'vanilla' homosexualities at the expense of less respectable homo-erotic practices (Eliason, Donelan and Randall 1992; GLAD 1994; McGregor 1996; Mason 1995). Cumulatively, these kinds of engagement with homosexuality produce not so much a ubiquitous or universal exclusion, but a pervasive atmosphere of inarticulation or silence (to momentarily invoke a different metaphor): a veil that is only broken by repeated representations of gay and lesbian ontologies.[4] This means that the decision to come out to others frequently involves a careful (although sometimes spontaneous) weighing of the likely rewards and possible repercussions. Many ingredients go into this somewhat unpredictable process: for example, personal experience, individual ideology, and the socio-political atmosphere at the time. On a more fundamental level, the act of coming out is deeply shaped by specificities of identity and corporeality, such as gender, age and ethnicity. These variables do not just influence the actual decision to disclose one's homosexuality, they literally mould the meaning of visibility. For example, certain acts, such as walking arm-in-arm, may be a greater signifier of homosexuality for men than for women, or more acceptable in some ethnic communities than in others. In turn, the age of the individuals involved affects the extent to which others even recognise that they are sexual beings with preferences and desires.

While the everyday silences of lesbians and gay men may contribute to the wider social and political opaqueness of homosexuality, such practices cannot be altogether portrayed as the oppressive product of a homophobic culture. The sexual privacy afforded by the closet also proffers a strategic means of control over the extent to which one is subjected to the undesirable implications of being marked as gay or lesbian in everyday life, such as disparagement, discrimination and hostility. Further, the hesitation to publicly identify as gay or lesbian does not only stem from the desire to avoid the more obvious forms of intolerance and inequity. It may also reflect an individual's belief that the very act of coming out entails an inevitable, even if unintended, disavowal of competing or contradictory aspects of identity; not to mention an investment in fixed and essential notions of sexuality. Once an individual makes a declaration of homosexuality there is no means to control or redress the ways in which that knowledge is interpreted by others, and little opportunity to challenge the standpoints from which it will be seen and then digested (Cohen 1991). In particular, the political imperative to 'stand up and be counted' may be outweighed by the risk that other facets of one's self, such as ethnic or racial identities, will be subsumed or 'white-washed' in the process (Omosupe 1991; Walker 1993). Quite simply, the rush to declare 'who we are' can bring with it an unintended series of assumptions about 'who we are not'. This is not to say that the shortage of unsullied public representations of homosexuality is not a prime mechanism in the processes of subjugation but, rather, to take seriously the idea that resistance is integral (rather than external or oppositional) to any given power relation (Foucault 1978). In this sense, the closet represents both a technique of self-surveillance and a strategy for resisting the surveillance of others; or, as Bordo suggests, 'the very same gesture that expresses protest . . . can also signal retreat' (1989: 21). This vacillation between the closet as an oppressive place of enforced secrecy, and a place from which to refuse the subjugatory implications of visible homosexuality (by encouraging the misrecognition of one's sexuality), should remind us that 'silence and secrecy are a shelter for power, anchoring its prohibitions', at the same time that they 'loosen its holds and provide for relatively obscure areas of tolerance' (Foucault 1978: 101).

In short, the closet is a rather contradictory and unstable place. Not only is it necessary to continually repeat the act of 'coming out' in order to actually 'be out' but, as Butler (1991) notes, what it means to be out at any given moment is inevitably dependent upon what it means to be closeted. Hence, one can never be completely in, nor completely out of, the closet. If we add to this discursive ambiguity the more personalised tension between the desire for recognition and the desire *not* to be recognised – to borrow from Skeggs' (1997) insights into identity among working-class women – the distinction between visibility and invisibility begins to look somewhat equivocal. The 'open secret' of homosexuality, the reality of living in and out of the closet at the same time, denotes a shifting, context-dependent and disputed line of demarcation between what it means to be visible in social and political terms, and what it means not to be visible. It is doubtful that homosexuality can be, unequivocally, one or the other.

Body maps

Vision has long been a metaphor for knowledge. In Foucauldian terms, and to repeat a point made in Chapter 1, things made visible are things that are 'shown' to knowledge or, as Rajchman puts it, '[t]o see is always to think . . . and to think is always to see' (1988: 92). In other words, how we see and how we know are inextricable from each other. It is not, therefore, surprising that visibility is one of the tropes through which we come to know homosexuality. Indeed, I have argued above that the construction of homosexuality as a discrete sexual preference that is capable of being concealed or exposed means that same-sex desire is always troubled by the ever-present possibilities of being visible or not visible, of being closeted or out, of speaking up or remaining silent, of being known or not known. If homosexuality is constructed in part through this trope of visibility, then what might this mean, in turn, for violence that is motivated by hostility towards this same sexuality? One suggestion is that the escalating visibility of lesbians and gay men in contemporary western culture has led to a rise in the prevalence of homophobia-related violence (Dean *et al.* 1992). Although this is an intriguing argument, my own approach does not follow this teleological route. Instead, I am interested to explore how the question of visibility might be entangled in the *implications* of violence. Indeed, if I were to momentarily take the risk of representing the relation between violence and visibility in linear terms, I might say that my interest lies at the other end of the cause-and-effect equation, that is, in considering how the trope of visibility shapes the 'effects' of violence, rather than the 'causes'.[5] To come to terms with the implications of violence in any collective sense, it is necessary to consider what it means for lesbians and gay men to know that homophobia-related violence is a tangible, if not always immediate, threat to their personal safety. In other words, if we accept that knowledge itself is the product of a 'mutual presupposition' (Deleuze 1988: 33) between materiality, on the one hand, and language and discourse on the other – that is, of the way in which they inform each other – then the knowledge that lesbians and gay men have of homophobia-related violence (as a material practice) is inevitably 'inscribed in a series of statements' (Kendall and Wickham 1999: 42) about visibility. I believe that the significance of this inscription becomes apparent if we take a closer look at the capacity of homophobia-related violence, as a knowledge, to mould lesbian and gay perceptions of personal safety.

Concerns about crime and violence in contemporary western societies, especially in urban regions, lead most people, and seemingly women in particular, to assess the danger to personal safety posed by particular spaces, situations and individuals (Pain 1997; Stanko 1993; Valentine 1992). These assessments become the basis for the construction of what have been called 'safety maps' (von Schulthess 1992). A safety map is an ever-changing, personalised, yet shared, matrix of attributes and relations that individuals employ to make their way in public and private space. In constructing these maps, individuals draw upon their knowledge of the ways in which specific variables render them vulnerable to personal danger. This conjunction of personal, spatial and temporal variables is likely to include: previous experience of violence; the degree to which an individual feels more or less vulnerable to violence because of their age, gender, ethnicity and the like; understandings of the risks associated with particular areas; the time of day; perceptions about the type of people likely to be encountered in particular areas or within particular social situations; popular discourse around violence and risk; the purpose an individual has for being at a particular place or with a particular group of people; perceptions about physical appearance and gesture; and so on. [6] Whilst the adoption of some form of safety map into our daily lives is so commonplace that most of us treat it as second nature, the actual *ways* in which we choose to map our safety are the product, in part, of the type of violence to which we believe we are vulnerable.

Like other forms of hate crime, an act of homophobia-related violence is symbolic (Cunneen *et al.* 1997; Whillock and Slayden 1995). It stands as a sign of the potential danger for all individuals who identify with the same target group/s as the victim. This argument has been well made in the context of gendered violence where feminist research has demonstrated that many women interpret a seemingly 'minor' or 'everyday' form of unwanted sexualised attention or aggression within the context of other, more serious possibilities. For example, encounters with flashing or obscene phone calls can generate concerns, not only about the incident itself, but also about 'what might happen next' (Kelly 1988). In particular, women's awareness of their vulnerability to certain types of violence, such as rape and sexual assault, shapes their perceptions of, and practices around, personal safety.[7] A similar process is evident in relation to homophobia-related hostility. Seemingly small incidents (such as homophobic remarks, name-calling or verbal abuse) can transform the generic hazards of heteronormativity into the tangible threat of more severe hostility. Although 'minor' incidents (which are disturbingly common according to the survey research cited in Chapter 2) are generally experienced as violating in themselves, their effects are magnified if individuals view them as part of a 'continuum' (Kelly 1988) that links supposedly lesser incidents with those that are of greater concern. Like sexual violence and racially motivated violence, the symbolism of homophobia-related violence is, therefore, contingent upon the extent to which an individual first, recognises their own vulnerability in the victimisation of others with similar identities or lifestyles, and second, interprets abusive, hostile and violent acts within a continuum of possible interconnected dangers.

Hence, the implications of symbolic crimes are not confined to those individuals who experience the violence itself. For many lesbians and gay men, the knowledge that they may be targeted for homophobia-related violence (or, indeed, anyone who thinks they may be) becomes a variable in the mapping of safety, whether they have directly encountered violence or not. Like all other variables, such knowledge makes its own particular contribution to the spatialisation of personal safety. In order to think about this contribution in empirical terms, and particularly the ways in which visibility configures gay and lesbian safety maps, I would like to introduce four excerpts drawn from my interview research. In these excerpts, each woman responds to a question about the ways in which she goes about maximising personal safety in her daily life, specifically safety from hostility or violence that is likely to be related to homophobia. Although the remarks are made by four different women, I wish to treat them as an aggregate form of commentary by discussing them collectively rather than taking each one in turn. Although each has a unique narrative, the accounts they provide are typical of research participants' understandings of the risk that homo-sexuality poses to personal safety. In other words, the material specificities they discuss vary greatly, but a common thread links them all.

Kim, 34 year old, Anglo-Australian, mother of two, recipient of government welfare payments:

> You just do little precautionary things. . . . The kind of strategies that you might employ when you know that you might be gonna cop a stone through the window. . . . Well, I took the bumper-sticker off my car that said something about 'gay love rights'. . . . We stopped holding hands at the shops . . . For a while I even drove the long way home so they [a group of young men at the local shops] wouldn't know where I lived.

Jennifer, 18 year old, Anglo-Australian student:

> Before I come home from a dyke bar I sometimes take off my jacket or brush my hair forward, depending on what I look like. I don't

worry about how much flesh I'm showing. When I go home I'm only worried about how much I look like a dyke. It freaks me out that my old man might be waiting for me. He suspects, but I don't want to give him the proof he needs to justify his own aggression.

Rose, 27 year old, Chinese-Australian doctor:

Sure, sometimes you make big conscious decisions, like, saying to yourself, 'No. I'd *never ever* hold hands in that part of town or in that racist, homophobic crowd. . . . But really it's the little things that you do to yourself every day, that you've gotten so used to doing that you barely realise. It's about not being *too* blatant. A little bit is okay.

Mel, 45 year old, Anglo-Australian postal worker:

I used to get hassled a lot because I looked like a dyke. Now I look straight it's a completely different thing. . . . Well, monitoring your clothes in the morning. If I wear this jacket with this butch haircut and those boots will everyone at work just find it too much? . . . Should I wear earrings to my sister's wedding to tone it down a bit and my god, what about a dress? . . . Setting up two bedrooms in your house, so your parents or, more importantly, friends of your kids won't realise you sleep together. That's a popular one.

Each of these women recounts a series of daily, localised practices designed to monitor, and often minimise, visible manifestations of their sexuality. Each situation calls for different precautionary responses to the conundrum of being 'too blatant'. These behaviours include: removing overt political paraphernalia; toning down the degree to which they look too much like a 'dyke'; not expressing intimate affection with a girlfriend or partner in front of others; not going to certain parts of town because they feel unsafe; going out of their way to ensure that people they don't trust won't find out where they live; and hiding the fact that they sleep together in their own house. Certainly, not all of these practices are a direct response to the presumed risk of violence. Most, however, are. While the behaviours themselves are often about what the women do with objects as diverse as cars, bedrooms and clothes, it is significant that the overall purpose of all of the strategies they describe is to reduce the degree to which they themselves are visible as lesbians, whether that visibility be in terms of personal demeanour, the places they go, or the daily details of their domestic lives. It is important to remember that many factors go into the construction of gay and lesbian safety maps overall. However, the prevalence of these strategies amongst lesbians and gay men suggest that homophobia-related violence, as a form of knowledge, engenders a distinct tendency to monitor one's own body for signs of homosexuality. Given the centrality of the body to the processes of self-surveillance, via which human subjects are subjugated, it is hardly unusual for individuals to adopt a plethora of bodily images, gestures and movements in response to the threat of violence. What is notable in this instance is that safety from homophobia-related violence is conceptualised primarily (albeit, not solely) as a question of the extent to which one is visible as a certain type of sexual subject in the eyes of others, as a homosexual in the eyes of the homophobe. If visibility is a key to safety from the hostility of homophobia then it is unavoidable that in mapping safety lesbians and gay men will be mapping their own bodies for manifestations of sexuality. Hence, we might usefully acknowledge the primacy of the body to the negotiation of safety from the specific problem of homophobia-related violence by thinking of this process as a form of 'body map' in itself: a cartographic matrix of practices for surveying, screening and supervising the times, places and ways in which one is manifest as a homosexual.

There is, of course, no such thing as *a* lesbian or gay body map. Practices for monitoring the visibility of one's homosexuality are refracted, not only by the shifting dynamics of the situation at hand, but also by relations of ethnicity, gender, class, and so on. As I mentioned earlier, these variables mediate the very meanings of visibility. However, they also fashion the components that go into gay and lesbian body maps, sometimes in contradictory ways. For example, during the course of my interview with Rose she suggested that, among the non-Asian population, extreme racism and homophobia often go hand-in-hand. This allows her to use what she calls her 'antenna for racism' to determine whether a group of people are not just likely to be racist but also homophobic. Yet, the very same ethnocentric assumptions that fuel the threat of racism can some-times operate to obscure what might otherwise be a visible expression of homosexuality. Rose puts it like this: 'Anglos are often so naive about other cultures that they think there's no such thing as Asian lesbians . . . I can hold hands with my girlfriend as much as I like in some places and they just think we're "nice Asian girls".' Not surprisingly, Rose is only too happy to 'exploit' these kinds of cultural assumptions when mapping her own safety. The realities of socio-economic difference also shape the extent to which different groups of lesbians and gay men feel the need to monitor their own visibility. Quite simply, the more money you have, the more options you have for choosing where you live, how you travel in your daily life, and where, and with whom, you spend your leisure time. While the signifiers of homosexuality may vary across different class contexts, the bottom line is that it is a lot easier to look 'blatant' when you are able to live and socialise in areas known as 'gay-friendly', or when the luxury of owning your own car allows you to avoid the everyday contingencies of public transport. Similarly, it is important to recognise that gender also frames the practices through which lesbians and gay men monitor their appearance and behaviour for visible expressions of sexuality. Given the prevalence of sexual violence against women, and the possibility of anti-homosexual sentiment leading to such violence, lesbians (like heterosexual women) have more reason than gay men to pay attention to the ways in which their physical appearance will be sexualised by heterosexual men. Yet, as with ethnicity and class, the interaction between gender and sexuality is unlikely to follow a straightforward formula. For example, while it is not unreasonable to expect that women's (supposed) greater fear of violence will produce more extensive practices of self-surveillance among lesbians than among gay men, other factors, such as gay men's apparent greater vulnerability to random homophobia-related assaults, may counter this. Although the details of such scenarios remain to be explored in any comprehensive manner, there is little doubt that the notion of visibility itself, and the practices through which it is charted, are the product not simply of homosexuality as an isolated identity but of the ways in which it is refracted by these (and other) subjectivities.

Stanko and Curry have demonstrated how a 'climate of unsafety' encourages gay men and lesbians to take responsibility for personal safety by self-policing their own behaviour. They suggest that homophobia-related violence 'leads to *a continuum of self-regulation,* whereby the physically threatening behaviour of the homophobe is intertwined with self-imposed regulation of self in heterosexual space' (1997: 525). I wish to pick up on the importance of this point, by suggesting that the discursive tension between homosexuality and visibility represents interacting axes upon which the specificities of various practices of self-regulation pivot. In other words, safety from the hostility of homophobia may be negotiated in a multitude of ways, but each negotiation inevitably turns on the question of visibility. The implications of knowing (and, of course, believing) that one may be subjected to physical violence or verbal hostility is found in the construction of body maps that incorporate an understanding of the hostile contingencies of displays of homosexuality; that is, body maps are the specific product of the integration of the trope of visibility into the broader safety maps that lesbians and gay men construct. If the corporeal practices that lesbians and gay men engage in to attain a sense of safety from homophobia-related violence are an effect of their knowledge of this hostility then, in an epistemological sense, it is possible that homophobia-related violence is always inscribed in – but never confined by – a series of statements about visibility.[8] Or, to relate this to my overall concern with the collective 'effects' of homophobia-related violence, the negotiation of visibility through the construction of lesbian and gay body maps may be an inevitable material implication of homophobia-related hostility, one that is not bound by the immediate and personal injuries inflicted by the act of violence itself.

Flouting danger

Like the woman at the international victimology conference who was resistant to the public witness of homosexuality, the perpetrators of homophobia-related violence (who appear to be primarily, but not exclusively, male) often seem to be more antagonistic towards unabashed and unashamed representations of gay and lesbian sexualities than they are toward homosexuality itself. It is not therefore surprising, as I have suggested above, that homophobia-related violence generates a tendency among lesbians and gay men to construct personal safety in terms that are framed by the question of visibility. The centrality of visibility to the 'body maps' that lesbian and gay men create in the pursuit of safety suggests that it is not possible to formulate the full social implications of homophobia-related violence in isolation from statements of sexual visibility. Nonetheless, this is not the same as saying that violence gives rise to a monolithic form of social invisibility.

Let me explore the significance of this distinction by considering what I call the 'holding hands' example. Among all the questions that I put to the women I interviewed, the one that received the most consistent response was a direct question about whether or not they tended to hold hands, or otherwise express intimacy, such as kissing, with a partner or girlfriend when they were in predominantly heterosexual spaces. Taking into account individual preferences around the public display of affection, and the fact that concerns about hostility and violence are just one aspect of broader concerns about disapproval and discrimination, the overwhelming response from this group of women was, 'it depends': it depends on the atmosphere and terrain of each and every situation as it arises; it depends on the gender and ethnicity of the people likely to be encountered; it depends on the possible repercussions; it depends on the short-term and long-term significance of any negative responses; it depends on staying attuned to any changes in the situation, and so on. No one said, 'I always feel safe enough to display such affection'. No one said, 'I never feel safe enough to display such affection'. The decision to hold hands or kiss was always a question of weighing up the risks and rewards. Even those women who saw themselves as 'blatant' about their sexuality exercised caution about the contexts within which they were so: 'I reckon I'm as out as anyone can be. But, yeah, I'm still careful about when I can afford to flaunt it. I'm not stupid, you know.' On the other hand, women who saw themselves as being relatively closeted also monitored and assessed situations for the degree of security they were likely to provide: 'Sometimes when I'm feeling *really* brave and things looks okay I'll grab my girlfriend's hand. It never lasts. But, hey, I did it!'

The correlation between the risk of hostility and the decision not to disclose one's sexuality – which can also be read as a correlation between being 'blatant' and being 'stupid' – is not a simple linear one. Danger does not necessarily signify a return to the closet. Many lesbians and gay men derive pleasure from being blatant about their sexuality and, moreover, from deliberately creating a bit of a spectacle. Russo has suggested that to make a sexual spectacle of oneself is a particularly feminine danger that invites one to be read as grotesque. In seems to me, however, that sexualised displays of homosexuality in men and women transgress the boundaries of decorum in ways that attract similar condemnation: to borrow from Russo, 'certain bodies, in certain public framings, in certain public spaces, are always already transgressive – dangerous and in danger' (1986: 217). In different ways, and to different degrees, lesbians and gay men may actively court this danger (and blame), in order to experience 'the pleasure of showing off, scandalizing, or resisting' (Foucault 1978: 45). For example, Helen, a woman I interviewed, described one of her favourite pastimes in these terms. In particular, Helen likes to shock groups of young men who cross her path. Pulling up in her car at the traffic lights often provides a perfect opportunity to do this: 'If there's a bunch of yahoos pulling up at the side, I can get quite bold and start passionately kissing my lover in the car. They'll wind down the window and say "Dirty lesos! Lesos!. . . You just can't get a man."' Helen then takes great delight as she 'leaves them for dead', by speeding off when the lights change to green. Sometimes they follow, sometimes they don't. For Helen, the thrill and amusement of this experience is the product not only of the sense of travesty that an open display of lesbian passion engenders but, more specifically, of evading the danger that the young men embody for her. By mocking their heterosexist insults she is able to trivialise and express contempt for the potential of homophobia-related hostility to injure her. Just as attempts to camouflage homosexuality represent both an oppressive silencing and a resistance to the trap of visibility, so too does this act of 'flaunting' homosexuality expose one to the possibility of homophobic repercussions, at the same time that it challenges the very ability of these repercussions to cause harm.

It is important to recognise that the pleasure of 'flaunting' one's sexuality may derive its effect, in part, from flouting, perhaps flirting with, danger. However, it is equally important to recognise, as suggested above, that blatancy is not the same as stupidity. Helen is always careful to stage her performances so that the risks to her safety do not outweigh the rewards. If her experience is in any way representative, such acts of deliberate affront are most likely to take place in situations where lesbians and gay men already feel safe enough to flirt with danger because they can control the outcome of the risks they take; for example: driving in their cars with their lovers; walking with a group of leather men; coming out to a violent father surrounded by friends; or dancing with thousands of other queers in a Mardi Gras parade, wearing nothing but body paint. Personal safety is a perception, as well as an embodied material condition. It cannot be procured or guaranteed once and for all. It is always a process of negotiation. To negotiate safety, lesbians and gay men (like everyone else) must find ways to continually reinforce and reproduce their own sense of it. It is possible that the integration into one's own body maps of controlled engagements with what it means to be unsafe is one method of doing this.

Managing safety

In their work on the policing of 'the responsible' homosexual Stanko and Curry (1997) suggest that the risk of violence is intertwined with the risk of self-exposure. Violence prevention strategies that pressure gay men and lesbians to 'pass' as heterosexual engender a form of self-regulation that supposedly allows individuals to manage potential harm. I am drawn to Stanko and Curry's use of the concept of management in this context. If the body maps that flow from gay and lesbian knowledges of homophobia-related violence are constituted by acts that seek both to avoid and to flout the danger of a visible homosexuality, then does the concept of 'management', especially 'self-management' offer a useful theoretical and linguistic tool for articulating these complexities? Might it be helpful to try to capture gay and lesbian attempts to corporeally map personal safety through the idea that visibility is 'managed' rather than, say, regulated?

In Foucauldian terms, the broad concept of regulation (in departure from, but subsuming, the notion of repression) captures most effectively the 'process of subjection' which *activates* or forms the subject' (Butler 1995: 230). In particular, the inscription of systems of knowledge (such as the classification of sexual desire into categories of homosexual and heterosexual) upon 'wayward populations' allows 'dysfunctional personalities' and 'behavioral deficiencies' to be understood as essential or self-evident properties of individuals (Rajchman 1988: 104). This process of reducing and containing human multiplicities to a 'tight space' (the category of homosexuality) facilitates the imposition of a *particular conduct on a particular human multiplicity*' (Deleuze 1988: 34).[9] This means that the choice to act in certain ways is shaped by the way in which subjects see themselves and others as certain types of individuals: '"[s]eeing" in this sense is part of doing' (Rajchman 1988: 94). In other words, once subjects are seen, and see themselves, in a particular light, their choices, decisions and actions are all affected by the parameters of these identity categories. They adapt to the cultural expectations attached to specific identities and restrict their behaviour accordingly. As we have already witnessed, it is not only formal systems of knowledge (such as sexology and psychology) that are deployed in the regulation of human multiplicities. Informal systems of knowledge (such as the exchange of anecdotes about homophobia-related hostility, rumours about unsafe spaces, and so on) are also crucial to the ways in which particular actions are taken up by subjects (Hunt and Wickham 1994). It is this merger of formal and informal knowledge systems that allows gay men and lesbians to know that they might be the object of someone else's homophobic hostility, irrespective of whether they have encountered that hostility directly themselves, and to employ this knowledge in the construction of their own maps for the pursuit of safety. It is via this imperative to normative obedience that subjects are regulated.

Certainly, the daily, localised decisions and embodied actions that lesbians and gay men engage in to negotiate safety can be well articulated as practices of self-surveillance in the wider regulatory processes of disciplinarity. We know, however, that subjects simultaneously defy this process. For example, the interview excerpts quoted above suggest to me that a safety map is not a blueprint for a secreted homosexuality; violence does not just function to coerce lesbians and gay men to stay in the closet (indeed, any such function will always be disrupted by the very instability of the closet itself). Safety is never a static condition but rather a context-dependent form of negotiation. In particular, safety from homophobia involves a continual process of monitoring and balancing the potential risks of disclosure with the potential rewards; assessments that, as I have suggested above, are always made through the conjunction of homophobia with other specificities. In any given situation, the way in which an individual has mapped out the meaning of safety may guide him or her toward a series of corporeal practices that effectively confine, conceal or exclude expressions of homosexuality. This much is clear. However, the imperative to map one's own safety is not only a matter of bridling, moderating or restricting bodily representations of homosexuality in order to 'make regular'. It is also an imperative towards 'looking after' these representations, by controlling and taking charge of them: practices that might involve not only regulating one's self-representations in order to conform but, also, refusing to regulate them in this way (a form of resistance in itself).

The collective implications of homophobia-related violence need to be formulated so as to account for these cartographical practices of compliance and defiance. This is where the concept of management might be useful. In a literal sense, the notion of management denotes the organising and handling of things, taking charge of situations and people. This involves strategies of self-regulation – moderation, correction and restriction – as well as a sense of command, stewardship, and the manipulation of events that comes with being in a position that demands, and allows, this kind of control. Although the relation between Foucauldian notions of management, regulation, discipline and governance is somewhat slippery and far from incontrovertible, I would like to briefly traverse some of this ground with the specific purpose of positioning the terms 'management' and 'self-management'. My purpose in seeking to flesh out these notions is not to make a pedantic point about the importance of semantic distinctions between concepts that are, to be honest, closely entwined with each other. More simply, I wish to suggest that the dictionary-type description of management that I have provided above hints at a more theoretical meaning of the concept, especially as it relates to the self, that might prove useful in the analysis of homophobia-related violence.

Management makes a brief appearance in Foucault's initial account of the disciplinary society (or, at least in English translations of it). Specifically, the kinds of self-monitoring practices that I have depicted above are, for Foucault, techniques that render the unpredictable, confusing multiplicities of human populations more 'manageable' (Foucault 1977: 219). While Prado (1995) suggests that the disciplines can therefore be 'glossed' as techniques for 'managing' people, a more precise interpretation of manage-ment really only becomes apparent within the context of Foucault's later work on governmentality.[10] If government is understood as a broad regu-latory strategy for the 'conduct of conduct' (Rose 1996b: 134), particularly as it relates to populations and nation states, then the notion of management most commonly signifies the techniques through which knowledge systems are brought to bear upon particular objects in order to achieve the overall objectives of government. Although governmentality has many components, one of the ways in which the 'collective mass' of human phenomena is controlled and managed is via the very 'depths' and 'details' of individual practices of self-surveillance (Foucault 1991: 102). In other words, the govern-ment of populations is not just a matter of the 'calculated management' of others (a form of 'management' which was explored in Chapter 3), but also of the small everyday 'technologies of the self' through which subjects 'experience, understand, judge and conduct themselves', and which are so often implemented through the body (Rose 1996b: 135). Hunt and Wickham (1994: 79) pick up on Foucault's use of management by referring to these more micro elements of government as 'self-management' (or self-government). It is significant that this 'managerialization' of identity and personal relations is not experienced exclusively as the imposition of a set of rules that serve the interests of others. Indeed, the very capacity of know-ledge systems to engender an imperative to self-management is determined by the extent to which this imperative is understood as a question of 'caring' for one's self (Gordon 1991).

The danger that homophobia-related violence, like other forms of violence, poses to one's physical and psychological integrity means that the safety practices that lesbians and gay men engage in are a matter of both regulating the ways in which one's self is vulnerable to violence, and of caring for the safety and security of that self. If we understand homosexuality as an object or thing to be governed in the pursuit of personal safety then, certainly, lesbians and gay men do chart their bodies for visible manifest-ations of homosexuality in ways that can only be described as an undesirable adaptation to the requirements of homophobic sentiment. But in constantly mapping their bodies for signs of homosexuality, lesbians and gay men are also able to exercise a form of control. They cope with the knowledge of violence by organising their bodies and optimising the ways in which others react to them. It seems to me that the concept of self-management may offer a fruitful formulation for recognising that this response to violence encompasses both the imperative to moderate and restrict the ways in which one is visibly homosexual, and the desire to carefully handle one's homosexuality as a means of looking after and caring for one's personal security and integrity. Self-management hints at the agency of subjects who do not just control themselves (or are controlled) in the face of danger, but who also 'take control' of certain situations, that is, subjects who literally subject things to *their* control. Gay men and lesbians may rarely be in a position to 'take charge' of the hostility that is committed directly against them, but as the 'managers' of their own visibility, many are able to take charge of the contexts that feed into and flow from their knowledge of such hostility.

Conclusion: managing the unmanageable

I have suggested that in avoiding or flouting danger, in negotiating safety, in hiding or flaunting sexuality, lesbians and gay men are involved in the complex daily management of a plethora of choices around the relation between homosexuality and visibility. As the corporeal spatialisation of these negotiations – what Foucault might call a diagram of 'the location of bodies in space' (1977: 205) – body maps resonate with panoptic principles of vision and visibility. They represent the collective implications of the knowledge that homophobia brings to the broader construction of a sense of personal safety. This includes, but is never confined to, a plethora of options for managing the ways in which one's homosexuality is recognisable, or visible, to audiences who may pose a threat. Irrespective of how a given individual experiences and responds to the question of personal safety, the knowledge of violence means that lesbians and gay men must grapple (whether regularly or irregularly) with the spectre of the closet; the kinds of management practices that are described above are only possible because visibility fashions our understandings of homosexuality and the choices available for negotiating safety. In short, I am suggesting that no matter how gay men and lesbians deal with the risks that homophobia poses to their safety, they are invariably drawn into an imperative to manage self-represent-ations of their sexuality towards desirable ends. If managing homophobia-related violence means managing one's homosexuality, then the risk of homophobia-related violence does not simply lie side-by-side with the risks associated with coming out. As Stanko and Curry suggest, the two are intertwined. The imperative to manage the visible representations of one's homosexuality suggests that the specifics of this entanglement lie in the fact that lesbian and gay knowledges of homophobia-related hostility are always infused with the homosexuality–visibility nexus. The very fact that at any given moment it might be possible to be anything less than 'blatant' about one's homosexuality inscribes the choices one has for negotiating safety. In this way, homophobia-related hostility, and the body maps it engenders, is inescapably configured by the 'trap of visibility'. Quite simply, it may be that to know of homophobia-related hostility is to manage visibility.

What, then, of the ambiguity of the trope of visibility? Whilst it is commonplace to represent the question of sexual visibility in dichotomous terms (visible/invisible, public/private, in/out, inside/outside, closet/freedom), as I have argued above, the meanings attached to being in or out of the closet are neither singular nor universal. To be closeted about one's sexuality can be a form of both acquiescence and control. Similarly, the decision to come out may be an act of resistance at the same time that it feeds into the 'trap' of visible sexualities. If, therefore, it is never possible to be completely closeted, it is likely that it is never possible to be completely safe from homophobia-related violence.[11] Further, even if it were possible, the equivocal nature of the closet means that every time lesbians and gay men grapple with the question of visibility they must grapple with the uncertainty and duplicity of the options available to them. Every small act of self-management, every body map, then, is a part not just of a larger diagram of the connection between homosexuality and visibility but, more specifically, of the flux and ambiguity of this relation. This, I suggest, means that the collective legacy of homophobia-related violence is found, not only in the harm and injury it inflicts on many individuals, nor in the personal and social veiling of a 'wayward' or 'unruly' population, but, moreover, in the capacity to incite this population to manage the equivocal and contested nexus between homosexuality and visibility, when the very troubled nature of that nexus is itself the source of much uncertainty and tension. The imperative to manage one's homosexuality is, in this instance, an imperative to manage the unmanageable.

A version of this chapter appeared as 'Body maps: envisaging homophobia, violence and safety' in *Social and Legal Studies* 10(1) March 2001, 23–44. Reprinted by permission of Sage Publications Ltd.

5

BACKLIGHT AND SHADOW

Constituting danger

Sticks and stones may break my bones.
But names will never hurt me.

This is a handy retort to have at one's disposal, one that we've probably all resorted to in the past to counter those inevitable schoolyard taunts. But, to be honest, I always thought it sounded a little lame. The thing you say when you've got no other defence, the words that inadvertently tell everyone that this is the best weapon you have to ward off an attack. If you have ever been called a name, you will know that it usually does hurt. It hurts in a different way to the pain of a physical attack. Unless a name actually has the capacity to hurt you it is not the kind of insult that this children's rhyme is talking about. It is something else. This was brought home to me recently by a Korean Australian student who told one of my classes a story about her 8-year-old son. Apparently, he came home from school one day, pleased and excited because he'd been given a new nickname: 'Ching Chong'. He kept singing it around the house, taking delight in the way that the words rolled off his tongue. Being familiar with the longer version of the name ('Ching Chong Chinaman') his mother thought it was probably intended as a racial slur, although she couldn't be certain. She decided not to tell him about her suspicions. Why spoil his fun? It wasn't hurting him. Not yet.

The happy ending to this story depends upon the fact that an 8-year-old boy is not aware of the history that enables these words to belittle or devalue the ways in which he is different from those who speak them. Such a boy does not feel the need to declare that 'names will never hurt me' because he has not yet imagined that this might be the intention. In contrast, when we respond to a recognised name by rebutting its ability to hurt us, we attempt to draw a line between what these words *may* do, and what we *allow* them to do. In consciously acting to deflect harm, we become the agents of our own defence. Our resistance, of course, is reliant upon the fact that we know, or assume, that the name was intended to single us out in some way and, most probably, to insult, impugn or affront us. We know these things by making experienced or instinctive calculations about the situation at hand. For example, to be called 'queer' will have a very different meaning according to who does the naming: is it a friendly gesture by another queer, or is it a troublesome slur by a potential queer-basher? In some instances, it may be difficult to be certain which of these interpretations is most apt. In other situations, however, the name is accompanied by behaviours that erase all uncertainty.

Acts of inter-personal violence, threats of violence and other forms of aggression and destruction (such as property damage) represent just such a situation. They hurt us by inflicting physical discomfort, pain, and, in some instances, severe injury, even death. They can also engender immediate and long-term emotional wounds in the form of anxiety, fear, anger, humiliation and so on. When we are named as homosexual, or as any 'type' of person, in such a hostile context, it is virtually impossible not to interpret the words in a denigratory fashion. Likewise, the words themselves provide a context through which we are able to construe the behaviour. That is, we know that the words are insulting because they are accompanied by hurtful practices, and we can guess at the ways in which these acts are intended to hurt us because of the language that accompanies them.

The question I explore in this chapter is: what happens to the knowledge of this hurt? This question is closely connected to recent debates over the power of language to wound, particularly hate speech as a mode of sub-ordination and subjectification. Unlike speech, however, less has been said about the constitutive capacity of physical violence. It is as if the overtly corporeal, and deeply destructive, nature of violence mitigates the need to recognise it as a form of discourse with performative and productive implications. The very fact that I ask this question is evidence of my belief that homophobic violence harms lesbians and gay men in discursive as well as corporeal terms. I suggest that the gist of this discursive injury cannot be confined to the particular insults that are hurled during an attack. Homophobia-related violence also marks the bodies of those it targets with signs of vulnerability and victimhood: signs that name homosexuality as being 'in danger' of hostility and violence. The issue at contest in my question is whether the injury implicit to this name insinuates itself into the normative processes through which lesbians and gay men are constituted as certain types of subjects.

If we do accept that homophobia-related violence makes a contribution to the processes of subject-formation, or subjectification, we must also consider the limits of, and constraints upon, this injurious production. How are these names understood and experienced in an empirical sense? Do individual lesbians and gay men draw a distinction between what homophobia-related violence does and does not do? If so, how? I attempt to come to terms with these issues by examining how the women I interviewed responded to the experience of being subjected to, or threatened with, homophobia-related violence. I focus upon how violence makes these women feel about themselves: how it affects their experiences of their own bodies, their identities, the way they appear to others, and their interactions with others. In doing so, I look specifically at the impact of violence on sexual identity, and its interaction with racial and gendered subjectivities. Whilst many women talked about the extent to which violence does, and does not, infiltrate their sense of self, it is notable that several women used the same words to do this. They spoke in terms of an empirical distinction between 'what' and 'who' they become, or do not become, in violence. This distinction presents an interesting, if thorny, way of thinking about the capacities and limits of violence.

To consider how we might interpret the distinction these women draw between 'who' and 'what' they are, I turn to some of the writings of political theorist and philosopher, Hannah Arendt. Arendt is probably best known for her work on totalitarianism and the Jewish pariah, as well as the politics of revolution and violence. However, she also wrote extensively on the human condition. Significantly, she formulated an account of the human subject by drawing upon the notions of 'who' and 'what' we are. For Arendt, 'who' we are signifies the on-going processes through which we form a particular identity. This is always a question of the things we say and do in relation to others. 'What' we are refers to the categories that are common to many of us, and that provide a framework within which 'who' we are emerges. Although Arendt was primarily concerned with political identity, recent feminist and poststructural interpretations suggest that some of her ideas might assist us in thinking about identity in a broader sense. This is especially so for those aspects of identity that we now recognise as deeply politicised in their own right, such as gender and sexuality.

Arendt has always been a controversial intellectual figure, attracting criticism from diverse political and philosophical quarters.[1] Although she has never been considered a friend of either feminism or poststructuralism, this does not mean that her work is necessarily irreconcilable with either school of thought. She is, in fact, linked to each, in various ways. For example, Arendt shares a certain intellectual history with Foucault: Nietzsche and Heidegger are two obvious influences that they have in common. In contrast to Foucault, however, her work on the human condition remained loyal to the kind of classical philosophical tradition that Foucault eventually rejected in his challenge to the modernist notion of the human subject. In terms of feminism, Arendt's intolerance of single-cause social movements led her to dismiss many of its aims and methods. This lack of support is reciprocated in the criticisms that feminists have made of Arendt's work, particularly her conventional definition of politics, her insistence on a public/private divide, and her rejection of the body as an important site of political struggle. Yet, as Young-Bruehl (1997) points out, some second-wave feminists responded to Arendt in a more positive manner, by employing her ideas, such as those on power and violence, toward their own projects. These kinds of mixed reactions to Arendt are not unusual. It is perhaps this ability to defy categorisation, as either a conservative or a radical thinker, which has brought about a recent resurgence of interest in her writing.

Although I have reservations about Arendt's model of the human subject, notably the ease with which it can be read as an endorsement of individualism, I believe that her distinction between 'what' and 'who' is helpful in interpreting and developing the point that my interviewees make. In particular, it provides us with a means of recognising both the capacities and limits of violent subjectification, as they are experienced in empirical terms. My intention is to adapt, rather than adopt, Arendt towards this end. In this sense, my reading of her work is deliberately narrow. I focus upon recent feminist interpretations of those aspects of her writing that are most pertinent to the question of identity. In thinking about identity as a question of 'what' and 'who' we are, I hope to recognise that violence has the capacity to *constitute* the meaning of homosexuality, without necessarily *determining* the subjectivities through which this identity category is experienced, rejected, reinvented and, generally, lived in an everyday sense.

My discussion in this chapter takes the injury and pain of violence very seriously, but refuses to treat the identity categories that pattern it as foundational or fixed. Instead of assuming that there are natural or predetermined victims of violence – as in the classic assumption that women are the inevitable objects of men's sexual violence – I attempt to think of violence as a process that maintains and reproduces this kind of thinking. In doing so, I follow a crucial feminist trend towards replacing deterministic accounts of violence with an interrogation of the ways in which particular discourses around violence 'script' the imaginable options for those who may occupy positions of victim or violator, and how they may be occupied. Much of this work has taken representations of violence in law, media, cinema, and fiction as its starting point (Young 1996; Hart 1994; Marcus 1992; Smart 1992). My own argument will pay attention to the constitutive capacity of actual incidents of violence.

In terms of my overall project in this book, it is worth noting that in earlier chapters, especially Chapters 2 and 3, I sought to highlight some of the discursive and corporeal contexts within which homophobia-related violence is enacted and experienced. In Chapter 4, I shifted from thinking about these contextual questions (where violence comes from) to thinking about the implications of violence (where violence goes). I now develop this question of implications by exploring the capacity of violence to effect certain things. At the risk of over-simplification, this involves looking at some of the products *of* violence, rather than violence *as* a product. What does violence do? As in previous chapters, I do this by drawing upon interview accounts of homophobia-related violence amongst women. I explore some of the gendered and racial dynamics of these accounts, and again take the liberty of extending my analysis to both lesbians and gay men.

Dangerous names

What words are used to insult lesbians and gay men in the context of homophobia-related violence? Dirty, faggot, lemon, butch, infected, man-hater, poofter are just some of the *less* pejorative ones that immediately come to mind. Sometimes the words used are generic, in the sense that they address both lesbians and gay men (such as homo or queer), sometimes they are gender-specific (such as butch leso or fairy), and sometimes they are coupled with other slights (such as leso wog). These names, especially those like queer that have been politically reclaimed in recent times, are open to a multitude of interpretations. Yet, when they are spoken in the context of an aggressive or violent situation it is impossible not to recognise the derisive tone of the intended message. Indeed, simply being called lesbian or gay in a hostile or less-than-supportive context – such as graffiti on your front door or whispers in the corridors of your workplace – implies that there is something about homosexuality that warrants scrutiny. The frequency with which lesbians and gay men report this kind of unwelcome attention, often characterising it as a form of abuse, suggests that 'pointing the finger' in this way is disparaging in itself. To acknowledge the injury of homophobia-related violence thus demands that we acknowledge not only the emotional and physical pain of an inter-personal assault, not only the distress of overtly derogatory statements, but also the insult that is intrinsic to being named as homosexual in unfriendly or hostile ways.

This injury is not simply a question of the words, phrases or sentences that are used in the violent incident itself. It is also a matter of the discourses that turn such insults into a particular type of statement. If, as Foucault (1972) suggests, statements emerge from the way in which events are articulated within associated fields of knowledge, the statements that violence makes will have much to do with the assumptions about homo-sexuality that it exposes. Of particular relevance to the social and legal contexts that frame homophobia-related violence in the west is the assumption that the disordered nature of homosexuality poses a danger to the sexual well-being of individuals, and to the body politic as a whole. Historically, homosexuality, particularly male homosexuality, has been said to endanger everything from the innocence of youth, to the fabric of the heterosexual family unit, to the growth and security of a nation. In many countries, this sense of dangerousness has been regulated through notions of sexual psychopathy and the imposition of criminal sanctions (Pratt 1997). However, as social anxiety over the dangerous individual has gradually been transposed into concerns about the innumerable risks that face particular populations (such as the risk of unemployment, cancer, or AIDS) we have seen a loosening of the formal prohibitions against homosexuality (Castel 1991; Lupton 1999b). [2] This does not mean that the notion of dangerousness has lost all significance, merely that its focus has become less a question of state intervention, and more a question of the practices through which individuals govern themselves and others. Homosexuality continues to resonate with notions of sexual and social danger. Nowadays, this is a more subtle matter of the danger that homosexuality poses to the discourses and institutions that keep regimes of sexual order alive and intact, such as the heterosexual family unit.

It is not unreasonable to expect that this association between homosexuality and dangerousness might provide a climate conducive to the commission of violence. For instance, as we saw in Chapter 2, much of the violence that is directed towards lesbians appears to be infused with perpetrator concerns that lesbianism poses a threat to the privileges that systems of sexual and gendered order accords to the heterosexual male. In responding to lesbian sexuality with a threat of violence of their own, perpetrators of homophobia-related violence unavoidably signal their belief that homosexuality in women is a danger to this regime and those who benefit from it.

Homosexuality is, however, a dangerous desire in more ways than one. Expressions of homosexuality may no longer have the dire religious or legal condemnation of previous historical periods but, depending upon the situation, they may still place lesbians and gay men at risk of individual and institutional censure. As a sign *of* danger, homosexuality thus *attracts* dangers of its own.[3] Inter-personal violence is one extreme, and potentially the most harmful, example of such danger. As we saw in Chapter 4, lesbians and gay men develop a series of safety strategies that enable them to manage the danger of homophobia-related violence; either by avoiding it altogether or by actively courting it so that they may flout its ability to harm them. This means that every time an act of homophobia-related violence makes a statement about the supposed dangers *of* homosexuality, it simultaneously illuminates the particular vulnerabilities of gay men and lesbians *to* the hostilities of a hetero-centric culture.

Let me explain how this might work in practice. To do this I'd like to draw upon the interview accounts of several different women. In these excerpts, each woman discusses her response to a personal experience of violence, or threat of violence, which had clear homophobic overtones. As we shall see, the anti-homosexual sentiment that is evident in these incidents is also shaped by specificities of gender and race. The first woman, Trish, refers to two incidents, one which involved physical violence by her ex-boyfriend, and one which involved an object being thrown from a passing car at her girlfriend and herself as they held hands on a busy city street. The second woman, Catherine talks of an incident where she was threatened by a group of young men in a park at night. In the third excerpt, Amelia discusses a physical assault by her ex-husband. Consider their comments:

Trish:

> Both times I've been attacked for being a leso and both times I felt
> like I had this big tattoo, well no, like they put this big tattoo on
> my body that said, 'Leso. Not a real woman.' or 'Lesbian. Beware!'
> Violence does not just push you around. It reminds you that you are
> someone who *can* be pushed around . . . When I talk about this stuff
> to other dykes and poofs they often go, 'Oh shit, that could happen
> to me'.

Catherine:

> It's like this nasty thing, this way of putting you down, belittling
> you and making you feel like being gay is a pretty dumb kind of
> thing to be. You know, like those old wives' tales that all homo-
> sexuals are lonely people. It may sound crazy but I think you feel
> littler and you look littler. You become littler. It's harder to hold
> your head high and walk tall.

Amelia:

> Because I had to go to the hospital after my ex-husband assaulted
> me a lot of people found out, people at work when I went back . . .
> Everyone was so nice to me but once they know you're a 'battered
> woman' that's how they see [you], victim, victim, victim! It makes
> you vulnerable in a way you weren't before . . . . I think it's there
> kind of subtly distorting the way people see you. Even if it isn't, you
> know, I still think it is . . . Me? Well, I became the 'Asian-girl-in-
> need-of-protection' . . . from my white husband. That's what the
> violence did to me. It made it easy for people to see me through
> these stereotypes.

To these women, the experience of violence is not just a physical pain. It is
also a painful knowledge. This knowledge comprises both the overt insults
that are hurled during the actual incident and a feeling of vulnerability that
comes with being violated in these ways. For Trish, this experience brands
her as someone with a troubled femininity and a dangerous sexuality: 'Not a
real woman'; 'Beware.' This interaction of sexual and gendered assumptions
reminds her that she is someone who not only *has* been pushed around, but
who *can* be pushed around, someone who might be in danger of hostile
condemnation in the future. For Catherine, this threat literally works its way
into her body to make her feel, look and act like a smaller or 'littler' person.
It diminishes her sense of sexual identity by naming homosexuality as a
suitable target for this kind of hostility. For Amelia, violence singles her out

in the eyes of others as a type of woman she doesn't want to be: a 'victim'; a 'battered woman'. This experience is very much the product of Amelia's understanding that Asian women in Australia are often perceived to be especially vulnerable to the abuse of white male partners. Whilst Amelia does not question the extent of this abuse, she suggests that it has produced a stereotype about Asian women that shapes the way that non-Asian people relate to her. She is not simply a woman who has been assaulted; she is a woman in need of special protection. Whether or not violence does invoke this stereotype is, as Amelia remarks, perhaps less significant than her belief that it has the capacity to do so. Together, Trish, Catherine and Amelia suggest that the pain of violation interacts with other experiences and corporeal specificities to produce a network of knowledges about violence and homosexuality. For example: violence can belittle the experience of one's own body and sexual desires; it can remind other lesbians and gay men about the dangers attached to homosexuality; and it may prompt others to look at lesbians and gay men as a group of people who are predisposed to attract such hostility.

Scarry (1985) has suggested that pain exposes the vulnerability of the body. If this is so, the body that experiences the pain of violence is a body that becomes marked by this sense of vulnerability: a transgressed body, a passive body, a body that is acted upon, a victimised body. In other words, violence is capable of rendering the bodies of its victims remarkable by implying that they are 'particularly vulnerable, passive, powerless or weak' (Lupton 1999b: 114). For Trish, Catherine and Amelia, this means that homophobia-related violence is a specific kind of danger that names them as victims, as people who are 'in danger' of such hostility; an objectified state of victimhood that is a far cry from the image of the homosexual as the potential perpetrator of social and moral misdeeds. Such danger is not only a question of the specific insults that are made during a violent incident. It is also a product of the sense of vulnerability that comes from the physical act itself. Hence, together, these women suggest that the injury of homophobia-related violence is simultaneously corporeal and epistemological. The pain of violence is something that they feel in their bodies, but it is also a form of knowledge that infiltrates their experiences of certain things. In particular, they suggest that to be named as someone 'in danger' of violence affects their sense of personal freedom and identity. More than this, they imply that this knowledge has the capacity to infiltrate understandings of homosexuality on a much wider scale.

These are provocative suggestions that, to my mind, raise several crucial questions. If we accept that homophobia-related violence marks its victims in this way, is the knowledge of this injury one of the means through which homosexual bodies thereby 'become invested with differences which are then taken to be fundamental ontological differences' (Gatens 1996: 73)? In other words, does the injury of violence fix itself to homosexuality, as a self-evident or natural characteristic of what it means to be homosexual? Does this, in turn, configure the imaginable options for how lesbians and gay men may occupy and live these subject positions? In short, does violence contribute to the processes of subjectification?

'What' are we in violence?

When I was a teenager we had a favourite saying that we would use when we wanted to point out that someone had broken some unwritten protocol of decorum or style. We would demand: 'What are ya?' The question was rhetorical. Simply by asking, we implied that there was something uncool or weird about the person's behaviour or appearance. Of course, the fact that we asked the question of each other so often meant that its power to insult us was fairly circumscribed. Significantly, we never thought to ask: 'Who are ya?' It just didn't have the same sting in it. This was probably because the latter is an appropriate form of address, and the former is not. 'Who' is a perfectly acceptable way of referring to individual people, identities and the like: 'I want to find out who I really am.' In contrast, 'what' is a less personalised reference to inanimate objects, things or categories: 'What type of person are you?'; 'What is she?' ('She is a doctor/Virgo/Jewish/gay', as the case may be). Hence, the different terminology in the questions 'what is your name?' and 'who are you?' Interestingly, the same answer may be given to both.

There is nothing essentially derisive about the word 'what'. It depends how you use it. When we used it as teenagers, we sought to categorise others in ways that could only be derogatory. There was no way of answering the question that resisted its negative innuendo, although attempts to counter one insult with another were popular. In some instances, we were able to achieve a more potent effect by combining the word 'what' with even less appropriate forms of address, such as the pronoun 'it'. To call another person 'it' is usually to imply that they have crossed the boundaries of acceptable human physicality or behaviour, perhaps, even, that there is something animalistic about them. These boundaries are deeply coloured with norms of physiology, sexual expression, racial appearance, cultural practices, gender image, and so on.

It not surprising, then, that words such as 'what' and 'it' are far from rare in incidents of homophobia-related hostility and violence. For example, one woman I interviewed, Lyn, recounted an incident that took place in her local supermarket on New Year's Eve. Lyn was walking down the aisle on her own, when she passed a woman shopping with her male partner. Upon seeing Lyn, the woman turned to her partner and loudly asked: 'Is that a boy or a girl? What is it?' When Lyn passed her a second time, the woman again said, with much emphasis: 'What *is* it?' Interpreting these remarks as a slur on both her gender image and her sexual preference, Lyn challenged the woman by unleashing a few derogatory comments of her own. The woman lashed out and kicked Lyn. A physical fight erupted.

Whilst it was this particular combination of language that Lyn found insulting, it is her subsequent response to this incident that is particularly revealing of the way in which an experience of violence can embody a knowledge that comes to imbue our understandings of homosexuality. This is what Lyn had to say on the matter:

Lyn:

> Whatever is behind that comment you know there is some kind of maliciousness behind it . . . It doesn't make me feel bad. It makes me feel discriminated against. It makes me aware of where I stand with other people in society. That I'm going to be, I'm going to be maybe pointed out, and tried to be the subject of someone's smart comment or humiliation and that's what they want to do. I find it threatening in that way. I mean I don't feel ashamed but I feel threatened . . . I mean you can be just . . . doing a common thing, walking down the street or you're in the marketplace and then all of a sudden this, this ugly thing can crop up from nowhere and remind you of *what* you are, *what* you are . . . It says something about your sense of freedom in a so-called free place, in a free society. [emphasis added]

Here again, we have the word 'what'. But this time it is Lyn who uses it. She suggests that homophobia-related hostility has the ability to threaten her by reminding her of 'what' she is. Homophobia doesn't tell Lyn anything new. It reinforces an existing knowledge, something which she may have pushed to the back of her mind, to the back of her life, for a while. Although Lyn might seek to distance herself from 'what' it is that violence says about her, as suggested by her use of the third person, she is, nevertheless, convinced that there is a message to be gleaned from the incident. But what is this message? What does it mean to say that violence reminds you of 'what' you are?

Arendt might respond by saying, if violence reminds you of what you are, it probably reminds you of the categories and characteristics that you share with others. In Arendt's (1958) account of the things that make us human (the human condition), 'what' we are refers to the characteristics that are common to us all, and through which we seek to describe ourselves. For Arendt, these are wide-ranging. They include corporeal specificities, sociological categories, cultural roles and interests, psychological traits and needs, as well as the historical circumstances into which we are born.[4] In other words, 'what' is about being a corporeally and historically specific type of person. It is, among other things, about being woman, man, heterosexual, homosexual, Anglo-Celtic, Asian, or Jewish: for example, Zerilli (1995) argues that signifiers of gender are always signifiers of 'what' we are.

Hence, 'what' we are encapsulates the sameness of normalised categorisations with the specificities of embodied traits. Arendt believed these embodied groupings to be descriptive, in the sense that being Jewish or being a woman was a pre-given fact. Yet, recent feminist readings of her work provide us with another interpretation. Central to this interpretation is Arendt's argument that human identity is the product of a series of actions rather than the expression of a pre-existing or essential condition. Although I will return to this point again shortly, it is important to outline it in part now, as it provides the context for understanding Arendt's notion of 'what'.

In *The Human Condition,* Arendt (1958) suggests that it is through speech and action – the things we do to insert ourselves into the world with others – that we develop a particular sense of self; as we shall see, Arendt refers to this sense of self as a question of 'who' we are. For Arendt, this takes place in the political realm of the public sphere, rather than the private sphere. Indeed, all identity formation for Arendt is public, in the sense that we become subjects through expression and communication with others; a process of inter-subjectivity between self and other. Although this favouring of the public over the private sphere, and the relegation of issues of embodiment to the latter, has attracted much criticism, it is worth noting that Arendt's confinement of political subjecthood to the public realm stems from her work on totalitarianism.[5] Arendt saw the persecution of Jews under Nazism as the product, in part, of the intervention of the state in questions of identity, and the bringing of a private matter, such as the Jewish body, into the realm of the polis. Her persistent location of the body in the private sphere is the product of her antagonism towards such undesirable politicisations of embodiment, and not an antagonism towards the body *per se* (Cocks 1995).

Arendt's account has been recently characterised by feminists as a performative model of the human subject.[6] This is because Arendt's subjects do not exist in a fixed or stable state of being. They take on identity through a continual, necessarily repetitive, process. This process is not 'external to or independent' to them but, instead, is one in which they 'actively take part' (Markus 1989: 126). Honig puts it like this:

> Arendt's actors do not act because of what they already are, their actions do not express a prior, stable identity; they presuppose an unstable, multiple self that seeks its, at best, episodic self-realization in action and in the identity that is its reward.
>
> (1995: 141)

It is this performative approach to identity that, in turn, has prompted Arendt's notion of 'what' to be interpreted, not so much as a description of natural or pre-given characteristics, but more as a signifier of the historically specific categories which construct these characteristics. For instance, Honig (1995) suggests that we might employ the notion of 'what' to recognise the group identities that emerge out of being thought to be a particular 'type' of person. Such groupings are agonistic, shifting and unstable rather than the fixed, individualised or homogeneous state that Arendt supposed them to be. In effect, this revitalised notion of 'what' denotes the classifications and categories that configure the performativity of identity. Significantly, identity is only ever formed within the framework of 'what' we are.

To return to the example of Lyn, these interpretations of 'what' we are provide us with a means of reading her comments more closely. Lyn suggests that hostility and violence remind her of the frequency with which lesbians are refused equal 'standing' with others. It tells her that this standing is such that some people may feel the need to point her out, to humiliate her by naming her as inferior in some way. Lyn goes on to suggest that this threat, and the feelings of vulnerability it evokes, engenders an awareness that she is not as free to openly express her sexuality as she believes she should, or could, be. Cumulatively, these messages make a statement that to be lesbian is to be discriminated against, to feel the threat of homophobia in certain situations. These dangers are part of 'what' being lesbian is to Lyn. This is more than a question of being labelled in undesirable ways. It is about the capacity of homophobia-related violence to infiltrate the ways in which Lyn recognises and experiences her sexuality.

This reading of Lyn's account has important implications for the broader question that I posed at the end of the last section: to what extent does the practice of violence contribute to the processes of subjectification? This, of course, begs the question of what I mean by subjectification. In Foucauldian terms, these processes are well established. They denote the double movement of becoming a subject through being subjected to the normative effects of discursively produced identities: 'subjection is a kind of power that not only unilaterally *acts on* a given individual as a form of domination, but also *activates* or forms the subject' (Butler 1995: 230). [7] In other words, subjectification involves the production, and performance, of identity through categories and groupings that tell us that we are certain types of individuals.

This is well illustrated in the cartography of Foucault's panoptic metaphor (described in more detail in Chapter 1). In structural terms, the panopticon is a building, often a prison, designed to allow large groups of people to be efficiently controlled and managed. In this structure, light shines through the windows in the outer wall to illuminate the occupants of each cell, to make them visible as 'small captive shadows' (Foucault 1977: 200). It is the knowledge that they are visible, and may be observed by those in authority at any moment, that compels these occupants to obedience. Foucault employed this panoptic image to illustrate the power relations of modern disciplinary societies. In the same way that the panopticon uses visibility to induce its occupants to manage their own behaviour, so too do disciplinary societies use formal and informal systems of knowledge to prompt us to look at, recognise and discipline our own bodies, and the bodies of others, in certain ways. Particular modes of 'binary division and branding' shape the knowledge systems through which we do this: 'mad/sane; dangerous/harmless; normal/abnormal' (Foucault 1977: 199). Thus, the panoptic gaze is able to coerce norms of behaviour, and reinforce systems of social order, because individuals judge and assess the way we look, act and feel according to these idealised and hierarchical delineations: 'the disciplines characterize, classify, specialize; they distribute along a scale, around a norm, hierarchize individuals in relation to one another and, if necessary, disqualify and invalidate' (1977: 223).

I have already suggested that 'what' we are can be understood as the group identities that emerge out of the idea that there are particular 'types' of individuals. In terms of subjectification, such group identities embody the divisions and classifications through which we are formulated as human subjects. We might thus envisage 'what' we are as a matter of backlight effect, of the way in which light shines through the outer wall of the panoptic structure to produce categories and typologies among its occupants. In terms of violence, 'what-ness' may provide an empirical way of thinking about the identity categories that become visible – the 'small captive shadows' – when the material and discursive knowledge of violence illuminates those it targets. For Lyn, this is a case of the ability of homophobia-related violence to construct her understanding of homosexuality, particularly lesbianism, as that which is vulnerable to violence, hostility and discrimination. In this way, violence is able to insinuate itself into her experience of being lesbian.

The point of subjectification, however, is that it is not simply the things that we experience directly that shape the way in which subject positions are formulated. Subjectification is about the capacity of particular knowledges to contribute to the construction of identity categories in general. Trish, Catherine and Amelia brought this to our attention in earlier interview excerpts. In different ways, each of these women suggests that violence does not only injure and insult those who are directly violated. Violence is also a form of knowledge that tells others 'what' groups of people are considered to be *appropriate* targets of such victimisation. This point has been well made in relation to other forms of hostility and violence, particularly sexual assault[8] and racist speech. For example, Matsuda has argued that racist words, threats and slurs are a form of injury in themselves, because they 'hit the gut of those in the target group' (1989b: 2332). The continual repetition of racist representations reinforces existing relations of subordination and domination, through their ability to function as a form of truth, not just for the person who spoke, not just for the people who identify with the particular group being targeted, but, significantly, for everyone who has ever been exposed to these ways of thinking:

> [A]t some level, no matter how much both victims and well-meaning dominant-group members resist it, racial inferiority is planted in our minds as an idea that may hold some truth. The idea is improbable and abhorrent, but it is there before us, because it is presented repeatedly. 'Those people' are lazy, dirty, sexualized, money-grubbing, dishonest, inscrutable, we are told. We reject the idea, but the next time we sit next to one of 'those people' the dirt message, the sex message, is triggered. We stifle it, reject it as wrong, but it is there, interfering with our perception and interaction with the person next to us. For the victim, similarly, the angry rejection of the message of inferiority is coupled with absorption of the message.
>
> (1989b: 2340)

Matsuda's image is poignant. It highlights the extent to which the accumulation of derogatory or vilifying names infiltrate the mechanisms through which we experience 'what' we are and 'what' we recognise others to be. In the context of homophobia-related violence, it suggests that the marks of violence – whether these are marks of 'danger', 'disorder' or 'dirtiness' – are capable of insinuating themselves into the formative processes through which sexual subject positions are defined. To this way of thinking, the violence of homophobia represents a body of knowledge that contributes to the recognition of 'what' homosexuality is.

If violence is able to mark the bodies of its victims, and potential victims, in this way, it follows that it must also codify the perpetrators of violence in analogous ways. To this end, Scarry argues that injured bodies are forms of substantiation that 'alert the observer' to the material reality and identity of those who claim the 'right' to dominate in this way (1985: 137–8). This suggests that the marks of injury do not just inscribe homosexuality with signs of being 'in danger' (an acted upon and violated object), they also inscribe the, primarily, heterosexual male, perpetrators of such violence as the bearers of the necessary strength and agency to do this, as bodies 'of danger' (acting, violating subjects). In this sense, the potential to be dangerous, to enact homophobia-related or other forms of violence, may be one of the discourses that name and define heterosexual masculinity; it may be one of the ways in which men experience and interpret, embrace or resist, their sexual and gendered identities, as well as being a knowledge through which others recognise, and respond to the image of 'the heterosexual male'. This means that violence is not simply a reflection or manifestation of heterosexual masculinity, but also a technique via which that identity can be performatively achieved.[9] In reproducing a presumed boundary between those who violate and those who are violated, violence may well be an act of differentiation through which we become sexual (and gendered, and raced) subjects. Or, to respond to the question that I posed at the end of the previous section, it seems to me that violence may be one of 'the means by which bodies become invested with differences which are then taken to be fundamental ontological differences' (Gatens 1996: 73). One way of thinking about these constitutive mechanisms is to envisage them as a question of 'what' violence makes us.

'Who' we are not in violence

I have suggested that the marks of homophobia-related violence are capable of configuring 'what' homosexuality is. The significance of this, for the way in which lesbians and gay men live the category of homosexuality in an everyday sense, is another question. Do lesbians and gay men simply experience their sexuality as a source of 'danger' or do they resist, reinvent and misrecognise this kind of signification? Do they distinguish between what homosexuality is, and who they are as homosexuals? That is, can we draw a line between what violence may, and may not do? If so, how?

Returning to Lyn's interview allows me to begin to reply to these questions. Remember, violence makes Lyn feel 'discriminated against', but it does not make her feel 'bad'. She is 'threatened' by it, but she says that this is not the same as feeling 'ashamed'. These distinctions seem to be grounded in Lyn's identification of homosexuality as a potential source of discrimination and hostility, and in her denial that this danger renders homosexuality intrinsically wrong or shameful. This kind of distinction was reinforced by many of the women I interviewed. I would like to introduce two further excerpts that I believe flesh out Lyn's comments in a particularly interesting manner. One of these excerpts comes from Amelia, who talks further about the ways in which she thinks people react to the knowledge that she was assaulted by her ex-husband, as well as some of her own responses to this. The other excerpt is from Samantha, who, at the time of interview, had never been subjected to homophobia-related violence, but was well aware of it as a general issue facing lesbians and gay men. She discusses how this knowledge affects her sense of sexual identity.

Amelia:

> Well, yeah, people might see me as a victim. He [her ex-husband] certainly saw me like that. That's *what* I am to them and sure I think to myself, God, is this victim stuff always a part of what it is to live your life as a lesbian, or even as a woman? . . . But in so many ways you show that you're not just *what* they think you are. It's hardly the last word on *who* you are. You talk to other people, you love other people, you have sex with other people and it's not like

110

this victim stuff. . . Besides homophobia can never dictate who I am. Sometimes being Asian is all that matters to me. That's *who* I am. [emphasis added]

Samantha:

> It's kind of like being told, 'We don't think you're as good as us, or we don't think you belong here with us'. But you know that really most of the time you don't feel that way. Most people you know don't relate to you that way. You only feel it when you come up against it, if you get what I mean. . .There's this other huge part of me that might be affected by all the hostility and violence that is directed towards gays, might be distressed, but later on, this other huge part of *who* I am takes control again and says, 'Fuck off, I know *who* I am!' [emphasis added]

Like Lyn, both of these women suggest that violence shapes the way they see themselves, by reminding them that homosexuality (in women) has a subordinate status in the eyes of many. This prompts them to experience their sexuality, at least in part, as a source of danger and vulnerability. Again, like Lyn, Amelia describes this sense of potential victimisation as a question of 'what I am', both to others and to herself. Significantly, however, all three women report limits to this oppression. They may live it, but they only live it in certain contexts, at certain times, or with certain people. The marks of vulnerability and danger that violence leaves are always exceeded or contradicted. Samantha refers to this excess as a question of 'who' she is. Amelia echoes this sentiment when she says that 'what' she is, including 'what' others think of her, cannot control the other facets of her identity, it cannot dictate 'who' she is. Whilst I do not wish to suggest that this language of 'what' and 'who' is representative of the way that all lesbians and gay men talk about violence, I would like to enlist the distinction itself. This is not so that I can argue that there is a real or deeper meaning to their words. More strategically, it is to use these words to articulate a practical method for recognising the experiential limits of violent subjectification.

To do this, I need to return to the model of the Arendtian subject, particularly feminist re-articulations of it, that I introduced earlier. I suggested that a performative take on Arendt's notion of 'what' the subject is, provides a means of recognising the capacity of violence to construct the category of homosexuality as a sexuality 'in danger'. So, too, is there a sense in which her notion of 'who' we are may be helpful in interpreting Samantha and Amelia's comments. As I have indicated, Arendt argues that we become human subjects through the things that we *do*, rather than because we simply *are* a certain way; for her this is a question of 'what we are doing' (1958: 6). If, as Arendt suggests, it is action that allows the actor to emerge

– there is no 'being' behind this doing – then identity must be something that we produce, not the expression of a pre-existing condition or essence (Honig 1995). Bickford puts it like this: 'That I act, and say particular things in particular situations in response to particular issue, shows me to be a certain who, a certain public self – or rather becomes part of the story through which my identity takes shape' (Bickford 1995: 317). This means that Arendt's subject is always a 'subject-in-process' (Zerilli 1995: 182); one who is in the continual act of becoming, rather than a fixed or stable state of being. Arendt signifies this process, the process through which we formulate an identity, as a question of 'who' we are. Action, for Arendt, corresponds to the 'human condition of plurality', to the fact that we each behave and think in distinct ways (1958: 9). In simple terms, this means that we enact 'who' we are through the things that we say and do *in relation to others*. Identity is thus a matter of inter-subjectivity, of the ways in which our interactions with, and differences from, others configure our sense of self. This is significant because it means that when we use the word 'who' to signify identity, this cannot be equated with an internal, essential or privatised sense of self.[10] Instead, it denotes an inter-subjective, what Arendt would call 'plural', understanding of identity.[11]

Central to Arendt's model is the fact that 'who' and 'what' function in an interlaced, but never polar, relation to each other. We only ever become 'who' we are through, and against, 'what' we are. Thus, identity is always configured, but only in part, by the various groupings that tell us 'what' type of person we are: '"What" we are creates a framework within which "Who" we are is formed and realised, but never conditions us absolutely' (Markus 1989: 121). In the original Arendtian account, we become 'who' we are through the 'freedom' of individuality and choice. Yet, recent readings of Arendt have reconstructed this freedom in terms of the ability of the subject – 'an embodied self with a variety of particular, inherited and culturally acquired traits' – to partially transcend its situation, on the basis that it is neither 'fully situated' nor 'fully autonomous' (Jacobitti 1996: 205). In other words, the freedom to become a certain 'who' is a question of the ways in which we move between, and beyond, the restrictive and imposed conditions of 'what-ness' (Cutting-Gray 1993; Dietz 1995).[12]

Arendt's notions of 'what' and 'who' provide us with a practical means of distinguishing between the ability of violence to manufacture an identity category, and its inability to condition the ways in which that category is incorporated into one's sense of self. Homophobia-related violence may configure 'what' the category of homosexuality is, but this does not mean that it completely conditions gay and lesbian subjectivities and identities ('who' they are). Subjectification is not simply about the imposition of a name upon an unsuspecting subject at a given moment. It is about the bodily gestures and habits through which we take up and reshape these names. As Rose states, we live our lives in a constant movement between practices that address us, on a daily basis, in different ways. This means that we become 'who' we are according to the ways in which techniques of 'discipline, duty and docility' encounter and compete with '[t]echniques of relating to oneself as a subject of unique capacities worthy of respect' (1996b: 140). It is this kind of everyday encounter that Samantha and Amelia talk about when they say that violent statements cannot account for the diversity and complexity of 'who' they are. They 'talk', 'love' and 'have sex' with other people, despite the 'victim' status that violence imposes on them. These ways of relating (as someone who is 'worthy of respect') engender other names that compete with violent statements: violence represents only one mode of knowledge via which homosexuality is experienced and recognised. Samantha, for example, suggests that although violence tells her that some other people believe her to be inferior because of her sexuality, this is not something that dominates her life. Most of the people with whom she regularly mixes do not see her in this light. She is really only aware of the negativity of homophobia when she is directly confronted by it. For Amelia, there is nothing permanent or stable about the sexual stereotypes that violence reproduces. These inscriptions can never completely determine 'who' she is, because they will always fail to obscure the significance of other, in this case, racial, subjectivities to her identity: 'Sometimes being Asian is all that matters to me. That's who I am.' The marks of vulnerability that violence leaves on Amelia's body may contribute to the idea that to be homosexual, or a woman, is to be in danger of violence. But these marks are contradicted by other marks, both positive and negative. Simply put, violence may construct a picture of 'what' homosexuality is, but it cannot describe 'who' people are as homosexuals.

To say that 'who' we are will always exceed the knowledge of 'what' we are, is to say that the authority of violence will always be met with resistance.[13] It will be modified and undermined by human plurality; contradicted, ignored, rejected, countered, overridden, and, in some instances, even welcomed. It is important to recognise that this resistance is not dependent upon human agency alone. Certainly, as Lyn, Amelia and Samantha suggest, lesbians and gay men do actively refuse the marks that violence leaves on their bodies. They fight back, throw a few insults of their own, or simply refuse to interpret violence as a sign of subordination. These actions contribute to the inability of violence to define gay and lesbian subjectivities. The point, however, is that violent subjectification will fail to account for 'who' they are, even if lesbians and gay men do not deliberately reject its names. This is because the limits of subjectification are not dependent upon the things that individuals consciously do. They are intrinsic to the process itself.

Butler (1997) discusses the limits of subjectification at length in the context of hateful, or vilifying, speech. Through a number of closely entwined arguments, she makes the overall point that subjectification is neither an efficient nor a highly successful process. Returning to, but revising, Althusser's work on interpellation, Butler reminds us that the attempt to name us in insulting terms is precisely that: an attempt. We may recognise ourselves in that name, but we may also misrecognise ourselves. The production may falter. The effect is as follows:

> [T]he name continues to force itself upon you, to delineate the space you occupy, to construct a social positionality. Indifferent to your protests, the force of interpellation continues to work. One is still constituted by discourse, but at a distance from oneself. Interpellation is an address that regular misses its mark, it requires the recognition of an authority at the same time that it confers identity through successfully compelling that recognition.
>
> (1997: 33)

In arguing that vilifying names may force themselves upon you, at the same time that they regularly miss their mark, Butler emphasises that subjectification is an on-going process, not something that happens in a single act. An identity is not something that one can just 'be' at any given moment. As I have discussed above, it is a 'kind of becoming or activity' that must be continually repeated in order to sustain an impression of natural authenticity (Butler 1990: 140, 112).[14] If language does act to bring its addressee into being – and this is highly debatable for Butler – its success is dependent upon the citation of these names over and over again and, hence, it is ever only provisional or momentary.[15] In effect, racist, homophobic or phallocentric names may act upon the subject to constitute 'identity through injury', but they do not confer this identity in a 'prescribed or mechanical way' that 'will remain always and forever rooted in its injury' (Butler 1997: 113, 246).

Butler's argument is helpful in clarifying my assertion that the distinction between 'what' and 'who' lies in the limits of subjectification itself; it neither depends upon, nor excludes, the deliberate actions of individuals. However, the difficulty that I have with Butler's claim is the ease with which these limits can be overstated. As a consequence, the injurious effects of insulting names tend to be diluted. Perhaps it is the fact that Butler restricts her argument to hateful words, rather than violent action, that prompts her to minimise the constitutive capacity of such names. Indeed, to make her case against the presumed success of linguistic subjectification, Butler emphasises the distinction between speech and action, particularly between hateful words and physical violence: 'When we say that an insult strikes a blow, we imply that our bodies are injured by such speech. And they surely are, but not in the same way as a purely physical injury takes place' (1997: 159).[16] For Butler, this difference is significant. It provides a basis for the distinction that she draws between action and speech; a distinction which enables her to suggest that, in contrast to violent action, which *is* itself an injury, violent language only *effects* an injury. This, in turn, opens up the space, seemingly not present in the case of physical violence, for the injurious implications of language to be misrecognised or resignified; that is, for the limits of subjectification to be realised.

The problem is that when we are talking about homophobia-related violence, there is no such thing as a 'purely physical injury'. Irrespective of whether the act itself is accompanied by words, it still has a discursive side to it. Otherwise, there is no basis upon which to connect the physical act to homophobic sentiment in the first place. Furthermore, whilst we could interpret Butler's distinction between hateful speech and hateful acts to mean that violence will succeed where speech fails – as if the injury of physical violence instantaneously constitutes its object – the point that I have made throughout this chapter is that the constitutive effects of violence are in no way confined to the physical harm that it inflicts. The ability of violence to inscribe the category of homosexuality is very much a question of the statements that it makes. The effects of a physical blow may be, as Butler suggests, different from the effects of a verbal blow, but both make a contribution to discourse; and, as such, both may be taken up, in different ways, in the process of subjectification.

I am thus concerned that Butler's emphasis on the limits of hostile subjectifications not be read to suggest that violence does not contribute to the ways in which the category of homosexuality is constructed. To say that subjectification regularly 'misses its mark' is not to say that the insult or injury of violence also misses it mark. Violence *does* name homosexuality in ways that are unwelcome, undesirable or insulting. Let us not be mistaken about this: violence contributes to the definition of 'what' homosexuality is. My point is that, as with all names, there are limits to the constitutive capacity of this insult. These limits are embodied in the ways in which the category of homosexuality is lived by lesbians and gay men, and recognised by others. The distinction that I have made between 'what' and 'who' gives us a practical means of acknowledging the successes and the failures of violence. It allows us to recognise that the injurious statements of violence can produce certain things, but, at the same time, there is much that they are not capable of producing; they cannot define 'who' we are as homosexuals.

Whilst I realise the permeability and fragility of this distinction, I find it helpful to reinforce its significance, in the context of subjectification, by returning to Foucault's (deceptively simple) metaphor of panopticism; the metaphor that he used to explicate the notion of disciplinary power that is at the core of his model of subject-formation. Remember, the panopticon is a structure whose basic function is dependent upon the very thing that will ultimately constrain the terms of its success: backlight effect. The panopticon is a circular-type building. Individual cells line the periphery. Each cell has a window on the outside and a window facing the centre. The building is designed to allow light to shine through the outer window and illuminate the cell. The inside window ensures that the inmates in each cell are visible from the tower in the centre of the panopticon. However, in coming from outside and behind, such light is incapable of flooding the cell with complete brightness. Instead, it renders the individuals in each cell visible only as 'small captive shadows' or silhouettes, never as fully featured subjects. The limitations of this backlight effect mean that disciplinary power is only capable of producing an imprecise, shifting and shadowy state of visibility, a subject position that is somewhere between complete darkness and complete light. In terms of violence, this opacity should remind us that, when we look at homosexuality through the statements that violence makes, we can only ever see an outline, a contour. There is always an excess, a contradiction, or a misrecognition – the things that violence cannot show us – which shape the ways this silhouette is occupied and transformed. Other names, other experiences, other knowledges will continually undo and rework the names that violence inscribes; '"who" the subject is depends as much on the names that he or she is never called' (Butler 1997: 41). Quite simply, to be *constituted* in violence is not to be *determined*.

Conclusion

Violence inflicts physical and emotional injury upon those it victimises. In the process, it makes injurious statements about these same people. The implications of these statements are not confined to those individuals who are directly violated. Violence also names groups of people in particular ways. For instance, despite the prevalence of discourses that characterise homosexuality as a danger to others, one of the legacies of homophobia-related violence is found in the marks of vulnerability that it leaves on the bodies of lesbians and gay men. Such violence makes a statement that to be homosexual is to be 'in danger' of violence and other forms of hostility.

This raises the question of whether such messages are capable of infiltrating the discursive processes by which notions of sexuality are constructed. My response to this question is both 'yes' and 'no'. I suggest that violence may mould 'what' we are, but it is unable to completely shape 'who' we are. The work of Hannah Arendt has proven useful in making this distinction. Arendt is a particularly pertinent choice here because of the way in which she articulates a model of the human subject, based upon her own differentiation between 'what' and 'who' we are. When lesbians and gay men state that violence is able to enforce a sense of 'what' they are, we might think of this as an epistemological injury, of the infiltration of the knowledge that they are 'in danger' of violence into their understandings of the category of homosexuality. If, however, we recognise identity as performative, rather than fixed, these representations of homosexuality remain continually open to the counter-authoritative processes of deconstruction.

Hence, when lesbians and gay men talk about the inability of violence to control 'who' they are, we might usefully think of 'who' as denoting not just their own agency to defy homophobic insults but, more fundamentally, the inability of violence to dominate their daily lives and interactions with others. In this way, the distinction between 'what' and 'who' accounts for both the constitutive successes and failures of violence; the things that violence can do, and the things it cannot do. It offers us with a means of acknowledging the capacities and limits of violence in an empirical sense, how it is experienced in the everyday. The idea that 'what' we are provides a framework for, but never a complete explanation of, 'who' we are, is important to this account. It suggests that violence represents a particular, and unwelcome, interpretation of the category of homosexuality, but it does not control how that identity category is experienced by lesbians and gay men, or recognised by others.

To my mind, these capacities and limits are well illustrated in Foucault's early work on subjectification, particularly in his use of the panopticon as a metaphor for disciplinary power. Whilst violent discourse may render the homosexual visible according to particular stereotypes, this visibility is always restricted by the inability of panoptic backlight to show us homosexuality in all its shades and configurations. The homosexual that we see through violence is a rather shadowy figure, a faint representation of what it means to be gay or lesbian in contemporary western cultures. The interactive, yet distinguishable, notions of 'who' and 'what' we become, or do not become, in violence, offer one means of articulating the limits of this backlight effect. That is, they enable us to see that subjectification fails at the same time that it succeeds, that subjectivity cannot be reduced to a matter of subject positions, and that it is crucial to distinguish between the capacity of violence to partially or momentarily *constitute* an identity category and its inability to *determine* how that category will be lived and reinvented everyday.

6

VIOLENCE

An instrument of power

Throughout this book I have explored some of the contexts for, and the implications of, homophobia-related violence. This research has raised some specific questions about both the practice of inter-personal violence and the concept of power. For example: Does violence oppress? What is power? Who has power? Is violence power? Each of these questions flows into a wider debate about the nexus between violence and power. In this chapter I seek to make a contribution to this debate. I do this by examining the different ways in which feminist theory and Foucauldian theory respond to these questions. Although much has been written about the divisions between feminism and Foucault on the question of power, only a small amount of this literature has been applied directly to the question of inter-personal violence. The chapter thus represents a culmination of, and conclusion to, some of the primary theoretical issues to emerge from earlier chapters. It offers an approach for conceptualising the nexus between violence and power in future research.

Feminist theory and Foucauldian theory are the two schools of thought with which I have engaged most consistently throughout this book. In different ways, my approach to homophobia-related violence is deeply indebted to both of these. They have shaped my interpretations of how violence is experienced, the kinds of discourses that facilitate its enactment, the effects that it has on the daily lives of lesbians and gay men, and its implications on a collective level. Although these are all issues that I have considered in preceding chapters, I have not commented directly on the ways in which the act of violence might be conceptualised as a question of power. In part, this is because I did not explore this in any detail with the women I interviewed. During interviews, I tended to take up the issue of power in a tangential way, for example, via a consideration of the notion of homophobia. It is these quite specific discussions that have highlighted, for me, the importance of thinking about the relationship between violence and power in a more theoretical way. Whilst feminist and Foucauldian theory provide me with a potential means of doing this, the difficulty is that when these paradigms are initially read with, and against, each other on the question of violence and power, a deep tension is exposed. For instance, although Foucault says little about violence, references to it at particular points in his writings on disciplinarity and governmentality mean that a lot is said, indirectly, about its relation to power.[1] Specifically, Foucault is usually interpreted as arguing that violence is *not* a form of power. Feminism, on the other hand, has successfully theorised violence, particularly men's violence towards women, as an expression *of* power, principally patriarchal power. These differences make it difficult to imagine how we might link the practice of violence with the concept of power, without choosing between feminist or Foucauldian theory.

As will be apparent from earlier chapters, I do not believe that this is a choice that we need to make. We are likely to close off important ways of thinking about violence if we do. Yet, it is exactly this kind of choice that is made, if not advocated, in much of the feminist literature on violence. In particular, research which prioritises women's experiences of violence sometimes positions Foucauldian and other poststructural theory as completely antithetical to a feminist analysis. Consider, for example, the influential work of Marianne Hester, Liz Kelly and Jill Radford. These writers, individually and together, have been responsible for some of the most groundbreaking and important research on gendered violence during the last two decades. In their 1996 book *Women, Violence and Male Power*, they make it clear that they believe that poststructural perspectives, including Foucauldian theory, are incompatible with a feminist account of violence. Poststructural theories are characterised as 'insidious' and 'unhelpful' forms of 'anti-feminism' that 'fail to engage with the actual, material realities of women's and children's lives' (8–9). Such theories are said to deny women's real experiences of violence and, in the process, to undermine feminism's fight against gendered violence.

These are strong accusations. To my mind, they are unnecessary accusations. By drawing such a clear line of demarcation between feminist theory and poststructuralism they imply that only certain forms of research are appropriate; for example, feminist thinking on violence can only be generated from the standpoint of women's experience. This closes off the possibility of bringing feminist and Foucauldian theory together to analyse violence. It is this very possibility that I have sought to pursue in this book. It should come as no surprise, then, that I wish to challenge these assertions. I believe that feminist accounts of violence have provided us with indispensable insights and understandings. But I also believe that we can learn much about various forms of violence by drawing upon Foucauldian and other poststructural theory. Of course, there is already a small and important body of feminist commentary that does this.[2] The existence of this research makes it clear that there is, in actuality, no clear-cut distinction between feminist theory and poststructuralism. Nonetheless, the myth of incompatibility remains strong. The vast majority of research that seeks to address and analyse men's violence towards women remains either uninterested in, or sceptical of, poststructuralism.[3]

In this chapter I explain the basis of my belief that feminist theory and Foucauldian theory are not incompatible paradigms for the analysis of violence. Initially, I do this by addressing the four questions that I have set out above: Does violence oppress? What is power? Who has power? Is violence power? These are questions that have arisen for me throughout the course of my research on women's encounters with homophobia-related violence. They are central to the ways in which feminist theory and Foucauldian theory each interpret the relation between violence and power. These questions are not mutually exclusive. By necessity, they overlap with, and pre-empt, each other. Negotiating them enables me to explore the character of the tension between these two schools of thought. (I spend more time on the latter because Foucault's comments on violence have received minimal attention.) As we shall see, this reveals some important conjunctions. Ultimately, however, it is the final question – is violence power? – that allows me to look most closely at the nature of the violence–power nexus (each of the earlier questions must be answered before I can hope to respond to this question). This leads me to argue that the tension between feminist theory and Foucault over the violence–power nexus is not so much a question of irreconcilable paradigms but, more specifically, of the lack of an identifiable path between the two models. In particular, I pick up on the idea, shared by both feminists and Foucault, that the nexus between violence and power is an *instrumental* one: violence is an instrument of power. Taking this path prompts me to ask a fifth, and final, question: What is an instrument? I respond to this question by arguing that the instrumental function of violence can be articulated as a question of *knowledge*. That is, of the capacity of violence to shape the ways that we see, and thereby come to know, certain things. This is not a panacea for some of the incommensurabilities between feminist theory and Foucauldian theory. But it does allow research to manoeuvre between the strengths of both, in order to conceptualise how the practice of violence relates to the concept of power.

Throughout this chapter I take the liberty of using the term feminist theory, or feminism, to refer to the feminist literature on men's violence towards women that does not engage with, or is sometimes antagonistic towards, poststructural theory. As I have indicated above, this does not include literature on violence that is informed by both feminist and poststructural perspectives. As such, it assumes a somewhat artificial distinction between feminist theory and poststructuralism. However, given the dominance of the former approach in the field of violence research I believe that the distinction is a helpful one to maintain for the purposes of the present discussion. My decision to focus on feminist, rather than anti-homophobic, theorisations of violence in this chapter probably also warrants some explanation. As I have indicated above, feminism has had a significant influence on my own research into homophobia-related violence towards women. But, more than this, feminist theory has provided us with one of the most extensive and careful articulations of the relationship between inter-personal violence and the concept of power. Its influence has been profound. Indeed, the literature on homophobia-related violence tends to follow the general lead of feminist theory in the sense that it conceptualises violence as an exercise *of* the power of sexual hierarchies.[4] The authority that feminist theory commands in the field of violence makes it a particularly fruitful avenue for the kind of questions I wish to ask. It also means that much of what I say about feminist theory is generally applicable to current concep-tualisations of the nexus between homophobia-related violence and power.

The discussion that follows is rather ambitious. It is, however, only intended to be schematic. It is an outline, a template, for how we might theorise the relationship between violence and power in a way that allows our research to incorporate both feminist and Foucauldian concerns.[5] It is fundamentally informed by my analysis of homophobia-related violence. I make occasional reference to other forms of violence, such as gendered violence and racist violence. This is in recognition of the fact that homophobia-related violence is configured by specificities of gender and race (in addition to others). It also serves to remind us that homophobic, gendered and racist violence are all undergirded by hierarchical constructions of difference that tie them to particular power relations in comparable ways.

Does violence oppress?

If feminist theory and Foucault agree on one thing, it is that violence is an oppressive behaviour. Oppression, in the sense that I use it here, refers to an unjust form of domination or subordination that operates by pressing down upon groups of individuals in a way that inflicts harm or unwelcome restrictions. Such domination is usually shaped by hierarchical constructions of difference, such as those of gender, sexuality or race.[6] For Foucault, it is the way in which violence acts upon the body that makes it oppressive. In acting 'directly and immediately' upon others, violence 'forces, it bends, it breaks on the wheel, it destroys, or it closes the door on all possibilities' (Foucault 1982: 789). The intensity of these sentiments echo a history of feminist argumentation around the forms of violence that are committed primarily by men against women, such as sexual and domestic assault (Russell 1975; Dobash and Dobash 1979; Hanmer and Maynard 1987; Bart and Moran 1993). Feminist theory has maintained that the hurt of this violence is oppressive, and not just painful, because it lies like a heavy weight on those women who are its targets. Violence dominates, not only by inflicting physical harm and injury, but also by engendering feelings of shame, worthlessness or guilt. Women's concerns and fears about violence can restrict everyday life, limiting pleasures and freedoms. In some instances, this can lead to a repressed sense of personal options and possibilities. It is not just the actual experience of violence that does this. The knowledge that one may be targeted for particular forms of violence also generates a series of self-regulatory strategies designed to minimise this perceived risk. Thus, for feminism, the oppression of violence is found in the ability of the act itself to repress the way that women act and experience their lives. In other words, the injury, or potential injury, of violence acts to constrain individuals, to stop them from doing things.

These arguments can be appropriated to explore the oppressive implications of homophobia-related violence (as I did in Chapter 4). For example, just as most women monitor the risk of sexual violence, so too do most lesbians and gay men monitor the risk of homophobia-related violence (lesbians may monitor both at the one time). The extent to which lesbians and gay men feel that they may be subject to this type of violence will shape the extent to which they feel it is safe to be open about their sexuality in particular situations. Of course, violence also engenders practices of resistance. In some cases, lesbians and gay men may deliberately flirt with the danger of violence. However, whether one capitulates to, or resists, the risk of violence, the effect is similar. It engenders an imperative to continually negotiate physical safety by managing certain aspects of oneself, such as monitoring one's body for visible signs of homosexuality. In this way, the perceived risk of violence exerts a subtle governing influence over those who directly experience it, and those who believe that they might.

In short, violence does not only restrain individuals from doing certain things, it also shapes their options for resisting those restraints. As Young (1991) suggests, in the broader context of gendered, homophobic and racist violence, it is the fact that groups of people not only experience violence, but also know that they are at risk of certain types of violence, that makes it a fundamentally oppressive practice. The difficulty of capturing the breadth and depth of these effects in any one concept is perhaps insurmountable. The notion of oppression may not provide us with an adequate analysis of these kinds of injuries, but it does go some way towards describing them. Whilst I do not advocate its use as an umbrella term for talking about the situation of women in general, or, for that matter, any group of people, I do think it allows us to depict the various harms of violence, particularly when situated within an analysis of power.

What is power?

Violence is an oppressive practice. Both feminist theory and Foucault agree on this. In terms of thinking about the violence–power nexus, this raises the question of how their respective theorisations of power account for oppression. This question highlights what is said to be one of the greatest sources of disparity between feminist and Foucauldian theory: how power is defined. This disparity has been the subject of intense debate over a number of years (Hartsock 1990; Ramazanoğlu 1993; Sawicki 1991). I have no desire to duplicate these arguments here. I do, however, wish to explore the different ways in which power is defined by feminist and Foucauldian theory, in order to consider what each can tell us about violence. Thinking about these different models of power has led me to believe that, although violence is an oppressive practice, it actually does *more* than oppress. Violence is also a productive practice. Hence, any attempt to theorise violence, through the concept of power, must be able to account for its oppressive and productive implications. Let me explain this assertion in more detail (in the next section, I will address the more precise question of whether violence *is* a form of power).

If power is defined as the domination of one group of people over another, it is quite easy to account for the oppressive effects of violence. The feminist definition of patriarchal power is a case in point. In this model, power is defined as a form of domination that subjugates women by blocking them from doing certain things or thinking in certain ways; women are controlled through demands for social conformity and obedience. Although there have been many feminist versions of power (Pringle 1995), the idea of patriarchal power as an autonomous and fundamental social structure that produces a coherent and stable set of relations by which men have dominance over women maintains considerable political purchase in violence research. This model of power quite comfortably incorporates the oppressive implications of violence because, like violence, it is said to directly act upon the bodies of women, to repress and prohibit. Although this way of looking at power, as a universal or seamless system of male domination, no longer commands the support it once did, there is little doubt it has been highly successful at exposing the ways in which violence flows into, and out of, unequal gender relations (Edwards 1987; Kelly 1988; Dominelli 1989; Stanko 1990).

In contrast to a feminist model of power, Foucault offers a methodology for thinking about power as a fundamentally productive process. Productive power is defined as a relation between forces that, in passing through discourse and material events, is constitutive of particular subject positions and the sense of self that is acquired in the negotiation of these positions. For instance, in arguing that the disciplinary society, which emerged throughout the seventeenth and eighteenth centuries, replaced an earlier, strictly sovereign one, Foucault (1977) asserted that the human body became regulated through systems of knowledge that defined and normalised it, according to historically specific categories; such as 'homosexual', 'feminine' or 'mad'. These discourses continue to act upon us, not so much to stop us from doing certain things, but to formulate us in certain ways. Foucault defines this productive model, in part, by contrasting it to what he calls the 'repressive hypothesis'. A repressive model is one that sees power as a question of prohibitions and limits that are placed upon the desires and actions of human beings: '[a]ll the modes of domination, submission, and subjugation are ultimately reduced to an effect of obedience' (1978: 85).

Here, power only ever acts *upon* a pre-given subject to oppress him or her; power does not act *to* formulate that subject. In comparison, Foucault's productive hypothesis seeks to articulate power as a question of subject-ification: the idea that we *become* a subject through being subjected to the normative effects of discursively produced identities. Foucault goes so far as to suggest that the repressive hypothesis, although an adequate account of older models of sovereign or juridical power, is 'utterly incongruous' with the disciplinary mechanisms of subjectification described in his own model of productive power (1978: 89).

The feminist version of power that I have described above has long been characterised as an example of Foucault's repressive hypothesis. Although many feminists have responded to Foucault's criticisms by appropriating the productive hypothesis, many who research violence, especially actual accounts of the experience of violence, have been indifferent to it (or have paid it only passing attention). This is not really surprising. Given the deeply oppressive nature of violence, I have no difficulty in understanding why feminists might be concerned about abandoning the repressive hypothesis – which allows us to recognise the limits and prohibitions that violence places on our lives – for an analysis that favours questions of productivity. [7] However, when we ignore the productive hypothesis we assume that the implications of violence can be adequately characterised as a matter of oppression.

As my arguments in previous chapters, especially Chapter 5, demonstrate, I am not convinced that this is so. Indeed, it is my reading of Foucault that initially prompted me to speculate about the ways in which violence might, like power, do more than oppress. For example, homophobia-related violence does not just act upon lesbian and gay bodies to restrict and constrain their actions. The things that we experience and know about violence also work their way *into* those bodies to shape our understandings of homosexuality itself. Violence marks lesbians and gay men with undesirable statements about their own vulnerability to violence; that is, with the idea that to be lesbian or gay is to be 'in danger' of violence. In turn, such violence is capable of making statements about the perpetrators of violence; for example, by defining heterosexual masculinity as a subject position that poses a danger to others. Although violence can never determine who we are – such definitions are continually modified, contradicted and resisted – the point is that violence has the ability to mould the ways in which we experience and recognise categories of sexuality. Put more simply, violence is capable of making undesirable or negative statements about those groups of people it targets and those groups of people who primarily perpetrate it. These messages infiltrate, albeit without dominating, the processes of subjectification through which we understand what it means to be one of those people.

Clearly, this interpretation of violence only makes sense within a Foucauldian model of power as productive. However, like most feminists who research violence, I am not prepared to abandon the question of oppression in order to undertake such an analysis. Violence demands that we recognise that its relation to power is both oppressive and productive. Yet, how can this be done if, as Foucault suggests, the repressive hypothesis, which underpins feminism's account of the oppression of violence, is irreconcilable with the productive hypothesis? How am I able to recognise the productivity of violence without denying its oppression?

Readers of Foucault will know, of course, that this is not a particularly difficult question to answer. A closer interpretation of his work readily reveals that the repressive and productive hypotheses do not, as he initially stated, and as some feminists also accepted, represent discrete polarities. The mechanisms of each may be quite dissimilar, but the functions are not mutually exclusive. In particular, it is not that disciplinary modalities of power have replaced all others, but rather that the juridical forms of power have been 'infiltrated' (1977: 216) or 'penetrated' (1978: 89) by disciplinary modes. Butler puts it like this:

> Although Foucault occasionally tries to argue that, historically, *juridical* power – power as acting on, subordinating, pregiven subjects – *precedes* productive power, the capacity of power to *form* subjects, it is clear . . . that the subject produced and the subject regulated or subordinated are one, and that the compulsory production is its own form of regulation.
>
> (1995: 230)

Foucault's notion of power does not fail to recognise oppression. Rather, it refuses to reduce power to a question of oppression alone (as the repressive hypothesis tends to do). Nor is it the case that productive power is never exercised 'over' an existing person. Instead, the point is that that person must 'be thoroughly recognised and maintained to the very end as a person who acts' and, thus, resists (Foucault 1982: 789). Indeed, in his articulation of bio-power, with its focus on embodiment, disciplinary power and juridical power are articulated as 'two absolutely integral constituents of the general mechanisms of power in our society' (1980: 108). Specifically, repressive discourses are said to be normalising technologies of power: 'Bio-power has incorporated the repressive hypothesis' (Dreyfus and Rabinow 1982: 142). Similarly, as these techniques of domination come to interact with techniques of the self in Foucault's account of the ways in which groups of people are governed (Burchell 1996), it becomes apparent that, just as the disciplinary society did not replace sovereignty, neither does his notion of governmentality replace the disciplines. Instead, sovereignty, discipline and government eventually function as a 'triangle', with the 'primary target' of managing the conduct of populations (Foucault 1991: 102).[8] In other words, there is no opposition between repressive and productive accounts of power, or as Butler says:

subjection is neither simply the domination of a subject nor its production, but designates a certain kind of restriction *in* production, a restriction without which the production of the subject cannot take place, a restriction through which that production takes place.

(Butler 1995: 230)

In effect, the Foucauldian model is particularly helpful for analysing violence because it recognises that power is both oppressive and productive. More specifically, it allows for the fact that the productive process of subjectification may take place *through* oppressive practices, such as violence. Although the feminist model of power does not address the question of subjectification in the same way, its contribution is crucial because of its ability to show us how violence oppresses. If we intend our research to come to terms with the various ways in which violence relates to power, we need to remain cognisant of the different emphases within both models.

Who has power?

The question of who, or what, possesses power brings to light another major distinction between Foucault and feminist theory that needs to be addressed in violence research. For Foucault, the question of who possesses power is a 'labyrinthine and unanswerable' one that we should not even ask (1980: 97).[9] To his way of thinking, power is not something that is held by individuals in an 'all-encompassing opposition between rulers and ruled' but, instead, emerges in the 'interplay of nonegalitarian and mobile relations' (1978: 94). To this end, power can be understood as a practice rather than a possession, an exercise rather than an attribute (Kendall and Wickham 1999). The depiction of power as a mobile relation is attractive because it offers us a means of analysing the ways in which regimes of difference – such as gender, sexuality and race – interact with each other to shape certain forms of violence. For example, we might categorise an incident of violence as homophobia-related because it is dominated by hierarchical understandings of heterosexuality and homosexuality, but, as we saw in Chapter 3, the enactment and experience of that violence is inevitably shaped by specificities of race and gender. Quite simply, different manifestations of power emerge in different contexts. This does not mean, however, that there is anything egalitarian about this mobility. Bordo provides a helpful interpretation of Foucault on this point when she comments that, 'no one may control the rules of the game' but 'not all players on the field are equal' (Bordo 1993: 191).

In contrast to Foucault, feminist theory has always been ready to name the sources and beneficiaries of power. Whilst feminism's historical preference for locating power in the hands of men may now seem to over-determine the issue, I believe that the 'who' question – who has power? – should remain on any agenda that investigates violence. Throughout this book I have argued that individuals assess their own experience and vulnerability to violence by identifying and managing the situations and groups of people that pose a risk to their personal safety. In turn, these assessments represent a form of knowledge that is capable of contributing to the way in which identities are constituted and re-constituted. This only happens because violence is able to send certain messages about the subjects and objects of violence. For example, take my argument in Chapter 2 that homophobia-related violence makes a statement about the disordered nature of lesbian sexuality, or my suggestion in Chapter 3 that acts of territorial violence function to remind us that Asians and/or homosexuals are not welcome in certain places. These statements are the products of hierarchical constructions of difference; for instance, of the relations between heterosexuality/homosexuality, Anglo/Asian, and the ways in which these differences interact with each other. This means that the actual or perceived identity of those who perpetrate, or are likely to perpetrate violence, is crucial to the experience of violation and to the ways others understand it. In this way, identity (and the differences that produce it) fundamentally shapes the oppressive and constitutive implications of violence. Goldberg makes this point well when he asserts, in the context of racial difference, that racist expressions maintain and rationalise relations of power by reminding their objects 'who it is that occupies the position of power' (1995: 270).

Foucault has indicated that power is tolerated, and thereby functions effectively, because it is able to 'mask a substantial part of itself' (Foucault 1978: 86). This may be so, but power does not necessarily make itself tolerable by concealing the inequalities and hostilities that pattern particular subject positions. We only have to think of the panoptic model of disciplinarity to realise that power is itself dependent upon the extent to which marginalised subjects are cognisant of the fact that they may be observed and defined by those who occupy more central, normative positions. It is not so much that positions of exploitation and profit do not exist or cannot be identified in a Foucauldian model. But, rather, that power is too 'diffuse' and 'enigmatic' to be confined to these positions, or to be held by the subjects who inhabit them (Foucault and Deleuze 1977: 213–14). The question 'who has power' may be, as Foucault suggests, ultimately unanswerable because it assumes that power is possessed by individuals, instead of acknowledging that power actually constitutes these individuals. Nevertheless, the point I wish to make is that the productive function of violence, including its oppression, is dependent upon the ability of that violence to tell us which subject positions are named as potential perpetrators of violence (e.g. categories of masculinity, whiteness or heterosexuality may be marked as dangerous) and which subject positions are named as vulnerable to violence (e.g. categories of femininity, homosexuality or Asian may be marked as 'in danger' of violence).

In terms of analysing violence, then, the 'who' question might be usefully reworked into a question about the ability of violence to tell us 'what' subject positions occupy positions of domination and subjugation.[10] This is not about seeking to prove that certain individuals *hold* unchanging or intrinsic power over other individuals. It is about naming the identity categories that are *coded* as the potential violators of corporeal and emotional integrity, and those that are coded as the potential victims.

Is violence power?

The idea that violence is intimately and inextricably entwined with power is an axiom of the feminist anti-violence movement. By articulating systems of male power as the cause and effect of men's violence towards women, feminist theory situates violence within wider social, economic and political inequalities of gender. This allows us to move away from a model that individualises and pathologises violence. The feminist formulation of the relation between male violence and male power is essentially two-sided. First, socio-political and psychological paradigms of gender inequality are said to be the cause of sexually and physically aggressive behaviours by men towards women. Second, in enforcing certain forms of individual and collective subordination, or obedience, violence is understood as a 'means of maintaining systems of oppression' (Kelly 1996: 37). Hence, violence is both an abuse of male power, and a form of support for the domination and control associated with that power.[11] The closeness of the feminist link between violence and power is demonstrated in the long-standing assertion that violence is 'essential' or 'key' to male dominance (Millett 1969; Brownmiller 1973; Daly 1978; Hester 1992; Hester *et al.* 1996). At the risk of over-simplifying things, it is thus possible to reduce the complex feminist arguments in this field to the idea that violence is both an effect of male power and crucial to the continuance of that power. Given that feminist theory defines this power as a matter of the dominance that one group of people (men) have 'over' another group of people (women), violence itself is often characterised as a form of power 'over' women.

Although this close alignment of violence and power has proven successful in highlighting, and challenging, violence as a systemic problem of unequal gender relations, it does embody a paradox that is important for thinking further about how we might conceptualise the violence–power nexus. On the one hand, feminist theory tends to assert that violence is a manifestation of male power. On the other hand, violence is said to be the product of the difficulty that patriarchy has in maintaining this power. For example, in arguing that 'men's gender power is ultimately backed by force', Kelly makes the point that this force is used 'when power is in jeopardy'. This means that gendered violence is the 'outcome of men's power as men and women's resistance to it' (1996: 37). Breines and Gordon made a similar point some time earlier, in the context of domestic violence, when they argued that violence, as a symptom of wider problems, is a sign of 'a power struggle for the *maintenance* of a certain kind of social order' (1983: 511). In this formulation, violence manifests at the weak points of male domination – where power is in jeopardy – rather than its sites of strength. It emerges out of a struggle between power and resistance.[12] Significantly, and to make a point that I will return to shortly, violence is thereby conceptualised as an *instrument* for maintaining existing relations of domination and subjugation. This hints at a fissure, or opening, in the otherwise close alliance that feminist theory posits between violence and power. It represents the possibility that violence might be something different *from* power, at the same time that it is closely tied *to* power. In other words, violence cannot be reduced to a question of unambiguous and unimpeded power. This begs the question of just how great this difference is. How much space is there between violence and power?

In *Discipline and Punish* and the first volume of *The History of Sexuality* Foucault writes as if the space between violence and power is immense. While juridical systems of power have historically relied on brute force to invoke obedience in their subjects, the 'new methods' of disciplinary power, graphically represented in the metaphor of the panoptic gaze, subjugate their subjects through techniques of surveillance, normalisation and codification. In his rejection of the repressive hypothesis, Foucault positions violence as the 'opposite extreme' of, and 'utterly incongruous' with, disciplinary power (1977: 208; 1978: 89). Although ultimately unsustainable, this power/ violence opposition is no more than the logical outcome of his model of power. As a productive relation between forces, power is dependent upon an acting and resisting subject: 'what defines a relationship of power is that it is a mode of action, which does not act directly, and immediately on others. Instead, it acts upon their actions: an action upon an action' (1982: 789). In contrast, violence, as we saw earlier, 'bends' and 'breaks' its object by acting directly and immediately upon the body, in order to minimise all opposition and resistance.

The problem with Foucault's rigid dichotomisation of power and violence lies not so much in the way power is defined, but more with the restricted meaning that he gives to violence. His tendency to bind physical force to sovereign power alone makes it easy to overlook the forms of violence that erupt in everyday relations between individuals. In a reminder of the importance of asking 'what' subject positions are coded as the bearers of power, MacCannell and MacCannell insist that Foucault is only able to dispute the linkage between violence and power by ignoring the fact that 'victims know that localised power in all its forms and applications remains supported by threats and actual use of violence and force' (1993: 212). Furthermore, and as I have previously argued, violence is both a corporeal injury which inflicts direct harm upon individual bodies, and a discursive statement that infiltrates the processes of subjectification through which these bodies are constituted; for example, by defining the homosexual as a subject 'in danger' of violence. Yet, the binary that Foucault creates between violence and power presumes a distinction between action and embodiment. Violence is only ever, and never more than, action upon the body. In contrast, power is conceptualised as action upon action. This appears to be limited in two ways. First, it does not recognise that violence is *more* than a material practice that oppresses by acting directly upon the body; that is, it fails to see the productive capacity of violence. Second, it assumes that the body that is violently acted upon is a static passive object that neither acts nor resists once it is violated; that is, it fails to recognise the ways in which individuals continually resist and subvert the effects of violence. Such premises are, in fact, irreconcilable with Foucault's broader thesis that corporeality and discourse infuse each other.

Despite Foucault's initial assertion that violence and power are mutually exclusive, traces of equivocation were evident from the very beginning. For example, he stated that it is only in 'principle', where it is free from the material realities of obstacle or resistance, that power can function without resort to violence (1977: 177). The central role that resistance eventually came to play in the productive hypothesis, may well have prompted him to consider the likelihood that, in practice, power will readily resort to violence. Whatever his reasoning, Foucault later modified his earlier opposition between violence and power. This is apparent in his 1982 article entitled 'The Subject and Power'. Here, he maintains that the exercise of power is 'always a way of acting upon an acting subject . . . a way in which certain actions modify others' (1982: 788–9).[13] Violence is still denied a key role in this formula, because of the assumed incompatibility between the body that is acted upon (as in the act of violence) and the body that acts (as in a relation of power). Violence neither constitutes the 'basic nature' or 'principle' of power: it is not essential to power. However, in this account 'passivity' now replaces power as the opposite of violence. This means that violence is no longer excluded from power relations altogether. Indeed, Foucault goes on to declare that violence, together with consent, may actually be indispensable to power. Power will always need one or the other:

> Obviously the bringing into play of power relations does not exclude the use of violence any more than it does the obtaining of consent; no doubt the exercise of power can never do without one or the other, often both at the same time.
>
> (1982: 789)

In this re-formulation, violence is neither indispensable to, nor exempt from, a given power relation. The exercise of power will always exceed, and in some ways contradict, violence. Violence is simply one strategy among others that power may employ. Here, Foucault no longer asserts that power never constrains or prohibits in the way that violence does. Rather, that it only does this at the points where it is most vulnerable; for example, where consent has failed or where resistance is strong. Such a situation might be characterised as a 'state of domination', a stable, asymmetrical relation of power that imposes limits and controls over the actions of those groups of people who are vulnerable to violence (Patton 1998: 68). When power is in a state of domination, it is still productive, but it is more likely to resort to oppressive practices, such as violence, to maintain the dominance that such productivity brings. It is significant that for Foucauldian theory, as for feminist theory, this link between violence and power is characterised as an *instrumental* one. In describing violence as an 'instrument', or a result, of power Foucault establishes a nexus between the two phenomena, while insisting that each does represent quite distinct practices and processes (1982: 789).

When read in this light, the differences between how violence is conceptualised within a feminist and a Foucauldian model of power seem less dramatic. Certainly, their respective interpretations of power are distinct. But, as I suggested earlier, they are neither incompatible with, nor mutually exclusive of, each other. Foucault's productive hypothesis incorporates the repressive hypothesis and, thereby, allows us to account for the processes of subjectification without abandoning the problems of oppression that concern feminist theory. In terms of violence, this means that we do not have to ignore the fact that violence controls and restricts the way we live our daily lives, in order to explore its (limited) capacity to constitute the very subject positions through which we interpret and experience these lives. Whilst it is important to recognise that violence and power are discrete phenomena in the sense that power functions quite effectively, perhaps most effectively, without violence, this should not be taken to imply that the operation of a given power relation necessarily excludes the practice of violence. Feminism knows this. Despite suggestions that violence is a sign *of* (male) power, it is probably more accurate to say that feminist theory understands violence as the product of a struggle between power and resistance. It emerges where power is in jeopardy. For Foucault, violence is also a form of oppression to which power resorts when its more subtle strategies falter. In this way, both feminist and Foucauldian theory suggest that violence is the outcome, or the result, of a struggle between power and resistance. Significantly, they each articulate this process as an instrumental one. Violence emerges out of a particular power relation in order that it may be put to use by this same power relation (or a closely associated one) to maintain certain forms of social order.

The idea of an instrumental nexus between violence and power represents a crucial site of convergence between feminist and Foucauldian theory. Despite their deep divisions, they each understand the practice of violence as something that is used in the exercise of power. For me, however, this raises a further question: in what sense is violence an instrument of power? How does power use violence? In the final section of this chapter, I would like to provide some tentative thoughts on this issue. In particular, I am interested in thinking about how we might articulate the notion of instrument so that it draws upon both feminist and Foucauldian insights. As we shall see, my answer to this question is deeply informed by the way in which the issue of *knowledge* has featured in the arguments that I have made throughout this book, arguments which I have sought to synthesise in this chapter.

What is an instrument?[14]

Taken literally, instruments are things that we use to do, to perform, and to produce other things. They are a means to an end. For instance, instruments often provide us with a method of looking at, and thereby seeing, things in ways that otherwise might not be apparent to us: as in a telescope, microscope, radar, speedometer, or, more simply, a ruler. Using instruments in this way is not simply a case of looking. In the act of looking, we are actively engaged in constructing how we know, and identify, the objects and events that we observe. That is, we constitute these phenomena, in part, according to the ways that we are able to see, and come to know, them. It is in this sense that we might say that knowledge is intrinsic to the exercise of Foucauldian power.[15] This is well illustrated in the centrality of knowledge to the panoptic metaphor, via which Foucault explicated his initial model of disciplinary power (which was subsequently incorporated into the productive hypothesis). As I have indicated, panopticism functions by exposing the bodies and behaviours of human subjects to historically specific systems of knowledge; this includes the formal knowledge of professions and institutions, as well as the informal knowledge of personal experience and social interaction. These knowledges operate like a lens through which we see, and thereby come to recognise, others and ourselves as certain types of individuals. For example, the construction of sexuality into hierarchical categories of homosexuality and heterosexuality shapes the ways in which we experience sexual desire and conduct our sexual lives. In taking up, reinventing and rejecting different identity categories we normalise and manage not just our own behaviour, but also the conduct of others. In this way, knowledge is integral to the processes of regulation through which particular subject positions are constituted and occupied. As the vehicle, or medium, through which we see the world, knowledge thus defines the 'channels' that enable power to function (Foucault 1978: 11).

Hence, one way of thinking about how violence might be an instrument of power is to recall this intimacy between knowledge and power in Foucauldian theory. In simple terms, we might say that knowledge is the link between violence, as a corporeal act and experience, and the hierarchies of difference that pattern a given power relation. Or, to put this another way, violence makes us know things according to the ways in which it makes contact with, or threatens to make contact with, our own bodies and the bodies of others.

It is helpful to separate the circularity of this process into two modes of operation. On the one hand, violence is the product of certain forms of knowledge. For example, the physical act of homophobia-related violence only makes sense within specific discourses that privilege some forms of sexuality over others. These same discourses interact with corporeal specificities to mould the way in which the bodily injury and emotional pain of violation is experienced and interpreted.[16] On the other hand, such violence generates its own form of knowledge. For example, it is the belief that homophobia-related violence is a genuine risk that prompts lesbians and gay men to monitor their bodies for signs that will make them vulnerable to violence. In this way, violence acts upon the bodies of lesbians and gay men to command them to obedience. Moreover, in leaving its unwelcome marks on these bodies, violence shows us which categories of people are vulnerable to violence and, by implication, which categories are likely to perpetrate violence: for example, by making a statement that to be homosexual is to be in danger of violence, or that to be a heterosexual male is to be a potential source of such danger. Such statements embody a knowledge that is capable of infiltrating the ways in which we experience, and recognise, these identity categories. Because this knowledge emerges from existing systems of sexual order, and the power relations that infuse them, it carries the kinds of undesirable messages that can readily be used to bolster these same systems and, thereby, maintain particular power relations.[17] In short, the knowledge that we have of violence is the instrument that connects corporeal injury and emotional harm (the oppression of violence) with the processes of subjectification (the constitutive capacity of power).

Violence is thus a deeply visceral knowledge with both oppressive and productive implications. Like all instruments, however, violence has its limits. As we have seen throughout this book, lesbians and gay men resist and subvert its command to obedience in a plethora of ways. The limits of violence are not confined to these individual modes of resistance. The capacities of violence cannot exceed the mechanisms of disciplinarity itself. Violence may contribute to the constitution of particular subject positions (for example, 'what' homosexuality is) but it can never determine the ways in which we take up and experience these positions ('who' we are as homosexuals).[18] The knowledge that violence represents must compete with other knowledges, other experiences and other power relations (the things that violence cannot show us). Like any piece of knowledge, it must be used over and over again in order to sustain a sense of authenticity. The outcomes of this process are unpredictable. The messages that violence contains may be ignored, re-invented or misrecognised. Just because power may use violence to bolster its own state of dominance does not mean that it is successful in stabilising that dominance. Indeed, if certain types of violence – such as homophobic, gendered or racist violence – emerge when power is in jeopardy, the very existence of such violence must function as a sign of the vulnerability or disintegration of that power.[19] This knowledge, in turn, is capable of undermining the authority of power by revealing its constant need for maintenance. In other words, to characterise violence as an instrument is to signify not only the knowledge that violence gives us about certain bodies, but also the things that violence reveals about a given power relation.

It is thus possible to think of instrumentality as a question of the things that violence shows us. This includes the moderated capacity of violence to mould the ways in which we experience, see and recognise the bodies of its objects and the bodies of its subjects. It also includes the tendency of violence to expose the limitations, failings and vulnerabilities of the powers that undergird it; there is much that violence is unable to conceal. In this way, the act of violence itself is a spectacle. This is not so much because violence provides us with a striking or eye-catching phenomenon to observe, but, more, because violence is a mechanism through which we distinguish and identify other phenomena. In panoptic terms, then, we can think of the act of violence as a lens, a metaphorical lens through which we see, and come to know, certain things. In this way, violence is not just something to look at. Violence also embodies a way of looking.

Conclusion

In this chapter I sought to bring together the major arguments of previous chapters by providing a framework for conceptualising the nexus between violence and power. I highlighted the contributions that feminist and Foucauldian theory make to our understandings of this nexus. Initially, I addressed a series of four questions: Does violence oppress? What is power? Who has power? Is violence power? These are questions that arose for me in the course of conducting research on homophobia-related violence. I believe that considering the ways in which feminist and Foucauldian theory each respond to these questions assists us to recognise that they are not irreconcilable paradigms for analysing the relationship between violence and power. But nor does this mean that either model, on its own, is capable of accounting for the complexities of this nexus. Feminism provides us with a means of connecting certain types of inter-personal violence, such as gendered violence or homophobia-related violence, to wider relations of subordination and domination. Indeed, feminism demands that we make this kind of link. However, the repressive model of power that continues to drive much feminist work in this field offers research little prospect of accounting for the ways in which violence does not only act upon bodies to make them obedient, but also functions to constitute the subject positions that these same bodies occupy. It is this limitation that prompts me, and many feminist researchers before me, to turn to the work of Foucault. Here, I find a model of power that does not exclude the repressive hypothesis but, rather, employs it as a technology in the productive processes of subject-ification. This assists me to conceptualise how an act of violence might not just operate to oppress, but may also contribute to the way in which we are formulated as certain kinds of individuals. This is crucial for research that hopes to fully account for the contexts, injuries and products of violence.

Despite their differences, both feminist and Foucauldian theory charac-terise the relationship between violence and power in similar terms. That is, they describe it as an instrumental nexus. This represents an important conceptual link that allows research to move beyond the question of whether violence is, or is not, a form of power. It offers a means of recognising, both the sense of distance between violence and power that we find in a Foucauldian model, and the sense of proximity between violence and power that is prioritised in a feminist model. Violence and power may be distinct, even oppositional, phenomena in a conceptual sense, but they are closely linked in practice. Power is not dependent upon violence. But it does often resort to using it. In particular, violence tends to arise out of the struggle between power and resistance, when power is in jeopardy of losing support or consent fails to be freely given. In short, to characterise violence as an instrument of power is to suggest that violence and power are separate from, but never mutually exclusive of, each other. Violence may not be intrinsic to power, but power is intrinsic to those forms of violence that are shaped by regimes of difference, such as those of gender, sexuality or race.

What, then, is the nature of this instrumentality? If we take my proposed pathway between feminist and Foucauldian theory, how might we think about the ways in which violence is an instrument of power? One way for research to conceptualise the instrumental link between violence and power is to articulate it as a question of knowledge. It is the knowledge that violence embodies – knowledge of pain, fear, danger, disorder and the like – that oppresses individuals. It is this same knowledge that, inevitably, makes some kind of contribution to the hierarchical way in which we recognise those groups of people who are the primary targets, and the primary perpetrators, of violence. Certainly, violence can never determine who we are, but it does leave an unwelcome mark upon our bodies. The paradox of violence, however, is that every time it is put to use in the exercise of power, its very presence alerts us to the fact that somewhere, in some way, that particular regime of power is in jeopardy. The template for conceptualising the nexus between violence and power that I have outlined here offers a means by which future research may acknowledge this.

NOTES

1 LOOKING THROUGH EXPERIENCE

1 According to Foucault, the idea itself did not originate with either member of the Bentham family. The theme of individual isolation and visibility was 'in the air' at the time (Foucault 1980:147).

2 Bentham's (1962) original design included elaborate systems of lamps and reflectors attached to the external window for illuminating the cells at night and tin tubes for ensuring that the slightest sound in the cells could be heard from the tower.

3 Foster draws a distinction between vision and visuality. Although he seeks to avoid associating the former with nature and the latter with culture, he uses vision to connote sight as a physical operation and visuality to refer to sight as a social fact (1988: ix). In some contrast, I use vision as an umbrella term to encompass the whole family of optic signifiers: visibility, evidence, the panoptic, observation, spectacle, and so on. My employment of the more specific notion of vision is primarily restricted to its highly contested claim as a metaphor for knowledge. In this context, observation is a means to vision.

4 Lincoln and Guba (1985) define positivism as comprising the following set of assumptions: all true knowledge is scientific; science is value-free and neutral; and science is capable of establishing a verifiable knowledge or truth about events. The identification of cause-and-effect relationships is at the heart of positivist social science, due to the assumed ability of such relationships to facilitate the prediction and control of events. Hence, Smart suggests that the 'problem' with positivism lies in the 'basic presumption that we can establish a verifiable knowledge or truth about events: in particular, that we can establish a causal explanation that will in turn provide us with objective methods for intervening in the events defined as problematic' (1990: 72).

5 I am not suggesting that there is a distinct fissure between those in the 'experience school' and those in the 'theory school'. Clearly, such a dichotomy is too simplistic and ignores commentators who straddle both camps, such as those working in and around cultural studies (although the extent to which these academics engage with the issue of violence, much less experiential accounts of violence, is minimal). I do wish to suggest, however, that a general, albeit far from all-encompassing, disjunction has emerged between feminist empirical research on gendered violence and feminist poststructural theory.

6 Although various forms of feminist empiricism also developed at the same time, these have posed a lesser challenge to core positivist traditions.

7 In responding to criticism, some standpoint feminists have replaced the idea of a singular feminist standpoint with multiple feminist standpoints. Some have qualified the extent to which feminist knowledge can be reduced to a question of women's experience; an interesting example of this is seen in the concessions that have been made regarding the ability of men to produce feminist-oriented research (Collins 1990; Harding 1993).

8 This is the case whether experience is being drawn upon to establish points of heterogeneity or points of homogeneity; for example, whether we use experience to establish commonalities among women or whether we use it to highlight differences between women.

9 It is not that the disciplines completely replaced juridico-political structures or sovereign modalities of power, but rather that these have been infiltrated by the disciplinary mode (Foucault 1977).

10 Diana Fuss refers to essentialism as 'a belief in true essence – that which is most irreducible, unchanging, and therefore constitutive of a given person or thing' (1989: 2).

11 Rajchman notes that, both in English and French, the word 'evidence' is derived from 'videre', meaning to see: 'In the course of its history, the word acquires the sense of proof, testimony, and clarity or indubitability to the mind' (1988: 93).

12 In contrast to those who have argued for a 'minimalist' (Longino 1990) or a 'strong' (Harding 1993) approach to objectivity, Haraway and others (Lazreg 1994; Lovibond 1994; Yeatman 1994) have argued that the 'partial perspective' of 'objective vision' should be understood as a signifier of accountability, rather than neutrality and transcendence. Although Haraway has argued that universalist knowledge claims be seen as a form of relativism in themselves, her definition of accountability as a form of critical and partial positioning has not been without its critics (Mangena 1994; Harding 1993).

13 Given that I do not believe that it is possible to remove all power differentials from the research environment, I attempted to remain mindful and respectful of the different roles that researcher and research participant each play in the research process. I interpreted my commitment to maintaining the integrity of the personal experiences told to me in interview, not as a need to shy away from representing and conceptualising these accounts within the context of my overall argument, but, rather, as a matter of acknowledging the different perspectives of each participant and not assuming that they need to be reconciled with my own or with each other.

14 I have, as is usual, used pseudonyms for these women. I define active participation as speaking when the tape-recorder was turned on. A small number of women involved in the focus groups either chose not to speak or are not fully audible on the tape.

15 A proportion of this interview material was initially examined, in quite different ways, in my doctoral thesis. Several interviews (and presentations) were conducted later and were not included in the thesis.

16 Of the forty-seven women who were interviewed individually, four had previously been involved in a focus group. I have counted these women only once.

17 A couple of these women stated that, although their current sexual and emotional lifestyles were lesbian, their broader sexual experiences should probably be characterised as bisexual.

18 I tape-recorded all of the interviews. I transcribed the first 10 per cent in full. I then selectively transcribed those segments of an interview that, at the time, I believed to be most relevant to the issues I wished to explore. For a discussion of selective transcription see Strauss and Corbin (1990). In this book I reproduce edited versions of these transcripts. For example, most 'umm' and 'ahs' have been removed. The women I interviewed were sent either a copy of the transcription or a copy of the tape-recording, as well as a publication I had written on homophobic violence. They were given the opportunity to comment on the interview content. Only a few participants took this opportunity. Their comments have been integrated into their original interview transcript.

19 Here Rose quotes Deleuze and Guattari.

20 Although statements about particular objects are legitimated within a wider discourse, they function, in turn, as the criteria through which that discourse is assessed and maintained (Bové 1990). Indeed, it is only when an event is validated as legitimate, within relevant discursive fields, that it is transfigured into a serious statement, that is, a statement capable of contributing to the corpus of power relations that maintain accompanying knowledge claims.

21 The notion of interpretive, or linguistic, repertoires that I use here has its origins in social psychology. However, there are counterparts in numerous other disciplines.

2 DISORDER

1 I draw this concept from parallel discussions about the 'risk of essence', see Fuss (1989).

2 Exceptions do appear from time to time, such as Schneider's (1993) study of workplace sexual assault against heterosexual and lesbian women.

3 For example, recent literature on domestic violence in lesbian relationships includes: Renzetti 1988; Lobel 1986; Taylor and Chandler 1995; Robson 1992; Kelly 1991, 1996.

4 Recent discussions of hate crime in both social and legal contexts include: Cunneen *et al.* 1997; Levin and McDevitt 1993; Whillock and Slayden 1995; Baird and Rosenbaum 1999; Lawrence 1999; Jacobs and Potter 1999.

5 The most common methodological limitations in this research are the absence of representative or random samples, and the lack of inter-survey uniformity in relation to the questions asked and the concepts operationalised.

6 I derive these figures from an examination of the following publications and empirical studies: Berrill 1990; Faulkner 1997; GLAD 1994; New Zealand Gay Task Force 1985; Mason and Palmer 1996; von Schulthess 1992.

7 In an Australian study of predominantly gay men, only 1.5 per cent of incidents took place at home, only 6 per cent knew the assailant, and 83 per cent of assailants were believed to be under 25 years old (Cox 1990).

8 Comstock (1991) compares violence towards lesbians with violence towards women as a whole in the United States. It should be noted that he does this by

contrasting a victim survey with the US national crime statistics (the latter represent crimes reported to the police). Australian research by Price Waterhouse Urwick (1995) suggests that gay men are at least four times more likely to experience an assault in a twelve-month period than other Sydney men, whilst lesbians were found to be six times more likely to experience an assault in a twelve-month period than other Sydney women.

9 Only a couple of women had never experienced any kind of hostile response to their sexuality. These women indicated that they were unlikely to experience hostility because they were extremely careful about the contexts within which they disclosed their sexuality.

10 As I saw in other heart-wrenching stories of social isolation, psychiatric institutionalisation, and solitary confinement at school, lesbianism is, to borrow the words of one young woman I interviewed, 'assumed to be containable if they just cut you off from others'.

11 Irigaray argues that this value is in no way intrinsic to woman. It is the functions she performs, particularly reproduction, that make her indispensable to man. Moreover, as a deeply hom(m)o-sexual social practice between men, this economy is only superficially heterosexual. Paradoxically, actual homo-erotic desire between men is purportedly forbidden because of its ability to challenge woman as the only necessary product of exchange: 'Once the penis itself becomes merely a means to pleasure, pleasure among men, *the phallus loses its power*' (Irigaray 1985: 193). In other words, the price that men pay for being the agents of exchange is forfeiture of the ability to serve as suitable commodities themselves.

12 This is irrespective of the fact that many women and men who are sexually attracted to members of their own sex do not consciously seek to reject gender roles, and may adhere to a conventional gender identity in all other aspects of their life.

13 Of course, interpretations of butch are context-dependent. To be called butch in an affirmative context can be a compliment.

14 Butler (1990), among others, has contested Wittig's associated call for lesbian and gay men to consciously rid themselves of the linguistic and political categories of woman and man. Identities constituted through exclusion are inevitably reliant upon the very categories they attempt to expel. Butler's concern emanates from the contribution such an identity makes to the reinforcement of compulsory heterosexuality. Although Butler's point is well taken, the angle to Wittig's argument that interests me here has less to do with the question of identity and more to do with her critique of conventional notions of sexual difference.

15 One interviewee suggested that the reason she attracted relatively high levels of hostility from men was because she 'looked like a dyke'. Whilst I do not wish to speculate about the extent to which a 'dyke look' equates with an 'unfeminine look' or a 'butch look', it may be that a 'dyke look' is less about the absence of femininity and more about the display of a mixture of gender codes. As with homophobia-related violence in general, it is possible that it is this sense of ambiguity that generates hostile repertoires around the question of gender. It is interesting to speculate about the possibility that those women who take on a hyper-masculine appearance may actually experience less violence. This may be not because they are genuinely mistaken for a boy or a man, but because

potential aggressors may view them as 'one of the boys', thereby suggesting that they are less of a threat to the rigid gender dimorphism of the straight mind.

3   DIFFERENT TERRITORY: A QUESTION OF INTERSECTIONALITY?

1   See Crenshaw (1991) and Abrams (1994). Although I do not directly address it here, I think it would be helpful to also explore the limitations of defining intersectionality as an anti-essentialist tool. For example, debates about the concept of essentialism itself, particularly as it relates to embodiment, suggest that we are sometimes too quick to categorise ways of thinking as essentialist, and to then dismiss them (Fuss 1989; Bell 1999). It seems to me that intersectionality is often used in violence discourse to overcome problems that might be more accurately described as universal or reductionist forms of analysis. See Grosz (1990) for a discussion of the ways in which feminist uses of the notion of essentialism relate to reductionism and universalism.

2   There are, of course, many other forms of difference that I could explore. Class, age and disability are obvious examples. Suffice to say that my focus upon race in this chapter, and its interaction with sexuality and gender, reflects the emergence of this variable among the women I interviewed. This reflected, in part, my own desire to examine this particular articulation of identity.

3   The category of Asian has a somewhat different meaning in the public discourse of Australia than it does, for example, in the United Kingdom. Non-Asian Australians tend to use Asian in a homogenising way to refer to those people whose heritage lies in the various countries of East Asia or South-East Asia, such as China, Japan, Korea, Vietnam, Malaysia, Singapore, Hong Kong, Indonesia, Thailand and the Philippines. It is less likely to be used to refer to someone of Indian or Pakistani heritage. As is apparent in the interview accounts used in this chapter, Asian is also deployed – less frequently but more strategically – by those women and men who are categorised as Asian by non-Asian Australians.

It is important to note that the question of race in this chapter is primarily confined to Asian–Anglo relations. Interviewees from other non-western, or non-English-speaking backgrounds also spoke of racism and ethnocentrism. Whilst the particulars of these experiences vary from those presented here, I believe that the theoretical points that I make about intersectionality can be applied to many racial and ethnic contexts. Although I did not interview any women who identified as Aboriginal Australian, questions of intersectionality have also been recognised in the context of violence and discrimination towards indigenous populations (Atkinson 1990a and 1990b).

4   This does not mean that the arguments presented here have no pertinence outside this national boundary, as if they must, or could, be completely confined to the immediate socio-political context from which they emerge. It does mean that whilst analytical insights may be appropriated from any empirical base, the material circumstances of that site will always mould the knowledge that is produced.

5   To say that violence is gendered, racist or homophobic is to suggest that it is invested with a hierarchical understanding of difference *between* subjects (e.g.

inter-personal distinctions of masculinity/femininity, whiteness/blackness, heterosexuality/homosexuality). I pick up on this issue later in the chapter.

6 For example, 'plural consciousness' (Mohanty 1991) or, in law, 'multiple consciousness' (Matsuda 1989a).

7 Although these young women appeared to be drunk at the time, this does not explain the particular ways in which their aggression manifested.

8 The Australian socio-political history is such that the vast majority of the population are, in global terms, relatively recent migrants or descendants of migrants from both English and non-English-speaking countries. As a nation, it thus bears the legacy of a history of violent colonisation and dispossession of the indigenous population. This has produced a drastic imbalance between the indigenous population and the colonising population (Gelder and Jacobs 1998). However, strong social, economic and political distinctions continue to operate between the various colonising groups. A dominant, yet ultimately unsustainable, division exists between those whose ethnic heritage is primarily Anglo-Celtic and English-speaking (usually from Great Britain) and those who come from other ethnic, national and linguistic backgrounds (for example, Italy, Greece, Turkey, Lebanon, or the various countries of Asia).

9 It is likely that the actions of these young Anglo women were also shaped by the specific football environment. For example, the territory of the Ladies may have a different significance in a football stadium than it does in a shopping complex or a nightclub. The football stadium continues to be less of a ladies space than these other environments.

10 As indicated, racialised readings of gender are not unique to Asian/non-Asian relations. Whilst the hyper-heterosexualisation of South-East Asian women by western culture can be contextualised within a history of masculine orientialism, it also shares some common ground with the sexualisation and/or masculinisation of black and indigenous women (hooks 1981; Elder 1993), as well as the pathologisation of lesbians (Hart 1994; Davies and Rhodes-Little 1993): a pathologisation that is magnified in the pejorative characterisation of the Black lesbian as 'bulldagger' (Walker 1993). The thread that links these stereotypes is the deployment of each toward the collective reproduction of white heterosexuality in normative terms.

11 A particular regime of difference may configure an act of violence even when the perpetrator and the victim share a sameness in this respect. For example, in So Fong's account, fixed and oppositional understandings of gender shaped the incident, even though the individuals who threatened her were women, not men.

12 The premise that regimes of gender are exclusive of regimes of race is the very same premise that, in according neutrality to whiteness, facilitates the othering of non-whiteness by aligning it, and it alone, with difference: an alignment that, as we have seen, is incapable of capturing the way in which regimes of difference shape violence across a diversity of racial specificities.

13 As discussed in Chapter 1, Cartesian dualism, or the mind/body split, accords superiority to the mind over the body. Within this paradigm, whiteness and masculinity have operated as metaphors for the superiority of the mind. Attempts to displace this opposition have implications for the deep association of the body with notions of femininity and blackness (i.e. as inferior).

14 Although the ontological status of the body in Foucault's work has been greatly

contested, Butler effectively draws upon his somewhat ambiguous treatment of the panoptic body to argue that the power of subjectification is a dual-sided process that 'not only unilaterally *acts on* a given individual as a form of domination, but also *activates* or forms the subject' (1995: 230). Butler interprets this to mean that the body is itself formulated through the play of power relations and calculated gazes. This prompts her to suggest that the panoptic version of the body is not to be understood as an 'independent materiality, static surface or site, which a subsequent investment comes to mark, signify upon or pervade', but, instead, as a on-going interaction between materiality and constitutive processes.

15 For Butler (1993), this is partly because materiality and language do not exist in opposition to each other. Rather, they are fields of meaning that are dependent upon each other in various ways. For example, it is only possible to make reference to materiality through the processes of signification. Signification, in turn, can only take place through corporeal functions, such as those of sight and hearing. This means that materiality can be neither fully reduced to language nor fully excluded from language. Or, as Grosz (1994) puts it, the body is not opposed to culture.

16 Inter-personal, or social, alterity functions in tandem with the more intra-personal understandings of alterity that interests psychoanalysis (Grosz 1994). Van Pelt (2000) argues that the former, more politically inspired, notion of social alterity (and its adoption in much feminist, anti-homophobic and anti-racist theory) tends to reproduce foundational and oppositional views of the self/other distinction; for example, by not actively contributing to the decon-struction of the white/black, man/woman, or heterosexual/homosexual binaries. Be this as it may, in both Chapter 2 and the present chapter, we have seen that these stratified versions of identity are very much a part of the discursive context through which certain violent behaviours are enacted and experienced. Articulating the way in which these different forms of alterity are mutually constitutive of each other makes its own contribution to their deconstruction.

17 Gatens (1996) uses the example of anorexia nervosa to illustrate the point that we always experience our own body through the way in which it appears to differ from other bodies.

18 As Bhabha (1994) makes clear, in the context of colonialism, the perpetrator's invocation of certain stereotypes does not represent a stable or fixed disciplinary gaze, but rather the need to fix an image of the victim as a means of establishing a secure identification. However, the violent policing of borders can never offer a secure point of identification because the 'ambivalence' of the subject who gazes, and the subject who is gazed upon, inevitably returns to disrupt the certainty of any territorial or identificatory gestures. I pick up on these issues in Chapter 5.

4 BODY MAPS: ENVISAGING HOMOPHOBIA, VIOLENCE AND SAFETY

1 The 8th International Symposium on Victimology, 'Victimisation and Violence: Strategies for Survival', August 1994, Adelaide, Australia.

2 Although Foucault may suggest that power in contemporary western societies is

better understood through relations of disciplinary surveillance, rather than through the spectacle of force and punishment, the way in which these mechanisms are themselves dependent upon visible sexual categories – which, in their less legitimate forms, represent a spectacle of their own – suggests that it might be more helpful to think of different forms of social spectacle as elements of, rather than oppositions to, surveillance. Indeed, as a model for the disciplinary society, the panoptic metaphor itself only functions as a form of surveillance through the production of visible types of subjects. In this sense, the relation between spectacle and surveillance is not so much a question of 'incompatibility', as of 'difference' (Foucault 1977: 199).

3 I use the phrase 'coming out' to refer to those times when individuals deliberately say or do something to indicate to others that they are gay or lesbian. An alternative, broader use of 'coming out' refers more to the self-recognition of one's homo-erotic desires.

4 Judith Butler (1991) has suggested that, in some contrast to gay men, the exclusion of the lesbian subject from western discourse itself is a form of violence that refuses her a site of prohibition from which to resist her own subjugation. Thus the lesbian is only thinkable and imaginable as an 'abiding falsehood'. Given the prominence of the lesbian subject in some contexts, such as the pornographic genre (Roof 1991), it is perhaps more helpful to characterise this as an exclusion from mainstream or legitimate discourse.

5 Although I believe that violence does have 'effects', I remain cognisant of the Foucauldian point that, in moving away from determinist assumptions, such 'effects' might be more appropriately understood as contingencies (Kendall and Wickham 1999).

6 Although personal safety concerns may be projected onto the figure of the 'unpredictable stranger' (Lupton 1999a), Stanko nonetheless reminds us that women's 'precautionary behavior occurs in public and private, [and is] aimed to minimize violence from strangers as well as loved ones' (1993: 160).

7 Research on violence against women has often highlighted women's 'fear' of violence. I have chosen not to use the notion of fear because I believe, at least in the context of homophobia-related violence, that it has a tendency to overstate and over-determine the problem. For a discussion of the rhetoric of fear in classic feminist texts on violence see Burton (1998).

8 A careful distinction must be noted here. Practices of self-surveillance are in no way determined only by the threat of hostility and violence. As some of the women above suggest, the concerns that prompt the self-regulation of visible representations of one's homosexuality exceed questions of violence or direct hostility. My suggestion that the knowledge of violence is inscribed in statements of visibility should not be taken to imply that the negotiation of visibility could be reduced to the negotiation of personal safety. Violence is never the sole factor in the decision not to disclose one's sexuality.

9 The imposition of conduct on subjects, in turn, allows for the 'ordering' of these multiplicities (Foucault 1977: 218).

10 Just as the disciplinary society does not replace sovereignty, neither does governmentality replace the disciplines. Instead, sovereignty, discipline and government function as a 'triangle', with 'its primary target the population' (Foucault 1991: 102).

11 As one interviewee put it: '[Y]ou can't totally avoid it. Unless you're gonna be totally insulated from the rough, the straight, the homophobic society, you know. You have to get in a leso taxi, you have to go to a leso bar, you have to go to a leso house . . . there is nowhere that you can go that [you] are guaranteed not to get homophobia.'

5 BACKLIGHT AND SHADOW: CONSTITUTING DANGER

1 For example, numerous aspects of Arendt's work have attracted sustained criticism. These include: her tendency to valorise individualism; her character-isation of Nazism as 'banal evil'; her conservation of the civil and institutional status quo in the face of disruptive or aggressive claims for minority rights; her refusal to politicise questions of gender; and her ethnocentric arguments around racial politics. Recent critiques can be found in: Feher 1989; Jacobitti 1996; Norton 1995; Young-Bruehl 1996; Pitkin 1994, 1995; Heller 1989; Hartsock 1983b.

2 Risk is a catch-all phrase that is often too broad to capture the specificities of the varied phenomena it is said to encompass. For this reason, I have chosen to talk about homosexuality and violence as a question of danger, rather than risk. This helps capture not only the historical association between homosexuality and danger, but also the serious harm and injury that violence can incur. We might think of this sense of danger as an intense, or even sexualised, form of risk. For further discussions of risk theory and 'the risk society' see Beck 1992 and Giddens 1991.

3 This is similar to the way in which HIV/AIDS discourse constructs gay men as both the source of risk for others and a risk to themselves.

4 For Arendt (1958), it is neither through our biological nor our psychological traits that we take on an identity of our own. These characteristics do not make us unique.

5 It is also important to note that, although Arendt prioritises the public sphere, she does not actually adhere to a conventional public/private dichotomy. Instead, she establishes a three-way distinction between the public, social and private spheres (Pitkin 1995).

6 In characterising Arendt's model as performative, Honig is, no doubt, influenced by Butler's (1990) work on the performativity of gender.

7 The power of subjectification acts upon the subject at the same time that it formulates that subject: 'power not only acts *on* the body, but also *in* the body . . . power not only produces the boundaries of a subject, but pervades the interiority of that subject' (Butler 1995: 234). According to Butler, it is through this discursively constituted 'psychic identity', or 'soul', that 'individuality' is rendered 'coherent' and 'totalized' (1995: 230). For Foucault, this soul eventually imprisons the body.

8 Some time ago, Carol Smart (1990, 1992) argued that law is more than an institu-tional site where discrimination is played out. Law is also a gendering strategy in its own right. Smart proposed that the rape trial provides us with an overt example of the way in which women's bodies become saturated with notions of sex

and sexuality that reinscribe the category of woman as the natural victim of (hetero)sexual assault. This capacity is not, of course, confined to the law. It permeates all institutional and professional commentary on sexual assault, including medicine, psychology, media, politics and so on. For Marcus, it is the very language of rape, its 'gendered grammar', that 'solicits women to position ourselves as endangered, violable, and fearful and invites men to position themselves as legitimately violent and entitled to women's sexual services' (1992: 389). Thus, Coward argues that the language of sex and violence promotes a 'view of the sexes as two species', where 'natural behaviour' is 'a world of male predators, aggressive animals who hunt the female of the species', who is 'passive and coy' (Coward 1987: 236). When brute force is fixed to male bodies, and passivity to female bodies, in this way, certain acts of violence, such as rape, become understood as something that is always 'done to the feminine other (whether its physical object be a woman, a man, or an inanimate object)' (de Lauretis 1989: 249).

With some exceptions (Cahill 2000), this line of argument focuses upon linguistic and visual representations of sexual violence, or, as in the case of Marcus, treats sexual violence as a 'linguistic fact'. The arguments thus come to rest upon an assumption that such representations can perform actions, or are a form of action, in themselves.

9 There is some interesting research on the ways in which both gendered violence and homophobic violence operate as a means of achieving heterosexual masculinity (Harry 1990; Jefferson 1994).

10 In Arendt's model, 'who' we are refers to a public, inter-subjective self, while 'what' we are is aligned with the 'private' sphere. It is Arendt's refusal to accord the body a legitimate place in the political realm that prompts her to associate 'what' with the private self, and 'who' with the public self. However, this disassemblage of orthodox public/private, group/individual, outer/inner binaries is said to open up possibilities for thinking about a human subject who is neither a seamless and harmonious whole, nor who is divided according to the arbitrary dichotomies traditionally associated with a mind/body split (Dietz 1995; Honig 1995).

11 As I have indicated, these pluralities cannot be reduced to a question of one's inner or private self, as if it is the truth of this inner self that enables one to resist 'what' one is. The difficulty with this kind of argument is that it assumes the primacy of a distinction between one's inner and outer self, with the former representing one's 'true' self. This is a distinction that has come to exist through historically and culturally specific disciplines, such as psychology and psychiatry (Bové 1990; Rose 1996a). Even if we were to accept the validity of an inner or psychic self, the problem is that it is these same 'psy' discourses that continue to authorise the kinds of normative judgements – healthy/unhealthy bodies, adjusted/maladjusted desires – that facilitate the pathologisation and denigration of homosexuality. As Diprose states, it is simply not possible to 'successfully oppose domination or exclusion by affirming some undiscovered truth of oneself', when that 'truth' is a product of the very discourses that maintain such domination in the first place (Diprose 1994: 280).

12 Arendt (1958) suggests that 'who' we are may well be beyond signification because, in attempting to communicate it, we always end up describing 'what' we are. Others may be better able than ourselves to see 'who' each of us is.

13 Of course, there are situations of violence so recurrent or so brutal that this does not happen, such as homicide or sustained abuse in domestic relationships. In such cases, the subject may be determined, or extinguished, by others' interpret-ations of 'what' they are. Arendt's notion of the pariah depicts a subject who is also determined by 'what' he/she is. However, Arendt defines a pariah as a state of exclusion from political community, and from the opportunity to publicly act in relation to others, because of one's outsider status. Implicit in being a pariah is a refusal to deny 'what' one is. Arendt reserves the contemptuous position of the 'parvenu' for those who seek to deny 'what' they are, and, in so doing, refuse the solidarity of group identity (Arendt 1967).

One of Arendt's criticisms of the women's movement was that it promoted a parvenu approach to liberation by assuming that women could just step into structures already established by men. Despite a certain inconsistency with her belief in participation politics, Arendt was convinced that for the oppressed to make political demands on their own behalf was not as effective a strategy as for others to recognise the importance of eliminating subjugation (Markus 1989).

14 Interestingly, Deleuze (1993) also develops a theory of 'becoming', in which he draws a distinction between becoming-the-same and becoming-other. However, this distinction is not central to the issues I discuss here.

15 If we accept that violence may constitute the subject in injurious way, we must also accept that it contains the ingredients for de-constitution of that subject; if a name 'acts once, it can act again, and possibly against its prior act' (Butler 1997: 69). Butler draws upon Derrida – who, she states, unlike Bourdieu, recognises that the failure of interpellation is intrinsic to the repeatability of marking and not just a social effect of a lack of authority on the speaker's behalf – to further argue that, like written marks, performative utterances, require repetition. In this repetition, the mark breaks with its historical context, so as to provide the opportunity for resignification and self-definition. In this way, words that wound can become the sites of resistance (1997: Chapter 4).

16 For example, Butler (1997) questions the presumption that racist, homophobic or misogynist speech is a form of action in itself, by exploring the differences between illocutionary and perlocutionary language. This distinction is drawn primarily from Austin, who defines illocutionary speech acts as those that do what they say, while perlocutionary speech produces effects. See pp. 2–24.

6   VIOLENCE: AN INSTRUMENT OF POWER

1 Although Foucault (1980) has stated that the modernist notion of the subject, rather than the question of power, was the primary focus of much of his work, analyses of power are extensive and prominent in this writing.

2 Feminist commentary on violence that takes up poststructural theory includes work by Smart 1992; Marcus 1992; Young 1996; Gavey 1989; Bell 1993; Hollway and Jefferson 1998; and Hart 1994.

3 I am reluctant to single out further examples of this literature. It is difficult to do so without implying that such research is somehow faulty or inferior. I do not wish to do this. Instead, I have singled out examples of feminist literature that *do* employ poststructural theory (see note 2). My approach to feminist research

that does not engage with this kind of theory is to cite examples in the context of particular arguments throughout this chapter. I believe that a perusal of recent journals and books in the field of gendered violence will verify the prevalence of this approach.

4 See, for example, Herek and Berrill 1992; Mason and Tomsen 1997. Many discussions of hate crime adopt a similar analysis of violence and power. See, for example, Cunneen *et al*. 1997; Levin and McDevitt 1993.

5 In creating this template of the violence-power nexus I draw heavily upon the arguments of previous chapters. I do not introduce any new interview material. This makes this final chapter more abstract in content and style than the rest.

6 Although the notion of oppression has fallen into disuse in recent years, it can be, as Grosz suggests, 'wrenched from humanist history and made to do the work of specifying, rendering visible, the issue of difference' (1995: 211). Grosz seeks to revitalise oppression in line with Foucauldian notions of domination and subordination that function outside of monolithic understandings of power.

7 The emphasis in some feminist writing on questions of violence and oppression has contributed to the claim that feminism can be characterised as a type of victim politics or 'ressentiment'. Be this as it may, it is a mistake to assume that accounts of gendered violence are, by the very nature of their subject matter, engaged in a valorisation of victimisation or oppression. For a discussion of ressentiment see Brown (1995).

8 The notion of government prioritises techniques of knowing and caring for oneself – over the subjugation that is emphasised in disciplinary power – in the processes of subjectification. Whilst this may 'imply a loosening of the connection between subjectification and subjection', it is not, as Burchell notes, a severance of this connection (1996: 20).

9 Foucault's entreaty to abstain from the 'who' question appears to assume an inseparability between 'who' and 'why': 'Who then has power and what has he in mind? What is the aim of someone who possesses power?' (1980: 97) It seems to me, however, that to ask, 'who' is positioned 'where', in a given moment, in a given power relation, requires neither that we ask 'why' power is exercised in a certain way, nor that we assume that individuals occupy fixed positions in that relation.

10 This distinction between 'who' and 'what' is derived from Chapter 5, where I argued that the process of violent subjectification is neither seamless nor inescapably successful. I suggested that it might be helpful to think about limits to the constitutive capacity of violence through a working distinction between 'who' and 'what' violence produces: where 'what' represents the normative categories of group identity formulated through knowledge of the dangers of violence, and 'who' represents the misrecognition and/or strategies of resistance via which the category of danger fails to define a sense of self. In other words, violence may produce a sense of 'what' homosexuality is, but it can never completely determine 'who' people are as homosexuals.

11 For example, see: Kelly 1988; Caputi 1991; Bart and Moran 1993; Miller and Schwartz 1995; MacKinnon 1983.

12 This is not only a question of the struggle for control that may take place between an individual man and woman. It refers more broadly to the on-going social and political interactions that characterise gender itself. Feminists have

argued that men's violence towards women may emerge from men's perception that they lack, or are losing, control over a particular woman or women in general. This is usually premised upon the understanding that such violence is an abuse of male power and is effective in bolstering such power.

13 For Foucault, the definition of power requires that the subject must still be able to act. In this way he distinguishes a relation of power from one of slavery, where the freedom to act is completely absent (Foucault 1982).

14 Like feminists and Foucault, Hannah Arendt (1969) has also described the nexus between violence and power as an instrumental one. Although Arendt discusses violence and power primarily in the context of politics, and her definition of power differs considerably from these two models, there are some interesting ways in which her ideas are similar to each. For example, like Foucault, she is at pains to distinguish violence from power. For Arendt, power cannot be reduced to a question of domination, but instead corresponds to the human ability to act and, particularly, to act in concert. Physical violence is an instrument of such power. Although Arendt also suggests that violence and power may be opposites, she places greater emphasis than Foucault does on the fact that power and violence are often found together; power often uses violence. This brings her closer to feminist theory on this point.

15 Feminist theory has also been concerned with the interaction of knowledge and power. This concern has focused upon the need to challenge patriarchal forms of knowledge, and to generate new and better knowledge in the interests of women (McNeil 1993).

16 See Chapters 2 and 3.

17 See Chapters 4 and 5.

18 This argument is detailed in Chapter 5.

19 I have partly borrowed this idea from Arendt (1969), who suggests that violence can only destroy power. It can never generate it. In part, this is because violence only emerges at those points where power is under threat.

BIBLIOGRAPHY

Abrams, Kathryn (1994) 'Title IV and the complex female subject' *Michigan Law Review* 92: 2479–540.

Ahmed, Sara (1998) 'Animated borders: skin, colour and tanning' in Margrit Shildrick and Janet Price (eds) *Vital Signs: Feminist Reconfigurations of the Bio/logical Body*, Edinburgh: Edinburgh University Press.

Alcoff, Linda (1991–2) 'The problem of speaking for others' *Cultural Critique* Winter: 5–34.

—— and Potter, Elizabeth (eds) (1993) *Feminist Epistemologies*, New York: Routledge.

Alexander, M. Jacquie and Mohanty, Chandra Talpade (1997) 'Introduction: genealogies, legacies, movements' in M. Jacquie Alexander and Chandra Talpade Mohanty (eds) *Feminist Genealogies, Colonial Legacies, Democratic Futures*, New York and London: Routledge.

Ang, Ien (1995) 'I'm a feminist but . . . "Other" women and postnational feminism' in Barbara Caine and Rosemary Pringle (eds) *Transitions: New Australian Feminisms*, St Leonards: Allen and Unwin.

—— and Stratton, Jon (1998) 'Multicultural imagined communities: cultural difference and national identity in the USA and Australia' in David Bennett (ed.) *Multicultural States: Rethinking Identity and Difference*, London: Routledge.

Anti-Discrimination Board of New South Wales (1992) *Discrimination: The Other Epidemic: Report of the Inquiry into HIV and AIDS-Related Discrimination*, New South Wales: Anti-Discriminatory Board of New South Wales.

Arendt, Hannah (1967) *The Origins of Totalitarianism* (3rd edition), London: George Allen and Unwin.

—— (1969) *Crises of the Republic*, Harmondsworth: Penguin Books.

—— (1958) *The Human Condition: A Study of the Central Dilemmas Facing Modern Man*, Garden City, New York: Doubleday Anchor Books.

Asquith, Nicole (1999) 'Sexuality at work: a study of lesbians' workplace experiences' *New Zealand Journal of Industrial Relations* 24(1): 1–19.

Atkinson, Judy (1990a) 'Violence against Aboriginal women: reconstruction of community law – the way forward' *Aboriginal Law Bulletin* 2(46): 18/05/2001, 6–9.

—— (1990b) 'Violence in Aboriginal Australia part 2' *Aboriginal and Islander Health Worker* 14(3): 7, 16, 20.

Baird, Barbara (1997) 'The role of the state in the regulation of sexuality: the police and violence against lesbians and gay men' *Flinders Journal of Law Reform* 2(1): 75–86.

Baird, Robert and Rosenbaum, Stuart (eds) (1999) *Hatred, Bigotry and Prejudice*, New York: Prometheus Books.

Bar On, Bat-Ami (1993) 'Marginality and epistemic privilege' in Linda Alcoff and Elizabeth Potter (eds) *Feminist Epistemologies*, New York: Routledge.

Bart, Pauline and Moran, Eileen Geil (eds) (1993) *Violence Against Women: The Bloody Footprints*, Newbury Park: Sage.

Beck, Ulrich (1992) *Risk Society: Towards a New Modernity*, London: Sage.

Bell, Vikki (1999) *Feminist Imagination*, London: Sage.

—— (1996) 'The promise of liberalism and the performance of freedom' in Andrew Barry, Thomas Osborne and Nikolas Rose (eds) *Foucault and Political Reason: Liberalism, Neo-liberalism and Rationalities of Government*, Chicago: University of Chicago Press.

—— (1993) *Interrogating Incest: Feminism, Foucault, and the Law*, London and New York: Routledge.

Benhabib, Seyla (1995) 'The pariah and her shadow: Hannah Arendt's biography of Rahel Varnhagen' in Bonnie Honig (ed.) *Feminist Interpretations of Hannah Arendt*, University Park, Pennsylvania: Pennsylvania State University Press.

Bentham, Jeremy (1962, first edition 1843) 'Panopticon, or, the inspection-house, &C' in *The Works of Jeremy Bentham (Vol. 4)*, New York: Russell and Russell.

Berrill, Kevin (1990) 'Anti-gay violence and victimization in the United States: an overview' *Journal of Interpersonal Violence* 5(3): 274–94.

Bhabha, Homi (1994) 'The third space' in Jonathan Rutherford (ed.) *Identity: Community, Culture, Difference*, London: Lawrence and Wishart.

Bickford, Susan (1995) 'In the presence of others: Arendt and Anzaldua on the paradox of public appearance' in Bonnie Honig (ed.) *Feminist Interpretations of Hannah Arendt*, University Park, Pennsylvania: Pennsylvania State University Press.

Bordo, Susan (1993) 'Feminism, Foucault and the politics of the body' in Caroline Ramazanoğlu (ed.) *Up Against Foucault: Explorations of Some Tensions Between Foucault and Feminism*, London: Routledge.

—— (1989) 'The body and the reproduction of femininity: a feminist appropriation of Foucault' in Alison Jaggar and Susan Bordo (eds) *Gender/Body/Knowledge: Feminist Reconstructions of Being and Knowing*, New Brunswick: Rutgers University Press.

Boswell, John (1980) *Christianity, Social Tolerance and Homosexuality*, Chicago: University of Chicago Press.

Bové, Paul A. (1990) 'Discourse' in Frank Lentricchia and Thomas McLaughlin (eds) *Critical Terms in Literary Study*, Chicago: University of Chicago Press.

Brah, Avtar (1993) 'Re-framing Europe: en-gendered racisms, ethnicities and nationalisms in contemporary Western Europe' *Feminist Review* 45: 9–29.

Breines, Wini and Gordon, Linda (1983) 'The new scholarship on family violence' *Signs: Journal of Women in Culture and Society* 8(3): 490–531.

Brenner, Claudia and Ashley, Hannah (1995) *Eight Bullets*, New York: Firebrand Books.

Brown, Beverley (1992) 'Symbolic politics and pornography' *Economy and Society* 21(1): 45–57.

Brown, Wendy (1995) *States of Injury: Power and Freedom in Late Modernity*, Princeton: Princeton University Press.

Brownmiller, Susan (1973) *Against Our Will: Men, Women, and Rape*, Harmondsworth: Penguin.

Burchell, Graham (1996) 'Liberal government and techniques of the self' in Andrew Barry, Thomas Osborne and Nikolas Rose (eds) *Foucault and Political Reason: Liberalism, Neo-Liberalism and Rationalities of Government*, Chicago: University of Chicago Press.

Burton, Nadya (1998) 'Resistance to prevention: reconsidering feminist antiviolence rhetoric', in Stanley French, Wanda Teays and Laura Purdy (eds) *Violence Against Women: Philosophical Perspectives*, Ithaca: Cornell University Press.

Butler, Judith (1997) *Excitable Speech: A Politics of the Performative*, New York: Routledge.

—— (1995) 'Subjection, resistance, resignification: between Freud and Foucault' in John Rajchman (ed.) *The Identity in Question*, New York: Routledge.

—— (1993) *Bodies That Matter: On The Discursive Limits of "Sex"*, New York: Routledge.

—— (1991) 'Imitation and gender insubordination' in Diana Fuss (ed.) *Inside/Out: Lesbian Theories, Gay Theories*, New York: Routledge.

—— (1990) *Gender Trouble: Feminism and the Subversion of Identity*, New York: Routledge.

Cahill, Ann J. (2000) 'Foucault, rape, and the construction of the feminine body' *Hypatia* 15(1): 43–63.

Cain, Maureen (1986) 'Realism, feminism, methodology and the law' *International Journal of the Sociology of Law* 14: 255–67.

Cameron, Deborah and Fraser, Elizabeth (1987) *The Lust to Kill*, Cambridge: Polity Press.

Caputi, Jane (1991) 'Men's violence against women: an international overview' *BN/SR* 34(6): 847–878.

—— (1988) *The Age of Sex Crime*, London: Women's Press.

Caraway, Nancie (1991) *Segregated Sisterhood: Racism and the Politics of American Feminism*, Knoxville: University of Tennessee Press.

Castel, Robert (1991) 'From dangerousness to risk' in Graham Burchell, Colin Gordon and Peter Miller (eds) *The Foucault Effect: Studies in Governmentality*, Chicago: University of Chicago Press.

Cheah, Pheng and Grosz, Elizabeth (1996) 'The body of the law: notes toward a theory of corporeal justice' in Pheng Cheah, David Fraser and Judith Grbich (eds) *Thinking Through the Body of the Law*, St Leonards: Allen and Unwin.

Cocks, Joan (1995) 'On nationalism: Frantz Fanon, 1925–1961; Rosa Luxemburg, 1871–1919; and Hannah Arendt, 1906–1975' in Bonnie Honig (ed.) *Feminist Interpretations of Hannah Arendt*, University Park, Pennsylvania: Pennsylvania State University Press.

Cohen, Ed (1991) 'Who are "we"? Gay "identity" as political (e)motion (a theoretical rumination)' in Diana Fuss (ed.) *Inside/Out: Lesbian Theories, Gay Theories*, New York: Routledge.

Collins, Patricia Hill (1990) *Black Feminist Thought: Knowledge, Consciousness, and the Politics of Empowerment*, Boston: Unwin Hyman.

Comstock, Gary (1991) *Violence Against Lesbians and Gay Men*, New York: Columbia University Press.

Coward, Roslyn (1987) *Female Desire: Women's Sexuality Today*, London: Paladin.

Cox, Gary (1994) *The Count and Counter Report: A Study into Hate Related Violence Against Lesbians and Gay Men*, Sydney: Lesbian and Gay Anti-Violence Project.

—— (1990) *The Streetwatch Report: A Study into Violence Against Lesbians and Gay Men*, Sydney: Gay and Lesbian Rights Lobby.

Crenshaw, Kimberley (1991) 'Mapping the margins: intersectionality, identity politics and violence against women of colour' *Stanford Law Review* 43: 1241–99.

Cunneen, Chris and Stubbs, Julie (1996) 'Violence against Filipino women in Australia: race, class and gender' *Waikato Law Review* 4(1): 131–54.

——, Fraser, David and Tomsen, Stephen (eds) (1997) *Faces of Hate: Hate Crime in Australia*, New South Wales: Hawkins Press.

Cutting-Gray, Joanne (1993) 'Hannah Arendt, feminism, and the politics of alterity: what will we lose if we win?' *Hypatia* 8(1): 35–54.

Daly, Mary (1978) *Gyn/Ecology: The metaethics of radical feminism*, London: The Women's Press.

Davies, Susanne and Rhodes-Little, Andrea (1993) 'History, sexuality and power: deconstructing the "Lesbian Vampire Case"' *Australian Cultural Studies* 12: 14–28.

Dean, Laura, Wu, Shanyu and Martin, John (1992) 'Trends in violence and discrimination against gay men in New York City: 1984 to 1990' in Gregory Herek and Kevin Berrill (eds) *Hate Crimes: Confronting Violence Against Lesbians and Gay Men*, Newbury Park: Sage.

de Lauretis, Teresa (1989) 'The violence of rhetoric: considerations on representations and gender' in Nancy Armstrong and Leonard Tennenhouse (eds) *Representation: Literature and the History of Violence*, London: Routledge.

—— (ed.) (1986) *Feminist Studies/Critical Studies*, Bloomington: Indiana University Press.

Deleuze, Gilles (1993) 'What is Becoming?' in C. V. Boundas (ed.) *The Deleuze Reader*, New York: Columbia University Press.

—— (1988) *Foucault*, London: The Athlone Press.

Dietz, Mary G. (1995) 'Feminist receptions of Hannah Arendt' in Bonnie Honig (ed.) *Feminist Interpretations of Hannah Arendt*, University Park, Pennsylvania: Pennsylvania State University Press.

Diprose, Rosalyn (1994) *The Bodies of Women: Ethics, Embodiment and Sexual Difference*, London: Routledge.

Dobash, R. Emerson, and Dobash, Russell P. (1979) *Violence Against Wives*, New York: The Free Press.

Dominelli, Lena (1989) 'Betrayal of trust: A feminist analysis of power relationship in incest abuse and its relevance for social work practice' *British Journal of Social Work* 19: 291–307.

Douglas, Mary (1966, reprinted 1994) *Purity and Danger: An Analysis of the Concepts of Pollution and Taboo*, London and New York: Routledge.

Dreyfus, Hubert L. and Rabinow, Paul (1982) *Michel Foucault: Beyond Structuralism and Hermeneutics*, Chicago: University of Chicago Press.

Dworkin, Andrea (1981) *Pornography: Men Possessing Women*, London: The Women's Press.

Dyer, Richard (1997) *White*, London and New York: Routledge.

Edwards, Anne (1987) 'Male violence in feminist theory: an analysis of the changing conceptions of sex/gender violence and male dominance' in Jalna Hanmer and Mary Maynard (eds) *Women, Violence and Social Control*, Hampshire: Macmillan Press.

Elder, Catriona (1993) 'It was hard for us to marry Aboriginal: some meanings of singleness for Aboriginal women in the 1930s' *Lilith* 8: 114–138.

Eliason, Michele, Donelan, Carol and Randall, Carla (1992) 'Lesbian stereotypes' *Health Care for Women International* 13: 131–43.

Faderman, Lillian (1991) *Odd Girls and Twilight Lovers: A History of Lesbian Life in Twentieth-Century America*, New York: Penguin Books.

—— (1981) *Surpassing the Love of Men: Romantic Friendships and Love Between Women from the Renaissance to the Present*, London: Junction Books.

Fanon, Frantz (1952, reprinted 1986) *Black Skin, White Masks,* London: Pluto.

Faulkner, Ellen (1997) *Technical Report: Anti-Gay/Lesbian Violence in Toronto: The Impact on Individuals and Communities: A Project of the 519 Church St Community Centre Victim Assistance Programme*, Ottawa: Department of Justice Research and Statistics Division/Policy Sector.

Feher, Ferenc (1989) 'The pariah and the citizen: on Arendt's political theory' in Gisela Kaplan and Clive Kessler (eds) *Hannah Arendt: Thinking, Judging, Freedom*, Sydney: Allen and Unwin.

Felton, Catrina and Flanagan, Liz (1993) 'Institutionalised feminism: a Tidda's perspective' *Lilith: A Feminist History Journal* 8: 53–9.

Flax, Jane (1987) 'Postmodernism and gender relations in feminist theory' *Signs: Journal of Women in Culture and Society* 12: 621–43.

Ford, Julienne (1975) *Paradigms and Fairy Tales: An Introduction to the Science of Meanings*, London: Routledge and Kegan Paul.

Foster, Hal (1988) 'Preface' in Hal Foster (ed.) *Vision and Visuality*, Seattle: Bay Press.

Foucault, Michel (1991) 'Governmentality' in Grahame Burchell, Colin Gordon and Peter Miller (eds) *The Foucault Effect: Studies in Governmentality*, Chicago: University of Chicago Press.

—— (1988) 'Technologies of the self' in Luther Martin, Huck Gutman and Patrick Hutton (eds) *Technologies of the Self: A Seminar with Michel Foucault*, Amherst: University of Massachusetts Press.

—— (1982) 'The subject and power' *Critical Inquiry* 8: 777–95.

—— (1980) 'Two lectures' in Colin Gordon (ed.) *Michel Foucault: Power/Knowledge*, Brighton, Sussex: Harvester Press.

—— (1978) *The History of Sexuality: An Introduction*, Middlesex: Penguin Books.

—— (1977) *Discipline and Punish: The Birth of the Prison*, England: Penguin Books.

—— (1972) *The Archaeology of Knowledge*, London: Tavistock Publications.

—— and Deleuze, Gilles (1977) 'Intellectuals and power' in Donald Bouchard (ed.) *Language, Counter-memory, Practice*, Ithaca: Cornell University Press.

Frankenberg, Ruth (1993) 'Growing up white: feminism, racism and the social geography of childhood' *Feminist Review* 45: 51–84.

Freud, Sigmund (1953) *On Sexuality: Three Essays on the Theory of Sexuality and Other Works (Vol. 7)*, London: Penguin Books.

Fuss, Diana (1989) *Essentially Speaking: Feminism, Nature and Difference*, New York: Routledge.

Garnets, Linda, Herek, Gregory and Levy, Barrie (1990) 'Violence and victimization of lesbians and gay men: mental health consequences' *Journal of Interpersonal Violence* 5(3): 366–83.

Gatens, Moira (1996) *Imaginary Bodies: Ethics, Power and Corporeality*, London: Routledge.

Gavey, Nicola (1989) 'Feminist Post-Structuralism and Discourse Analysis' *Psychology of Women Quarterly* 13: 459–75.

Gelder, Ken and Jacobs, Jane (1998) *Uncanny Australia: Sacredness and Identity in a Postcolonial Nation*, Carlton South: Melbourne University Press.

Giddens, Anthony (1991) *Modernity and Self-Identity*, Cambridge: Polity Press.

Gilligan, Carol (1982) *In A Different Voice: Psychological Theory and Women's Development*, Cambridge, Massachusetts: Harvard University Press.

GLAD (Gay Men and Lesbians Against Discrimination) (1994) *Not A Day Goes By: Report on the GLAD Survey into Discrimination and Violence against Lesbians and Gay Men in Victoria*, Melbourne: GLAD.

Goldberg, David Theo (1995) 'Afterword: hate, or power?' in Rita Kirk Whillock and David Slayden (eds) *Hate Speech*, California: Sage.

Gordon, Colin (ed.) (1980) *Michel Foucault: Power/Knowledge: Selected Interviews and Other Writings 1972–1977*, Brighton: The Harvester Press.

—— (1991) 'Governmental rationality: an introduction' in Grahame Burchell, Colin Gordon and Peter Miller (eds) *The Foucault Effect: Studies in Governmentality*, Chicago: University of Chicago Press.

Grosz, Elizabeth (1995) *Space, Time and Perversion: The Politics of Bodies*, St Leonards: Allen and Unwin.

—— (1994) *Volatile Bodies: Towards a Corporeal Feminism*, St Leonards: Allen and Unwin.

—— (1990) 'Conclusion: a note on essentialism and difference' in Sneja Gunew (ed.) *Feminist Knowledge: Critique and Construct*, London: Routledge.

Gunew, Sneja and Yeatman, Anna (1993) 'Introduction' in Sneja Gunew and Anna Yeatman (eds) *Feminism and the Politics of Difference*, St Leonards: Allen and Unwin.

Hage, Ghassan (1998) *White Nation: Fantasies of White Supremacy in a Multicultural Society*, Annandale: Pluto Press.

Hale, Jacob (1996) 'Are lesbians women?' *Hypatia* 11(2): 94–121.

Hanmer, Jalna (1990) 'Men, power, and the exploitation of women' in Jeff Hearn and David Morgan (eds) *Men, Masculinities and Social Theory*, London: Unwin Hyman.

—— and Maynard, Mary (eds) (1987) *Women, Violence and Social Control*, Hampshire: Macmillan Press.

—— and Saunders, Sheila (1984) *Well-Founded Fear*, London: Hutchinson.

—— Radford, Jill and Stanko, Elizabeth (eds) (1989) *Women, Policing and Male Violence*, London: Routledge.

Haraway, Donna (1990) 'A manifesto for cyborgs: science, technology, and socialist feminism in the 1980s' in Linda J. Nicholson (ed.) *Feminism/Postmodernism*, New York: Routledge.

—— (1988) 'Situated knowledges: the science question in feminism and the privilege of partial perspective' *Feminist Studies* 14(3): 575–99.

Harding, Sandra (1993) 'Rethinking standpoint methodology: "What is strong objectivity?"' in Linda Alcoff and Elizabeth Potter (eds) *Feminist Epistemologies*, New York: Routledge.

—— (1986) *The Science Question in Feminism*, Ithaca: Cornell University Press.

Harry, Joseph (1990) 'Conceptualizing anti-gay violence' *Journal of Interpersonal Violence* 5(3): 350–58.

Hart, Lynda (1994) *Fatal Women: Lesbian Sexuality and the Mark of Aggression*, Princeton: Princeton University Press.

Hartsock, Nancy (1990) 'Foucault on power: a theory for women?' in Linda J. Nicholson (ed.) *Feminism/Postmodernism*, New York: Routledge.

—— (1983a) 'The feminist standpoint: developing the ground for a specifically feminist historical materialism' in Sandra Harding and Merrill Hintikka (eds) *Discovering Reality: Feminist Perspectives on Epistemology, Metaphysics, Methodology, and the Philosophy of Science*, Dordrecht: Reidel.

—— (1983b) *Money, Sex, and Power: Toward a Feminist Historical Materialism*, New York: Longman.

Hekman, Susan J. (1999) *The Future of Differences: Truth and Method in Feminist Theory*, Cambridge: Polity Press.

Heller, Agnes (1989) 'Hannah Arendt on the "vita contemplativa"' in Gisela Kaplan and Clive Kessler (eds) *Hannah Arendt: Thinking, Judging, Freedom*, Sydney: Allen and Unwin.

Herek, Gregory (2000) 'The psychology of sexual prejudice' *Current Directions in Psychological Science* 9(1): 19–22.

—— (1990) 'The context of anti-gay violence: notes on cultural and psychological heterosexism' *Journal of Interpersonal Violence* 5(3): 316–33.

—— (1986) 'On heterosexual masculinity: some psychical consequences of the sexual construction of gender and sexuality' *American Behavioral Scientist* 29(5): 563–77.

—— and Berrill, Kevin (1992) (eds) *Hate Crimes: Confronting Violence Against Lesbians and Gay Men*, Newbury Park: Sage.

Hesse, Mary (1980) *Revolutions and Reconstructions in the Philosophy of Science*, Bloomington: Indiana University Press.

Hester, Marianne (1992) *Lewd Women and Wicked Witches: A Study of the Dynamics of Male Domination*, London and New York: Routledge.

——, Kelly, Liz, and Radford, Jill (eds) (1996) *Women, Violence and Male Power*, Buckingham: Open University Press.

Hollinsworth, David (1995) 'Aboriginal Studies – an epistemological no go zone?' in Penny van Toorn and David English (eds) *Speaking Positions: Aboriginality, Gender and Ethnicity in Australian Cultural Studies*, Melbourne: Department of Humanities, Victoria University of Technology.

Hollway, Wendy and Jefferson, Tony (1998) '"A Kiss is Just a Kiss": date rape, gender and subjectivity' *Sexualities* 1(4): 405–23.

Honig, Bonnie (1995) 'Toward an agonistic feminism: Hannah Arendt and the politics of identity' in Bonnie Honig (ed.) *Feminist Interpretations of Hannah Arendt*, University Park, Pennsylvania: Pennsylvania State University Press.

hooks, bell (1981) *Ain't I a Woman: Black Women and Feminism*, Boston: South End Press.

Howe, Adrian (1997) 'More folk provoke their own demise: (homophobic violence and sexed excuses: rejoining the provocation law debate, courtesy of the homosexual advance defence)' *Sydney Law Review* 19(3): 336–65.

Human Rights and Equal Opportunity Commission (HREOC) (1991) *Racist Violence: Report of the National Inquiry into Racist Violence in Australia*, Canberra: Australian Government Publishing Service.

Hunt, Alan, and Wickham, Gary (1994) *Foucault and Law: Towards a Sociology of Law as Governance*, London: Pluto Press.

Hunter, Joyce (1990) 'Violence against lesbians and gay male youths' *Journal of Interpersonal Violence* 5(3): 295–300.

Irigaray, Luce (1985) *This Sex Which Is Not One*, Ithaca: Cornell University Press.

Jacobitti, Suzanne Duvall (1996) 'Thinking about the self' in Larry May and Jerome Kohn (eds) *Hannah Arendt: Twenty Years Later*, Cambridge, Massachusetts: MIT Press.

Jacobs, James and Potter, Kimberly (1999) *Hate Crimes: Criminal Law and Identity Politics*, New York: Oxford University Press.

Jefferson, Tony (1994) 'Theorising masculine subjectivity' in Tim Newburn and Elizabeth Stanko (eds) *Just Boys Doing Business? Men, Masculinities and Crime*, London: Routledge.

Jeffreys, Sheila (1985) *The Spinster and Her Enemies: Feminism and Sexuality 1880–1930*, London: Pandora.

Jenness, Valerie and Broad, Kendal (1994) 'Anti-violence activism and the (in)visibility of gender in the gay/lesbian and women's movements' *Gender and Society* 8(3): 402–23.

Kelly, Liz (1996) 'When does the speaking profit us?: reflections on the challenges of developing feminist perspectives on abuse and violence by women' in Marianne Hester, Liz Kelly and Jill Radford (eds) *Women, Violence and Male Power*, Buckingham: Open University Press.

—— (1991) 'Unspeakable acts' *Trouble and Strife* 21: 13–20.

—— (1988) *Surviving Sexual Violence*, Cambridge: Polity Press.

Kendall, Gavin, and Wickham, Gary (1999) *Using Foucault's Methods*, London: Sage.

Kinsey, Alfred, Pomeroy, Wardell and Martin, Clyde (1953) *Sexual Behavior in the Human Female*, Philadelphia: W. B. Saunders.

—— (1948) *Sexual Behavior in the Human Male*, Philadelphia: W. B. Saunders.

Kinsman, Gary (1987) *The Regulation of Desire: Sexuality in Canada*, Montreal: Black Rose Books.

Kristeva, Julia (1982) *Powers of Horror: An Essay on Abjection*, New York: Columbia University Press.

Kuhn, Thomas (1962) *The Structure of Scientific Revolutions*, Chicago: University of Chicago Press.

Laqueur, Thomas (1989a) 'Amor Veneris, vel Dulcedo Appeletur' in Michael Feher (ed.) with Ramona Naddaff and Nadia Tazi *Fragments for a History of the Human Body: Part Three*, New York: Zone.

—— (1989b) 'The social evil, the solitary vice and pouring tea' in Michael Feher (ed.) with Ramona Naddaff and Nadia Tazi *Fragments for a History of the Human Body: Part Three*, New York: Zone.

Lawrence, Frederick (1999) *Punishing Hate: Bias Crimes under American Law*, Cambridge, Massachusetts: Harvard University Press.

Lazreg, Marnia (1994) 'Women's experience and feminist epistemology: a critical neo-rationalist approach' in Kathleen Lennon and Margaret Whitford (eds) *Knowing the Difference: Feminist Perspectives in Epistemology*, London: Routledge.

Lehne, Gregory (1976) 'Homophobia among men' in Deborah S. David and Robert Brannon (eds) *The Forty Nine Percent Majority: The Male Sex Role*, New York: Addison-Wesley.

Lennon, Kathleen and Whitford, Margaret (1994) *Knowing the Difference: Feminist Perspectives in Epistemology*, London: Routledge.

Lesbian and Gay Anti-Violence Project (1992) *The Off Our Backs Report: A Study into Anti-Lesbian Violence*, Darlinghurst, Sydney: Gay and Lesbian Rights Lobby Inc.

LeVay, Simon (1996) *Queer Science: The Use and Abuse of Research into Homosexuality*, Cambridge, Massachusetts: MIT Press.

Levin, Jack and McDevitt, Jack (1993) *Hate Crimes: the Rising Tide of Bigotry and Bloodshed*, New York: Plenum.

Lincoln, Yvonna, and Guba, Egon (1985) *Naturalistic Inquiry*, Newbury Park: Sage.

Lobel, Kerry (1986) (ed.) *Naming the Violence: Speaking Out About Lesbian Battering* (Report of the National Coalition Against Domestic Violence Lesbian Task Force), Seattle: Seal Press.

Lockhart, Lettie and White, Barbara W. (1989) 'Understanding marital violence in the Black community' *Journal of Interpersonal Violence* 4(4): 421–36.

Longino, Helen (1990) *Science as Social Knowledge: Values and Objectivity in Scientific Inquiry*, Princeton: Princeton University Press.

Lorde, Audre (1982) *Zami: A New Spelling of My Name*, New York: The Crossing Press.

Lovibond, Sabina (1994) 'The end of morality?' in Kathleen Lennon and Margaret Whitford (eds) *Knowing the Difference: Feminist Perspectives in Epistemology*, London: Routledge.

Lupton, Deborah (1999a) 'Dangerous places and the unpredictable stranger: constructions of the fear of crime' *Australian and New Zealand Journal of Criminology* 32(1): 1–15.

—— (1999b) *Risk*, London: Routledge.

MacCannell, Dean and MacCannell, Juliet Flower (1993) 'Violence, power and pleasure: a revisionist reading of Foucault from the victim perspective' in Caroline Ramazanoğlu (ed.) *Up Against Foucault: Explorations of Some Tensions Between Foucault and Feminism*, London: Routledge.

McGregor, Craig (1997) *Class in Australia*, Ringwood: Penguin.

McGregor, Fiona (1996) 'I am not a lesbian' *Meanjin* 55(1): 31–46.

McIntosh, Mary (1992) 'The homosexual role' in Edward Stein (ed.) *Forms of Desire: Sexual Orientation and the Social Constructionist Controversy*, New York: Routledge.

MacKinnon, Catherine (1987) *Feminism Unmodified: Discourses on Life and Law*, Cambridge, Massachusetts: Harvard University Press.

—— (1983) 'Marxism, method and the state: toward feminist jurisprudence' *Signs: Journal of Women in Culture and Society* 8(4): 635–58.

McNeil, Maureen (1993) 'Dancing with Foucault: feminism and power-knowledge' in Caroline Ramazanoğlu (ed.) *Up Against Foucault: Explorations of Some Tensions Between Foucault and Feminism*, London: Routledge.

Mama, Amina (1989) *The Hidden Struggle: Statutory and Voluntary Sector Responses to Violence against Black Women in the Home*, London: London Race and Housing Research Unit.

Mangena, Oshadi (1994) 'Against fragmentation: the need for holism' in Kathleen Lennon and Margaret Whitford (eds) *Knowing the Difference: Feminist Perspectives in Epistemology*, London: Routledge.

Marcus, Sharon (1992) 'Fighting bodies, fighting words: a theory and politics of rape prevention' in Judith Butler and Joan W. Scott (eds) *Feminists Theorize the Political*, New York and London: Routledge.

Markus, Maria (1989) 'The "anti-feminism" of Hannah Arendt' in Gisela Kaplan and Clive Kessler (eds) *Hannah Arendt: Thinking, Judging, Freedom*, Sydney: Allen and Unwin.

Martin, Biddy and Mohanty, Chrandra Talpade (1986) 'Feminist politics: what's home got to do with it?' in Teresa de Lauretis (ed.) *Feminist Studies/Critical Studies*, Bloomington: Indiana University Press.

Mason, Angela and Palmer, Anya (1996) *Queer Bashing: A National Survey of Hate Crimes Against Lesbians and Gay Men*, United Kingdom: Stonewall.

Mason, Gail (1997a) '(Hetero)sexed hostility and violence toward lesbians' in Sandy Cook and Judith Bessant (eds) *Women's Encounters with Violence: Australian Experiences*, Thousand Oaks: Sage.

—— (1997b) 'Sexuality and violence: questions of difference' in Chris Cunneen, David Fraser and Stephen Tomsen (eds) *Faces of Hate: Hate Crime In Australia*, New South Wales: Hawkins Press.

—— (1995) '(Out)Laws: acts of proscription in the sexual order' in Margaret Thornton (ed.) *Public and Private: Feminist Legal Debates*, Melbourne: Oxford University Press.

—— and Tomsen, Stephen (1997) *Homophobic Violence*, Sydney: Hawkins Press.

Matsuda, Mari (1989a) 'When the first quail calls: multiple consciousness as jurisprudential method' *Women's Rights Law Reporter* 11(7): 297–300.

—— (1989b) 'Public response to racist speech: considering the victim's story' *Michigan Law Review* 87: 2320–81.

May, Larry and Kohn, Jerome (1996) *Hannah Arendt: Twenty Years Later*, Cambridge, Massachusetts: MIT Press.

Millbank, Jenni (1996) 'From butch to butcher's knife: film, crime and lesbian sexuality' *Sydney Law Review* 18(4): 451–73.

Miller, Jody and Schwartz, Martin D. (1995) 'Rape myths and violence against street prostitutes' *Deviant Behavior: An Interdisciplinary Journal* 16: 1–23.

Millet, Kate (1969) *Sexual Politics*, London: Rupert Hart-Davis.

Mirza, Heidi Safia (1997) (ed.) *Black British Feminism: A Reader*, London: Routledge.

Mohanty, Chandra Talpade (1991) 'Cartographies of struggle: third world women and the politics of feminism' in Chandra Talpade Mohanty, Ann Russo and Lourdes Torres (eds) *Third World Women and the Politics of Feminism*, Bloomington: Indiana University Press.

Moraga, Cherrie (1983) *Loving in the War Years*, Boston: South End Press.

Morin, Stephen and Garfinkle, Ellen (1978) 'Male homophobia' *Journal of Social Issues* 34(1): 29–47.

National Coalition of Anti-Violence Programs (1999) *Anti-lesbian, gay, transgender and bisexual violence in 1999: A report of the National Coalition of Anti-Violence Programs*, internet address: <http://www.aup.org/ncavp1999/NCAVP%201999%20report.pdf>

New Zealand Gay Task Force (1985) 'Survey on anti-gay/lesbian violence', unpublished research results, Wellington and Christchurch.

Norton, Anne (1995) 'Heart of darkness: Africa and African Americans in the writings of Hannah Arendt' in Bonnie Honig (ed.) *Feminist Interpretations of Hannah Arendt*, University Park, Pennsylvania: Pennsylvania State University Press.

Omosupe, Ekua (1991) 'Lesbian/bulldagger' *differences: A Journal of Feminist Cultural Studies* 3(2): 101–11.

Padgug, Robert (1992) 'Sexual matters: on conceptualizing sexuality in history' in Edward Stein (ed.) *Forms of Desire: Sexual Orientation and the Social Constructionist Controversy*, New York: Routledge.

Pain, R. (1997) 'Social geographies of women's fear of crime' *Transactions of the Institute of British Geographers* 22: 231–44.

Pallotta-Chiarolli, Maria (1992) 'What about me?: a study of Italian-Australian lesbians' in Karen Herne, Joanne Travaglia and Elizabeth Weiss (eds) *Who Do You Think You Are? Second Generation Immigrant Women in Australia*, Broadway: Women's Redress Press.

Patel, Pragna (1997) 'Third wave feminism and black women's activism' in Heidi Safia Mirza (ed.) *Black British Feminism*, London and New York: Routledge.

Pateman, Carole (1988) *The Sexual Contract*, Cambridge: Polity Press.

Patton, Paul (1998) 'Foucault's subject of power' in Jeremy Moss (ed.) *The Later Foucault: Politics and Philosophy*, London: Sage.

Pharr, Suzanne (1988) *Homophobia: A Weapon of Sexism*, Little Rock: Chardon Press.

Pitkin, Hanna Fenichel (1995) 'Conformism, housekeeping, and the attack of the blob: the origins of Hannah Arendt's concept of the social' in Bonnie Honig (ed.) *Feminist Interpretations of Hannah Arendt*, University Park, Pennsylvania: Pennsylvania State University Press.

—— (1994) 'Justice: on relating private and public' in Lewis P. Hinchman and Sandra K. Hinchman (eds) *Hannah Arendt: Critical Essays*, Albany: State University of New York Press.

Plummer, Kenneth (1981) 'Homosexual categories: some research problems in the labelling perspective of homosexuality' in Kenneth Plummer (ed.) *The Making of the Modern Homosexual*, London: Hutchinson.

Potter, Jonathan and Wetherell, Margaret (1987) *Discourse and Social Psychology: Beyond Attitudes and Behaviour*, London: Sage.

Prado, C.G. (1995) *Starting with Foucault: An Introduction to Genealogy*, Boulder: Westview Press.

Pratt, John (1997) *Governing the Dangerous: Dangerousness, Law and Social Change*, Leichhardt: The Federation Press.

Price Waterhouse Urwick (1995) *Out of the Blue: A Police Survey of Violence and Harassment of Gay Men and Lesbians*, NSW Police Service.

Pringle, Rosemary (1995) 'Destablising patriarchy' in Barbara Caine and Rosemary Pringle (eds) *Transitions: New Australian Feminisms*, St Leonards: Allen and Unwin.

Probyn, Elspeth (1998) 'Dis/connecting the parts: rethinking the politics of the body' *Asian Women* 6: 1–18.

—— (1996) *Outside Belongings*, New York: Routledge.

Radford, Jill, and Russell, Diana (1992) (eds) *Femicide: The Politics of Women Killing*, Buckingham: Open University Press.

Rajchman, John (1988) 'Foucault's art of seeing' *October* Spring: 89–117.

Ramazanoğlu, Caroline (1993) (ed.) *Up Against Foucault: Explorations of Some Tensions Between Foucault and Feminism*, London: Routledge.

Raymond, Janice (1986) *A Passion for Friends: Towards a Philosophy of Female Affections*, Boston: Beacon Press.

Razack, Sherene (1994) 'What is to be gained by looking white people in the eye? Culture, race, and gender in cases of sexual violence' *Signs: Journal of Women in Culture and Society* 19(4): 894–923.

Read, Daphne (1989) '(De)Constructing pornography: feminisms in conflict' in Kathy Peiss and Christina Simmons (eds) *Passion and Power: Sexuality in History*, Philadelphia: Temple University Press.

Reason, Peter, and Rowan, John (eds) (1981) *Human Inquiry: A Sourcebook of New Paradigm Research*, Chichester: John Wiley and Sons.

Reinharz, Shulamit (1979) *On Becoming a Social Scientist: From Survey Research and Participant Observation to Experiential Analysis*, San Francisco: Jossey-Bass.

Renzetti, Claire (1988) 'Violence in lesbian relationships: a preliminary analysis of causal factors' *Journal of Interpersonal Violence* 3(4): 381–99.

Rich, Adrienne (1980) 'Compulsory heterosexuality and lesbian existence' *Signs: Journal of Women in Culture and Society* 5(4): 631–60.

Roberts, Helen (ed.) (1981) *Doing Feminist Research*, London: Routledge and Kegan Paul.

Robson, Ruthann (1992) *Lesbian (Out)Law: Surviving Under the Rule of Law*, New York: Firebrand Books.

Roof, Judith (1991) *A Lure of Knowledge: Lesbian Sexuality and Theory*, New York: Columbia University Press.

Rose, Nikolas (1996a) *Inventing Our Selves: Psychology, Power, and Personhood*, Cambridge: Cambridge University Press.

—— (1996b) 'Ideology, genealogy, history' in Stuart Hall and Paul Du Gay (eds) *Questions of Cultural Identity*, London: Sage.

Rosenau, Pauline Marie (1992) *Postmodernism and the Social Sciences: Insights, Inroads, and Intrusions*, Princeton: Princeton University Press.

Rothenberg, Paula (1990) 'The construction, deconstruction, and reconstruction of difference' *Hypatia* 5(1): 42–57.

Rubin, Gayle (1975) 'The traffic in women: notes on the "political economy" of sex' in Rayna Reiter (ed.) *Toward an Anthropology of Women*, New York: Monthly Review Press.

Russell, D. (1975) *The Politics of Rape: The Victim Perspective*, New York: Sten and Day.

Russo, Mary (1986) 'Female grotesques: carnival and theory' in Teresa de Lauretis (ed.) *Feminist Studies/Critical Studies*, Bloomington: Indiana University Press.

Ryan, Caitlin and Futterman, Donna (1998) *Lesbian and Gay Youth: Care and Counselling*, Columbia: Columbia University Press.

Safe Neighbourhoods Unit (1992) *Violence Against Gay Men in Lewisham*, London.

Said, Edward (1978, reprinted 1991) *Orientalism*, London: Penguin.

Sawicki, Jana (1991) *Disciplining Foucault: Feminism, Power and the Body*, New York: Routledge.

Scales-Trent, Judy (1990) 'Commonalities: on being black and white, different and the same' *Yale Journal of Law and Feminism* 2: 305–27.

Scarry, Elaine (1985) *The Body in Pain: The Making and Unmaking of the World*, New York: Oxford University Press.

Schneider, Beth E. (1993) 'Put up and shut up: workplace sexual assaults' in Pauline Bart and Eileen Geil Moran (eds) *Violence Against Women: The Bloody Footprints*, Newbury Park: Sage.

Scott, Joan (1991) 'The evidence of experience' *Critical Inquiry* 17(4): 773–99.

Sedgwick, Eve Kosofsky (1990) *Epistemology of the Closet*, Berkeley: University of California Press.

Skeggs, Beverley (1997) *Formations of Class and Gender*, London: Sage.

Smart, Carol (1992) 'The woman of legal discourse' *Social and Legal Studies* 1: 29–44.

—— (1990) 'Law's power, the sexed body and feminist discourse' *Journal of Law and Society* 17(2): 194–209.

Smith, Dorothy (1987) *The Everyday World as Problematic: A Feminist Sociology*, Boston: Northeastern University Press.

Southall Black Sisters (1994) *Domestic Violence and Asian Women: A Collection of Reports and Briefings*, London: Southall Black Sisters

Spelman, Elizabeth (1988) *Inessential Woman: Problems of Exclusion in Feminist Thought*, Boston: Beacon Press.

Spivak, Gayatri Chakravorty (1988) 'Can the subaltern speak?' in Cary Nelson and Lawrence Grossberg (eds) *Marxism and the Interpretation of Culture*, London: Macmillan.

Stanko, Elizabeth (1993) 'Ordinary fear: women, violence, and personal safety' in Pauline Bart and Eileen Geil Moran (eds) *Violence Against Women: The Bloody Footprints*, Newbury Park: Sage.

—— (1990) *Everyday Violence: How Women and Men Experience Physical and Sexual Danger*, London: Pandora.

—— and Curry, Paul (1997) 'Homophobic violence and the self "at risk": interrogating the boundaries' *Social and Legal Studies* 6(4): 513–32.

Stanley, Liz and Wise, Sue (1983) *Breaking Out: Feminist Consciousness and Feminist Research*, London: Routledge and Kegan Paul.

Stasiulis, Daiva and Yuval-Davis, Nira (1995) 'Introduction: beyond dichotomies – gender, race, ethnicity and class in settler societies' in Daiva Stasiulis and Nira Yuval-Davis (eds) *Unsettling Settler Societies: Articulations of Gender, Race, Ethnicity and Class*, London: Sage.

Stein, Edward (1992) 'Introduction' in Edward Stein (ed.) *Forms of Desire: Sexual Orientation and the Social Constructionist Controversy*, New York: Routledge.

Strauss, Anselm and Corbin, Juliet (1990) *Basics of Qualitative Research: Grounded Theory Procedures and Techniques*, Newbury Park: Sage.

Stubbs, Julie and Tolmie, Julia (1994) 'Battered woman syndrome in Australia: a challenge to gender bias in the law?' in Julie Stubbs (ed.) *Women, Male Violence and the Law*, Sydney: The Institute of Criminology Monograph Series No. 6.

Taylor, Joelle and Chandler, Tracey (1995) *Lesbians Talk: Violent Relationships*, London: Scarlet Press.

Tomsen, Stephen (1997) 'Sexual identity and victimhood in gay-hate murder trials' in Chris Cunneen, David Fraser and Stephen Tomsen (eds) *Faces of Hate: Hate Crime In Australia*, Sydney: Hawkins Press.

Valentine, Gill (1992) 'Images of danger: women's sources of information about the spatial distribution of male violence' *Area* 24: 22–9.

van den Boogard, Henk (1989) 'Blood furious underneath the skins…on anti-homosexual violence: its nature and the needs of the victims' in Dennis Altman (ed.) *Homosexuality, Which Homosexuality? Essays for the International Scientific Conference on Lesbian and Gay Studies*, London: GMP.

van Pelt, Tamise (2000) 'Otherness' *Postmodern Culture* 10(2): e-journal: <http://muse.jhu.edu/journals/postmodern_culture/v010/10.2vanpelt.html>

Vicinus, Martha (1989) '"They wonder to which sex I belong": the historical roots of the modern lesbian identity' in Dennis Altman (ed.) *Homosexuality, Which Homosexuality?: Essays for the International Scientific Conference on Lesbian and Gay Studies*, London: GMP Publishers.

Von Schulthess, Beatrice (1992) 'Violence in the streets: anti-lesbian assault and harassment in San Francisco' in Gregory Herek and Kevin Berrill (eds) *Hate Crimes: Confronting Violence Against Lesbians and Gay Men*, Newbury Park: Sage.

Waldby, Catherine (1996) *AIDS and the Body Politic: Biomedicine and Sexual Difference*, London and New York: Routledge.

Walker, Lisa (1993) 'How to recognize a lesbian: the cultural politics of looking like what you are' *Signs: Journal of Women in Culture and Society* 18(4): 866–90.

Weeks, Jeffrey (1990) *Coming Out: Homosexual Politics in Britain from the Nineteenth Century to the Present* (revised edition), London: Quartet Books.

Weinberg, George (1972) *Society and the Healthy Homosexual*, New York: St Martin's Press.

Weiss, Gail (1999) *Body Images: Embodiment as Intercorporeality*, New York and London: Routledge.

Whillock, Rita Kirk and Slayden, David (1995) *Hate Speech*, California: Sage.

White, Rob (1997) 'Immigration, nationalism and anti-Asian racism' in Chris Cunneen, David Fraser and Stephen Tomsen (eds) *Faces of Hate: Hate Crime in Australia*, Sydney: Hawkins Press.

Wilson, Melba (1993) *Crossing the Boundary: Black Women Survive Incest*, London: Virago.

Wittig, Monique (1992) *The Straight Mind and Other Essays*, Boston: Beacon Press.

Yeatman, Anna (1994) 'Postmodern epistemological politics and social science' in Kathleen Lennon and Margaret Whitford (eds) *Knowing the Difference: Feminist Perspectives in Epistemology*, London: Routledge.

Young, Alison (1996) *Imagining Crime*, London: Sage.

Young, Iris Marion (1991) *Justice and the Politics of Difference*, Princeton: Princeton University Press.

—— (1990) *'Throwing Like A Girl' and Other Essays in Feminist Philosophy and Social Theory*, Bloomington: Indiana University Press.

Young-Bruehl, Elisabeth (1997) 'Hannah Arendt among feminists' in Larry May and Jerome Kohn (eds) *Hannah Arendt: Twenty Years Later*, Cambridge, Massachusetts: MIT Press.

Yue, Audrey (1996) 'Colour me queer' *Meanjin* 55(1): 87–99.

Zerilli, Linda M. G. (1995) 'The Arendtian body' in Bonnie Honig (ed.) *Feminist Interpretations of Hannah Arendt*, University Park, Pennsylvania: Pennsylvania State University Press.

INDEX

action/speech 114–15, 146n16
affection, demonstrations in public 44, 55, 89
Ahmed, Sara 71, 72, 73
Alexander, M. Jacquie 58
alterity 75–6, 142n16; *see also* otherness
Althusser, Louis 114
ambiguity, gender 54–5, 139–40n15
androcentrism 18
anorexia nervosa 142n17
anti-empiricism 17
anti-essentialism 59, 64, 140n1
anti-feminism 119
anti-racism 64
anti-violence 128
Arendt, Hannah 144n1; feminism 98–9, 146n13; human condition 105–6, 111–12; identity 98–9, 112, 144n4; instrumentality of violence/power 148n14; pariah 146n13; public self 145n10; subject 10, 99, 106, 111–12, 116; violence/power 148n14, 148n19; who/what terms 145n12
Asian identity 66–7, 68, 140n3
Asquith, Nicole 44
assault: physical 2, 40, 45, 53–4, 101–2, 104–5, 139n8; sexual 5, 41, 47–8, 99; verbal 44, 45, 96–7, 100, 104, 108–9, 114, 117
Australia: Asian identity 62–3, 66–7, 68, 140n3; Chinese identity 62–3, 74, 96; gay men 138n7; homophobia-related violence 9, 35–7; multiculturalism 67; racism 7–8, 58–9, 60; socio-politics 141n8

battered woman syndrome 38

Bentham, Jeremy, panopticon 13–14, 15, 19–20, 33, 136n1, 136n2
Bhabha, Homi 142n18
Bickford, Susan 112
biological difference 72–3
bio-power 125
blatant homosexuality 86, 89–90, 94
bodily gestures 112–13
body: Butler 142n14; culture 75, 76; difference 75, 77; exchanges 75–6; experience 142n17; Foucault 75, 123–4, 141–2n14; Grosz 46, 47, 142n15; perpetrators 73–4; safety 54; social constructionism 66; survivor 54; transgressed 103; violence 130; vulnerability 113; *see also* corporeality; physical appearance
body maps 87–8, 89, 93–4, 95
body/mind dualism 72–3, 74, 141n13
Bordo, Susan 82, 126
Breines, Wini 128–9
Brown, Wendy 4, 147n7
Burchell, Graham 125, 147n8
butch identity 50–2, 53, 68–9, 139n13
Butler, Judith 25; action/speech 114–15, 146n16; body 142n14; closet 82–3; dirt 45; on Foucault 125; heterosexuality 49, 52; identity 65, 70, 114; interpellation 146n15; lesbian exclusion 143n4; materiality 142n15; subject 91, 107, 126; subjectification 113–14; on Wittig 139n14

categorisation: identity 74–5, 112, 117, 132; lesbians 53; sexuality 8, 21–4; verbal insults 104
Chinese identity 74, 96